CAMBRIDGE GREEK AND LATIN CLASSICS

HOMER

ILIAD

BOOK XXIV

EDITED BY

C. W. MACLEOD

University Lecturer in Greek and Latin Literature and
Student of Christ Church, Oxford

CAMBRIDGE UNIVERSITY PRESS

CAMBRIDGE

LONDON   NEW YORK   NEW ROCHELLE
MELBOURNE   SYDNEY

Published by the Press Syndicate of the University of Cambridge
The Pitt Building, Trumpington Street, Cambridge CB2 1RP
32 East 57th Street, New York, NY 10022, USA
296 Beaconsfield Parade, Middle Park, Melbourne 3206, Australia

First published 1982

Printed in Great Britain at
the University Press, Cambridge

Library of Congress catalogue card number: 81-12208

British Library Cataloguing in Publication Data
Homer
[Iliad. Book 24]. Iliad, book XXIV. – (Cambridge Greek and Latin classics)
I. Title   II. MacLeod, Colin   III. Iliad, book XXIV
883'.01   PA4020.P24
ISBN 0 521 24353 X hardcovers
ISBN 0 521 28620 4 paperback

CONTENTS

[v]

To
ALBIO CASSIO
OLIVER TAPLIN

οἵτινες οὐκ ὤκνησαν ὁμόφρονα θυμὸν ἔχοντες
ἴσον τῶν ἀγαθῶν τῶν τε κακῶν μετέχειν.

PREFACE

This commentary has two main purposes. First, to give some at least of the help which unpractised readers might want in tackling *Iliad* 24. Second, to show in detail, over a continuous stretch of his poem, something of Homer's skill and greatness. I have not ignored 'analytic' and 'formulaic' criticism; and I believe I have learned something from them. But I do not share their assumption that the *Iliad* is not a designed and significant whole, or not the work of a deeply thoughtful poet who repays close study as much as Sophocles or Dante or Shakespeare. Ruth Finnegan's *Oral poetry* (Cambridge 1977), and her Penguin Anthology, have made it clear both how diverse and how subtle or reflective oral poetry can be. I have attempted a commentary because that seemed the best way to bring out how variously Homer's art is manifested and how firmly it is sustained; questions of style and expression, as well as of overall structure, have therefore claimed a good deal of attention. I have also introduced more parallels than might be expected from later authors, in order to show how Homer's language, artistry and thought are comparable to theirs. The greatest poet of ancient Greece is too often treated as if he were not a part of Greek civilization.

A word on (1) the arrangement and (2) the limits of this book.

(1) It seemed necessary to discuss at length the place of Book 24 in the *Iliad* and the qualities of Homer's style. As a result, many observations that a reader might expect to find in the commentary proper figure in the Introduction. I have not made cross-references to the Introduction in the commentary simply because they would have had to be so many as merely to confuse and irritate. I have, however, divided the Introduction into small and distinct sections so that it can be readily consulted. It remains true, I think, that the commentary will give better value if a reader approaches it after a careful look at the Introduction.

(2) Some of my omissions are deliberate. In particular, there is one matter I should mention here, the supposed 'Odyssean' character of *Iliad* 24. As far as language in the narrower sense is concerned, *Iliad* 24 is no more 'un-Iliadic' than parts of the poem which by universal agreement are 'old': see Beck 102–6; Stawell 94–103. As for places where *Iliad* 24 was thought to be drawing on the *Odyssey*, these have

been brilliantly discussed by Reinhardt 469–506. At times he overstates his case: some correspondences presumably have a common source in the epic tradition (though I suspect that the tradition was not quite so wonderfully capacious as some modern scholars seem to think). But where there is any chance of defining the relation between a passage of *Iliad* 24 and one in the *Odyssey*, in every case it seems natural to suppose that the *Iliad* passage came first. In the commentary I have registered the parallels between *Iliad* and *Odyssey* and, where appropriate, tried to show why the *Iliad* passage is the earlier one; I have abstained from such comment where it seemed pointless. The humane spirit of *Iliad* 24 has also sometimes been considered peculiarly 'Odyssean': that belief I try to counter in sections 1 and 2 of the Introduction. It is harmless enough to speak of some aspects of *Iliad* 24 as 'Odyssean' if we mean simply that they resemble prominent aspects of the *Odyssey*. Thus the gods' concern for morality among men – a dominant theme in the *Odyssey* – plays a part in *Iliad* 24 which it does not in the rest of the poem; or the meeting of Hermes and Priam with its probing exchanges (the words πειρᾶσθαι/πειράζειν are a sort of *Leitmotiv* in the *Odyssey*) and its dramatic irony is of a type common in the later work. But it is a truism, though one often ignored where Homer is concerned, that a poem, however vast its scope, is not a total display of the poet's art or world: it is the result of a deliberate selection. What matters, then, is to see why 'Odyssean' features have a proper place in the *Iliad* where they occur.[1]

I have been helped, more than by any other writings, by three books, all of them German. Wolfgang Schadewaldt's *Iliasstudien* and Karl Reinhardt's *Die Ilias und ihr Dichter* taught me to see the *Iliad* as a deep and complex unity rather than a glorious patchwork or a baffling muddle; and few works of classical scholarship combine sensitive perception with tough argument so well as they do. Götz Beck's dissertation, *Die Stellung des 24. Buches der Ilias in der alten Epentradition* carefully applies their insights to Book 24 (though without the distinction of their style) as well as discussing many questions of detail. A commentator on Homer does not have an ample stream of previous comment to draw on, which made his work especially helpful. All three books have yet, it seems to me, to be fully absorbed and appreciated

---

[1] For a plain and thoughtful account of these problems and the whole 'Homeric question' see C. G. Hardie, *G. & R.* 3 (1956) 118–30.

by English-speaking scholars: it gives me the more pleasure to ac-
knowledge that *senz'essi non fermai peso di dramma*.

It is also a pleasure to record something of what this book owes to
friends and colleagues nearer home. A number of typists, including my
wife, worked cheerfully and accurately on a repulsive manuscript:
Philippa Lanchbery, Glenys McGregor, Melissa Palmer, Catherine
Ross and Carolyn Stapleton. Malcolm Willcock generously put at my
disposal a draft of what he has written on *Iliad* 24 in his commentary
on the whole work. Some friends read parts of my work in typescript
and made valuable criticisms: Michael Comber, Mary Lefkowitz,
Hugh Lloyd-Jones, Anna Morpurgo Davies, Christopher Pelling and
Agathe Thornton. I should also like to thank those who attended a class
on *Iliad* 24 which I held in Oxford University in Hilary Term 1980:
their contributions sharpened my wits and stiffened my resolve for the
final stages of my work. The editors of this series greatly improved all
my drafts with their patient and thoughtful advice. A special word of
thanks is due to Oliver Taplin who read the whole book in typescript
and offered a wealth of comment which continually drew my attention
away from trivia to *seria*; and he was always ready with guidance and
encouragement when I needed them.

I am very grateful to the staff of the Cambridge University Press for
their efficiency and courtesy, and to Robin Hankey for his help in
reading the proofs.

Finally, I must thank my teacher and my college. From Eduard
Fraenkel's formidable seminars on Greek and Latin texts I first learned
what scholarship meant, and from his friendship, what it could give to
a man: I only hope that some faint afterglow of his inspiring work and
presence may be felt in this book. For the last twelve years I have had
the good fortune to work as a tutor in Christ Church. This has allowed
me, without the need to prove that I was up to anything, gradually
to explore my ignorance and pick at my confusions; and what I have
received in the way of help, tolerance, instruction and friendship from
colleagues, pupils and staff is too much to describe. I simply register
it with gratitude.

Christ Church, Oxford   C.W.M.
September 1980

INTRODUCTION

1. THE ILIAD AS A TRAGIC POEM[1]

When the Greek envoys arrive at Achilles' tent in *Iliad* 9, they find him, now that he is no longer himself winning glory in battle, singing 'the tales of famous men' (189 κλέα ἀνδρῶν).[2] It is not hard to see that the *Iliad* too is such a tale. It relates the deeds of men who are treated as historical; and like history in ancient and modern times, it aims both to record something notable from the past and to make what it records come alive in the imagination. These qualities are embodied by the Sirens in *Od.* 12 who represent poetry in an extreme and sinister form: they know everything that happens on earth, including the saga of which the *Iliad* is part, the tale of Troy (189–91), and their song charms or bewitches their hearers.[3] So too Odysseus praises the bard Demodocus in *Od.* 8. 487–91 with these words:

> Δημόδοκ᾽, ἔξοχα δή σε βροτῶν αἰνίζομ᾽ ἁπάντων·
> ἤ σέ γε Μοῦσ᾽ ἐδίδαξε, Διὸς πάϊς, ἤ σέ γ᾽ Ἀπόλλων.
> λίην γὰρ κατὰ κόσμον Ἀχαιῶν οἶτον ἀείδεις,
> ὅσσ᾽ ἔρξαν τ᾽ ἔπαθόν τε καὶ ὅσσ᾽ ἐμόγησαν Ἀχαιοί,
> ὥς τέ που ἤ αὐτὸς παρεὼν ἤ ἄλλου ἀκούσας.

'Demodocus, you are to be praised above all men. Either the Muse, daughter of Zeus, or Apollo must have taught you. For you sing so finely of the fate of the Greeks, all that they did and endured and

---

[1] In these first two sections I am particularly indebted to two writers: as regards *Od.* 8 and Homer's 'poetics', to W. Marg, *Homer über die Dichtung*[2] (Münster 1971) and 'Das erste Lied des Demodokos' in the *Festschrift* for F. Jacoby, *Navicula Chilonensis* (Leiden 1956) 16–29; and as regards the spirit of the *Iliad* as a whole, to S. Weil, 'L'Iliade, ou le poème de la force' in *La source grecque* (Paris 1953) 11–42; there is an English translation of this essay in her *Intimations of Christianity among the ancient Greeks* (London 1957). I know of no better brief account of the *Iliad* than this. See now also J. Griffin, *Homer on life and death* (Oxford 1980).

[2] The same phrase is used in *Od.* 8.73 of Demodocus' themes; cf. ἔργ᾽ ἀνδρῶν τε θεῶν τε in *Od.* 1.338 of Phemius' (whose name is formed from φήμη = 'report').

[3] Cf. *Od.* 11.334 = 13.2; 17.518–21; *H.H.Ap.* 161. Plato, *Rep.* 607c–d speaks of the bewitching effect of poetry, and especially of Homer himself.

1

toiled, as if you had been there yourself or heard it from one who was.'

Line 491 recalls *Il.* 2.485 where the Muses are addressed: 'you are present (πάρεστε) and you know everything'. The Muses are 'present' or Demodocus seems to have 'been there himself', because not only is poetry's subject-matter historical, but it has the quality of realism or authenticity.[1]

But this is far from an adequate account of the purpose of the *Iliad*. A further look at *Od.* 8 will help to frame a true notion of Homer's epic. The songs of Demodocus are of course something less than the *Iliad*: they are only 'lays', selections from the corpus of legend, not a grand architectonic poem. But in so far as they span the whole tale of the fall of Troy (and include the doings of the gods), they hint at a larger whole. Moreover, they may be regarded both as a complement to the *Iliad*, in that they recount stories which are closely connected with it but lie outside the scope of the narrative, and as a reflection upon the *Iliad*, in that they embody in a condensed and significant form some of its major themes and aims.[2]

The first song of the Phaeacian singer (72–82) tells of a quarrel between Odysseus and Achilles. The dispute caused Agamemnon to rejoice, because of a prophecy Apollo had given him at Delphi just before the expedition left for Troy. This episode, it is clearly implied, happened near the beginning of the war; and what the god foretold must have been that Troy would fall soon after 'the best of the Greeks' had quarrelled. What Agamemnon did not know is that it is his own quarrel with Achilles nearly ten years later which was meant. As Odysseus hears this tale, he weeps and groans, while the Phaeacians are delighted by it (83–92). Here, then, are two important motifs from the *Iliad*: the quarrel of the two 'best' men as the beginning of a series of troubles (Book 1),[3] and the deception by a god of the Greek leader (Book

---

[1] In later criticism, this quality was called ἐνάργεια ('vividness'); the scholia sometimes find it in Homer in matters of detail: e.g. 4.473, 6.467. It is often thought proper to history too: see [Longinus], *De subl.* 15.1 and Russell ad loc.; Hor. *Od.* 2.1.17 and Nisbet–Hubbard ad loc.

[2] Much the same goes for the tales of Nestor and Menelaus in *Od.* 3 and 4, Odysseus' conversations with Achilles, Agamemnon and Ajax in *Od.* 11 and the suitors' with Agamemnon in *Od.* 24.

[3] A quarrel caused by a god's anger also begins Nestor's tale in *Od.* 3.130ff. A divine quarrel (over the famous 'apple of Discord') began the series of

2) – or more broadly, men's unwitting fulfilment of a divinely determined pattern of events: *Od.* 8.81–2 τότε γάρ ῥα κυλίνδετο πήματος ἀρχὴ | Τρωσί τε καὶ Δαναοῖσι Διὸς μεγάλου διὰ βουλάς ('the beginning of trouble for Trojans and Greeks was surging on, by the plan of Zeus') echoes *Il.* 1.2–5 μυρί᾽ Ἀχαιοῖς ἄλγεα... |... Διὸς δ᾽ ἐτελείετο βουλή ('ten thousand sufferings for the Greeks... and the plan of Zeus was achieved'). Here too is the proper response of its audience: they are to be pleased, like the Phaeacians, but also moved; for Odysseus' tears reveal what a participant, and so also a fully sympathetic hearer of Homer's poem, would feel about such a tale.[1]

The second song of Demodocus (266–366)[2] is in lighter vein. It tells of the adultery of Aphrodite with Ares, and of how Hephaestus took his revenge and received his compensation, against a varied background of sententious disapproval and rumbustious humour from the other gods, and it ends with Aphrodite going off to be cosseted by the Graces in Cyprus. Both the Phaeacians and Odysseus are delighted by it (367–9). The theme of the song fits firmly into the *Odyssey*: the unfaithful wife on Olympus contrasts with Penelope, the faithful wife on earth. But that the divine action should echo in tones of fun what is deeply serious among men is typical of the *Iliad*: perhaps the most striking example is the quarrel of Zeus with Hera which follows Agamemnon's with Achilles in Book 1. The gods' dispute returns to laughter, whereas the human beings' ends in increased resentment and brings 'ten thousand sufferings'. Moreover, the story of Ares and Aphrodite is a close relative to the deception of Zeus in *Iliad* 14. Sexual pleasures and misdemeanours have no place in the life of the Iliadic hero:[3] the Greeks have their concubines and the Trojans their wives,

events leading to the Trojan War, which were narrated in the post-Homeric *Cypria*.

[1] Cf. Eumaeus' reaction to Odysseus' story in *Od.* 14.361–2: 'Poor stranger [ἆ δειλέ, the same words with which Achilles responds to Priam's appeal in *Il.* 24.518], you have stirred my heart [i.e. to pity, cf. the same words in *Il.* 24.467] as you told of all your sufferings and wanderings'; for Odysseus' tales are in effect poems: cf. H. Fränkel, *Early Greek poetry and philosophy* (Oxford 1975) 10–15.

[2] On this tale, cf. W. Burkert, *R.M.* 103 (1960) 130–44; on its conclusion, Griffin 200–1.

[3] When Paris carries off Helen to bed in *Il.* 3, his words of desire (441–6) closely resemble Zeus's to Hera in Book 14.313–28. But Helen has been constrained by Aphrodite's power, whereas Hera has used it; and Paris in the *Iliad* is less than a true hero.

4 INTRODUCTION

but the women of the poem either suffer themselves or else are the cause of suffering and death. The ease and gaiety of the Olympians, then, sets in relief the passion and painfulness of mortal existence; but it can also amuse and refresh the poet's listeners.

The third song of Demodocus completes and culminates the series. This time Odysseus solicits a tale from the poet about what he openly names as one of his own triumphs, the Trojan horse (492–8). Demodocus complies, following the story through to the sack of Troy and giving prominence to Odysseus' part in it (499–520). One might have expected that having heard himself duly represented as an epic hero, Odysseus would rejoice in this performance too. But his reaction is to weep, as he did after the bard's first song:

> ταῦτ' ἄρ' ἀοιδὸς ἄειδε περικλυτός· αὐτὰρ 'Οδυσσεὺς
> τήκετο, δάκρυ δ' ἔδευεν ὑπὸ βλεφάροισι παρειάς.
> ὡς δὲ γυνὴ κλαίῃσι φίλον πόσιν ἀμφιπεσοῦσα,[1]
> ὅς τε ἑῆς πρόσθεν πόλιος λαῶν τε πέσῃσιν,
> ἄστεϊ καὶ τεκέεσσιν ἀμύνων νηλεὲς ἦμαρ·
> ἡ μὲν τὸν θνήσκοντα καὶ ἀσπαίροντα ἰδοῦσα
> ἀμφ' αὐτῷ χυμένη λίγα κωκύει· οἱ δέ τ' ὄπισθε
> κόπτοντες δούρεσσι μετάφρενον ἠδὲ καὶ ὤμους
> εἴρερον εἰσανάγουσι, πόνον τ' ἐχέμεν καὶ ὀϊζύν·
> τῆς δ' ἐλεεινοτάτῳ ἄχεϊ φθινύθουσι παρειαί·
> ὡς 'Οδυσεὺς ἐλεεινὸν ὑπ' ὀφρύσι δάκρυον εἶβεν. (521–31)

Thus sang the famous singer; but Odysseus' heart melted, and tears dropped from his eyes and wetted his cheeks. As a woman weeps, falling to clasp her husband who has fallen in defence of his city and his people, to keep off the day of pitiless doom for his town and his children: seeing him in his death-throes, she clings to him, shrilly wailing; but the enemy, striking her back and shoulders from behind with their spears, lead her off to slavery, to toil and groaning; and her cheeks melt with most pitiful grief – just so did Odysseus pour down pitiful tears from his eye-lids.

The simile brings out the workings of pity in Odysseus' mind: he weeps *like* a woman whose husband has died in defence of his city and who is taken into captivity – she is, in effect, Andromache – because it is as

[1] The echo of πέσῃσιν in ἀμφιπεσοῦσα is a very fine detail: the mourning wife's gesture re-enacts the husband's death; cf. 3 (i) (a) below on Il. 22.405–6.

if her suffering has through the poet's art become his own.[1] Homer's narrative and comparison represent what Gorgias later expressed in the elaborate figures of his oratory:

ἧς (sc. τῆς ποιήσεως) τοὺς ἀκούοντας εἰσῆλθε καὶ φρίκη περίφοβος καὶ ἔλεος πολύδακρυς καὶ πόθος φιλοπενθής, ἐπ' ἀλλοτρίων τε πραγμάτων καὶ σωμάτων εὐτυχίαις καὶ δυσπραγίαις ἴδιόν τι πάθημα διὰ τῶν λόγων ἔπαθεν ἡ ψυχή. (*Helen* 9)

A fearful *frisson*, a tearful pity, a longing for lamentation enter the hearers of poetry; and as words tell of the fortune and misfortune of other lives and other people, the heart feels a feeling of its own.

So the song which was to glorify the hero is felt by the hero himself as a moving record of the pain and sorrow he helped to cause. Once again this recalls the *Iliad*, whose central subject is not honour and glory, but suffering and death:

μῆνιν ἄειδε, θεά, Πηληϊάδεω Ἀχιλῆος
οὐλομένην, ἣ μυρί' Ἀχαιοῖς ἄλγε' ἔθηκε,
πολλὰς δ' ἰφθίμους ψυχὰς Ἄϊδι προΐαψεν
ἡρώων, αὐτοὺς δὲ ἑλώρια τεῦχε κύνεσσιν
οἰωνοῖσί τε δαῖτα, Διὸς δ' ἐτελείετο βουλή. (1. 1–5)

Sing, goddess, of the anger of Achilles, the deadly anger which caused ten thousand sufferings for the Greeks, which sent many souls of mighty heroes to Hades and made their bodies a dinner for dogs and birds, in fulfilment of the plan of Zeus.

This programme is pursued consistently throughout the poem. Fighting in the *Iliad* is for the heroes concerned a way of gaining glory; but in seeking glory, they always face death – indeed, they seek it not least *because* of impending death (12.322–8). The many killings in the poem

---

[1] This exactly corresponds to the common Greek conception of pity as a sentiment caused by seeing that another's troubles are the same as troubles we might endure or have endured ourselves: cf. Soph. *Aj.* 121–6; *O.C.* 560–8; Hdt. 1.86.6; Thuc. 5.90–1; Arist. *Rhet.* 1385b13ff. The Greeks also carefully distinguish between the feeling evoked by our own suffering or the suffering of those very close to ourselves, and by others' suffering (Hdt. 3.14; Arist. *Rhet.* 1386a17–28); only the second kind is proper material for tragedy (Hdt. 6.21.2). See also below on *Od.* 8.577–80.

are meant to evoke horror and pathos, not bloodthirsty glee;[1] and one of war's characteristic epithets is 'tearful' (δακρυόεις, πολύδακρυς). In the greatest duels of all the gods determine the outcome in such a way that it is human helplessness, not heroic strength and prowess, which most strikes us: Zeus pities his son Sarpedon, but still leaves him to his death at Hera's insistence; the same happens to Hector, who is, moreover, tricked by Athena; and Patroclus is benumbed, befuddled and disarmed by Apollo before Euphorbus and Hector finish him off.

The first time that Odysseus wept Alcinous had tactfully relieved and concealed his guest's sorrow by starting the games (94–103). This time, however, he cannot forebear to discover who the stranger is and what causes his tears (577–80):

> εἰπὲ δ' ὅ τι κλαίεις καὶ ὀδύρεαι ἔνδοθι θυμῷ
> Ἀργείων Δαναῶν ἰδὲ Ἰλίου οἶτον ἀκούων.
> τὸν δὲ θεοὶ μὲν τεῦξαν, ἐπεκλώσαντο δ' ὄλεθρον
> ἀνθρώποις, ἵνα ᾖσι καὶ ἐσσομένοισιν ἀοιδή.

'Tell me why you are weeping and groaning in your heart as you hear of the fate of the Greeks and Troy. It was the gods who brought it about: they spun destruction for those people, so that future generations might have a song.'

With these words the Phaeacian king, who is detached from the events concerned, tries to comfort Odysseus. They recall the words that Helen, a participant, speaks with chagrin in the *Iliad* (6.357–8):

> ...οἷσιν ἐπὶ Ζεὺς θῆκε κακὸν μόρον, ὡς καὶ ὀπίσσω
> ἀνθρώποισι πελώμεθ' ἀοίδιμοι ἐσσομένοισιν.

'...on whom [i.e. herself and Paris] Zeus put an unhappy lot, so that we might be a theme for songs in the future.'

Poetry gives pleasure[2] – how should it not? – as well as inspiring pity;

---

[1] On pathos, see Griffin, ch. 4. Horror, which ancient critics tend to couple with pity (e.g. Plato, *Ion* 535c, on Homer; Gorgias, loc. cit.; Arist. *Poet.* 1453b5 φρίττειν καὶ ἐλεεῖν), is aroused in Homeric battle-scenes by the many descriptions of mortal wounds and by the boasting of conquerors over their dead or dying enemies.

[2] τέρπειν is regularly used of the effect of poetry; see *Il.* 1.474; *Od.* 1.347; 8.91, 368, 429; 17.385. Likewise of the Sirens' song (*Od.* 12.188). The bard Phemius carries the significant patronymic Τερπιάδης (*Od.* 22.330).

but for those who live out what poets retail, the suffering which makes the stuff of the poem is merely bitter experience. However, to listen to poetry is not only to find pleasure. In *Od.* 1 Penelope asks Phemius to stop singing of the return of the Greeks from Troy because that stirs up her longing for Odysseus: she wants his song to be a drug or spell (θελκτήρια, cf. p. 1 n. 3 above) that will soothe her grief;[1] but Telemachus replies (353–5)

σοὶ δ' ἐπιτολμάτω κραδίη καὶ θυμὸς ἀκούειν·
οὐ γὰρ Ὀδυσσεὺς οἶος ἀπώλεσε νόστιμον ἦμαρ
ἐν Τροίῃ, πολλοὶ δὲ καὶ ἄλλοι φῶτες ὄλοντο.

'Let your heart endure and listen. Odysseus was not the only one who lost his homecoming in Troy; many other men were undone.'

If poetry gives comfort, it should be not just by affording a captivating distraction, but rather by helping us to feel whatever sorrows we have as part of a common lot, and so to endure them more bravely.[2]

What emerges from *Od.* 8, as from the opening lines of the *Iliad* itself, is a conception of tragic poetry:[3] human passion and blindness, which lead to suffering, death and loss of burial; behind it all, the will of the supreme god, and above it all, the Olympians, only too man-like in everything but their freedom from pain and mortality. Moreover, there is an awareness of the paradox that pain, as recorded in art, can give pleasure[4] – and not only of this aesthetic paradox, but also of the fact it rests on, namely the difference between art and life, tragedy and suffering. At the same time, for Homer, people can get not only

---

[1] Cf. Hes. *Theog.* 55, 98–103.

[2] Cf. Timocles, *CAF* II 453 = Athenaeus 223b on the usefulness of tragedy: it teaches us that someone has always suffered worse than ourselves. Likewise Polybius (1.1.2) on history.

[3] Cf. the scholion on 1.1 (μῆνιν ἄειδε)...τραγῳδίαις τραγικὸν ἐξεῦρε προοίμιον ('he has created a tragic proem to a series of tragedies').

[4] For treatments of this paradox in antiquity, see Gorgias, *Helen* 9, quoted above; Plato, *Ion* 535b–536d; *Philebus* 47e–48b; *Republic* 605c–606b; Timocles, *CAF* II 453.5–7; Augustine, *Confessions* 3.2. Modern treatments are discussed by T. R. Henn, *The harvest of tragedy* (London 1956) 43–58. Likewise Homer notes, with a pointed oxymoron, how *remembered* suffering can give pleasure when recounted as a story: *Od.* 15.399–400 (Eumaeus to Odysseus) κήδεσιν ἀλλήλων τερπώμεθα λευγαλέοισι | μνωομένω· μετὰ γάρ τε καὶ ἄλγεσι τέρπεται ἀνήρ... ('Let us take pleasure in each other's grim sorrows by recalling them; for a man enjoys even suffering when it is over'); cf. *Od.* 23.301–8.

refreshment and enjoyment from poetry, but also knowledge of their own condition and so ability to live with it better.

The poetics implicit in Homer himself, rather than any preconceived notions of 'oral' or 'heroic' poetry, should guide our reading of his work. The *Iliad* is concerned with battle and with men whose life is devoted to winning glory in battle; and it represents with wonder their strength and courage. But its deepest purpose is not to glorify them, and still less to glorify war itself. What war represents for Homer is humanity under duress and in the face of death;[1] and so to enjoy or appreciate the *Iliad* is to understand and feel for human suffering. The greatest of all critics of poetry rightly called Homer 'the path-finder of tragedy' (*Republic* 598d).[2]

2. BOOK 24 AND THE SPIRIT OF THE ILIAD

To some critics it has seemed that the spirit of compassion which works upon both gods and men in *Il.* 24 and pervades its poetry was a reason for denying that it belonged to the original design of the poem. But if the description of suffering and the evocation of pity are the very essence of poetry as Homer conceives it, then Book 24 is a proper complement and conclusion to the rest. To illustrate a little further how it is that, I consider (i) two major episodes from earlier in the *Iliad* in connection with Book 24 and (ii) the main events of Book 24 in relation to the body of the poem.

(i) (*a*) The meeting of Hector with Andromache in Book 6[3] is one of the chief pillars which uphold the edifice of the *Iliad* (cf. 723–76 n.), and it embodies something essential to the spirit of the poem. Hector and Andromache can foresee his death and the fall of Troy: they live in the consciousness of their doom. But Hector's premonitions and his love for his wife and son do not stop him returning to battle; for his

---

[1] See further 3 (i), p. 22 n. 2.

[2] Cf. 595c. For the view of Greek tragedy implied here, and an excellent exegesis of Gorgias, *Helen* 9, cf. O. Taplin, *Greek tragedy in action* (London 1978) 159–71; also Vickers, *passim*.

[3] On this episode and the contrast between Achilles and Hector cf. Schadewaldt, *HWW* 207–33, 257–63.

personal honour and his role as defender of the city require him to fight
(6.441–6). In Book 22, as he resolves to stand against Achilles, the same
motives find even more tragic expression: because in Book 18 he refused
Polydamas' advice to lead the Trojans back into the city, he must now
cover the shame that he feels for that act of folly with a hero's death;
but thus he seals the fate of Troy whose only saviour he is. So he can
only pity his wife, and the words which lovingly echo her appeal to him
are also an expression of helplessness:

> ἀλλ' οὔ μοι Τρώων τόσσον μέλει ἄλγος ὀπίσσω,
> οὔτ' αὐτῆς Ἑκάβης οὔτε Πριάμοιο ἄνακτος
> οὔτε κασιγνήτων, οἵ κεν πολέες τε καὶ ἐσθλοὶ
> ἐν κονίῃσι πέσοιεν ὑπ' ἀνδράσι δυσμενέεσσιν,
> ὅσσον σεῦ, ὅτε κέν τις Ἀχαιῶν χαλκοχιτώνων
> δακρυόεσσαν ἄγηται, ἐλεύθερον ἦμαρ ἀπούρας. (6.450–5)

'But it is not so much the Trojans' future sufferings that matter to
me, or even Hecuba's or King Priam's or my brothers', those brave
men so many of whom have fallen in the dust at the hands of the
enemy, as *you*, when one of the bronze-shirted Greeks will lead you
along in tears, taking away your freedom.'

> Ἕκτορ, ἀτὰρ σύ μοί ἐσσι πατὴρ καὶ πότνια μήτηρ
> ἠδὲ κασίγνητος, σὺ δέ μοι θαλερὸς παρακοίτης. (429–30)

'*You*, Hector, are my father and mother and brother, and *you* are my
young husband.'

> σοὶ δ' αὖ νέον ἔσσεται ἄλγος
> χήτεϊ τοιοῦδ' ἀνδρὸς ἀμύνειν δούλιον ἦμαρ.
> ἀλλά με τεθνηῶτα χυτὴ κατὰ γαῖα καλύπτοι,
> πρίν γέ τι σῆς τε βοῆς σοῦ θ' ἑλκηθμοῖο πυθέσθαι. (462–5)

'And for you it will be fresh suffering, with such a husband lost, to
face slavery. I pray that the earth may be heaped over me before
I hear of *you* crying for help, *you* being dragged off.'

> ...ἔμ' ἄμμορον, ἦ τάχα χήρη
> σεῦ ἔσομαι· τάχα γάρ σε κατακτενέουσιν Ἀχαιοὶ
> πάντες ἐφορμηθέντες· ἐμοὶ δέ κε κέρδιον εἴη
> σεῦ ἀφαμαρτούσῃ χθόνα δύμεναι. (408–11)

'I, poor wretch, shall soon be bereft of *you*; for soon the Greeks will all rush upon you and kill you. It will be better for me, when I have lost *you*, to go under the earth.'

Likewise, his prayer for his son, that he should be another and better warrior (476–81), is that of a hero, and of a man who is doomed together with his family. At the same time as Hector voices the imperatives of his ethics, he fulfils a necessity: Troy must fall, and his sense of honour will help to cause its fall; and his son will not in fact live to realize his father's hopes. Almost to the last he vainly tries to turn his eyes away from this destiny; he prays that he will be dead and insensible before his wife is taken into captivity and that his son will bring her joy (6.464–5, 480–1); he hopes to drive away the Greeks for good (8.527–9) and to slay Achilles (16.860–1; 18.305–9); he dreams, when he finally meets him, that he might obtain mercy from his implacable enemy (22.111–20).

From Book 18 onwards, Achilles is more fully and calmly aware than Hector of his future. The fantasy of escape he had toyed with in Book 9 (356ff.) is a thing of the past, and unlike Hector when he goes out to succeed in battle he is fully aware of his coming death: contrast 19.420–1 (Achilles to his horse):

> Ξάνθε, τί μοι θάνατον μαντεύεαι; οὐδέ τί σε χρή.
> εὖ νυ τὸ οἶδα καὶ αὐτὸς ὅ μοι μόρος ἐνθάδ' ὀλέσθαι

'Xanthus, why do you prophesy my death? There is no need; I know full well myself that I am doomed to die here'

with 16.859–61 (Hector to the dying Patroclus):

> Πατρόκλεις, τί νύ μοι μαντεύεαι αἰπὺν ὄλεθρον;
> τίς δ' οἶδ' εἴ κ' Ἀχιλεύς, Θέτιδος πάϊς ἠϋκόμοιο,
> φθήῃ ἐμῷ ὑπὸ δουρὶ τυπεὶς ἀπὸ θυμὸν ὀλέσσαι;

'Patroclus, why do you prophesy my sudden destruction? Who knows but Achilles, son of fair-tressed Thetis, may not first lose his life struck by my spear?'

He sees, moreover, the universal law that no one can escape suffering; and in the light of this understanding he pities and consoles Priam.

But for all his insight and fellow-feeling he does not protect his own
father or spare Priam's children:

> ...οὐδέ νυ τόν γε
> γηράσκοντα κομίζω, ἐπεὶ μάλα τηλόθι πάτρης
> ἧμαι ἐνὶ Τροίῃ, σέ τε κήδων ἠδὲ σὰ τέκνα. (24.540–2)

'...and I do not care for him [i.e. Peleus] in his old age, because I
am sitting in Troy, far from my homeland, bringing trouble and grief
to you and your children.'

Achilles lives out a necessity: the warrior suffers in being the cause of
suffering, and he must die young, and far from home and parents, like
those he kills. Achilles is helpless, as Hector was in Book 6; but first in
facing his death with clear foreknowledge, and then in ignoring the 'last
infirmities of noble mind', renown and revenge, he comes here to a
deeper consciousness of the human condition.

(b) Again in Book 6, Glaucus and Diomede meet on the field of
battle.[1] Diomede challenges the other to tell him if he is a man or a
god. Glaucus replies in a long speech which tells the story of his
grandfather Bellerophon; the two men thus discover that they are ξεῖνοι
πατρῷοι (i.e. Bellerophon received hospitality from Diomede's
grandfather, Oeneus, and exchanged gifts with him), and so they part
in peace after each has presented the other with his armour. Glaucus'
speech is far more than an amiably discursive account of his ancestry.
For the tale of Bellerophon sums up the relation of man to the gods.
Bellerophon was the descendant of a god; the gods gave him beauty
and valour, and they helped him through dangers and difficulties to
gain glory and prosperity as the conqueror of the Chimera and the
Solymi, and as the son-in-law of Proetus. But all that changed:

> ἀλλ᾽ ὅτε δὴ καὶ κεῖνος[2] ἀπήχθετο πᾶσι θεοῖσιν,
> ἤτοι ὁ κὰπ πεδίον τὸ Ἀλήϊον οἶος ἀλᾶτο,
> ὃν θυμὸν κατέδων, πάτον ἀνθρώπων ἀλεείνων·
> Ἴσανδρον δέ οἱ υἱὸν Ἄρης ἆτος πολέμοιο
> μαρνάμενον Σολύμοισι κατέκτανε κυδαλίμοισι·
> τὴν δὲ χολωσαμένη χρυσήνιος Ἄρτεμις ἔκτα. (200–5)

[1] On this episode cf. Andersen 96–107.
[2] I.e. like Lycurgus (cf. 140 ἐπεὶ ἀθανάτοισιν ἀπήχθετο πᾶσι θεοῖσιν), but also like
men in general.

'But when he too fell foul of the gods, then he wandered lonely over the Aleian plain, eating his heart out, shunning the paths of men; and his son Isandros, as he fought against the famous Solymi, was killed by Ares, the insatiable warrior, and his daughter by Artemis of the golden reins.'

By now it is clear that the opening of Glaucus' speech was no mere fanfare; rather it appropriately leads into the account of human life, aware of suffering and death and infused with pity, which is contained in the story of Bellerophon:

> Τυδεΐδη μεγάθυμε, τίη γενεὴν ἐρεείνεις;
> οἵη περ φύλλων γενεή, τοίη δὲ καὶ ἀνδρῶν.
> φύλλα τὰ μέν τ' ἄνεμος χαμάδις χέει, ἄλλα δέ θ' ὕλη
> τηλεθόωσα φύει, ἔαρος δ' ἐπιγίγνεται ὥρη·
> ὡς ἀνδρῶν γενεὴ ἡ. μὲν φύει ἡ δ' ἀπολήγει. (145–9)

'Great-hearted son of Tydeus, why do you ask what is my lineage? The generations of men are like leaves: the wind scatters the leaves to the ground, and the flourishing wood makes others grow when the beauty of spring follows. So one generation of men grows up and another ceases.'

This is, moreover, a complement to the proud conclusion of the speech (207–10): Glaucus goes to win glory in battle and do credit to his ancestors precisely because he knows human life is short and insecure (cf. Sarpedon in 12.322–8).

The whole episode is also fully appropriate in its larger context. This is the end of Diomede's *aristeia*, the section in which he is the prominent and triumphant warrior. At the beginning of the *aristeia* Athena gave him special powers and permission to fight Aphrodite (5.1–8, 121–32); later she encourages and enables him to fight Ares (5.825–34); and he discomfits both the goddess and the god. But warning voices are also heard. Dione, as she consoles her wounded daughter Aphrodite, hangs threats and admonitions over the Greek hero (5. 405–15);[1] and when

---

[1] Later myths about Diomede do not present anything that corresponds to Dione's premonitions. It looks, indeed, as if Homer were being deliberately vague; but her words are no less effective for that, since they indicate a general truth about the relation of man to the gods. (They also express a helpless mother's hostility to one who has harmed her daughter.)

he attacks Aeneas, although he knows that Apollo is protecting his adversary, the god thrusts him back with the words (5.440–2)

> φράζεο, Τυδείδη, καὶ χάζεο, μηδὲ θεοῖσιν
> ἶσ' ἔθελε φρονέειν, ἐπεὶ οὔ ποτε φῦλον ὁμοῖον
> ἀθανάτων τε θεῶν χαμαὶ ἐρχομένων τ' ἀνθρώπων.

'Beware, son of Tydeus, and withdraw. Do not try to share the gods' pride; for the race of immortal gods and the race of earth-bound men cannot be equal.'

Diomede himself, when he sees that Hector is accompanied by Ares, retires and tells the Greeks to do likewise (5.600 – 6). Finally, in his own speech to Glaucus (6.123–43), he is anxious not to do battle with a god, and tells the cautionary tale of Lycurgus who was blinded for the injuries he did to Dionysus. So the hero's *aristeia* is ultimately designed to remind him and us that men are less than the gods, and that divine favour, whatever glory it may give to an individual, never removes him from the common condition.[1] This thought is vividly represented, with a touch of dry humour, at the end of the episode. Glaucus exchanges his armour, which is golden, for Diomede's, which is of bronze, because 'Zeus took away his wits' (234). The gods, as ever, prevail over human wishes or calculations.

In Book 24 the gods give honour to both Hector and Achilles; but they have let Hector die, they will let Achilles die, and soon they will let Troy fall. This is, for Homer, a typical piece of human history, and indeed Achilles, explaining Priam's troubles to the old man and knowing his own end is not far off, tells how human beings can never avoid some portion of suffering, and are always subject to the gods (525–51): ἀλλ' ἐπὶ καὶ τῷ θῆκε θεὸς κακόν (24.538) corresponds to ἀλλ' ὅτε δὴ καὶ κεῖνος ἀπήχθετο πᾶσι θεοῖσιν (6.200). Here, as in the speeches of Glaucus and Diomede, there is endurance and sadness, but no bitterness, no railing or cringing: the passage displays in fact a virtue often denied to the archaic Greeks, humility. This is also the fullest and deepest expression in words of Achilles' pity for the suppliant; for pity, as Homer and the Greeks represent it, is a sense of shared human

---

[1] Similarly, the deception of Zeus, which has in common with Book 5 a humorous irreverence in its portrayal of the gods, including the supreme god, ends in a reinforced affirmation of Zeus's authority (15.4ff.).

weakness. And it is pity which is at the heart of Homer's conception of poetry.[1]

(ii) The plot of Book 24 may be roughly divided into three parts: (a) the gods show pity, (b) a man accepts a supplication, (c) a lament and burial are achieved. All these three actions contrast with what the poem has represented to us up till now.

(a) In the course of the *Iliad* single gods sometimes feel pity for the men they love or save their lives in moments of danger. But as a group, the gods are set apart from human beings and even, in the last analysis, indifferent to them. So Hephaestus can say, in reconciling Zeus and Hera (1.573–6)

ᾗ δὴ λοίγια ἔργα τάδ' ἔσσεται οὐδ' ἔτ' ἀνεκτά,
εἰ δὴ σφὼ ἕνεκα θνητῶν ἐριδαίνετον ὧδε,
ἐν δὲ θεοῖσι κολῳὸν ἐλαύνετον· οὐδέ τι δαιτὸς
ἐσθλῆς ἔσσεται ἦδος, ἐπεὶ τὰ χερείονα νικᾷ.

'It will be an intolerable plague if for mortals' sake you two quarrel in this way and stir up wrangling among the gods. There will be no joy in our noble banquets when such base behaviour prevails.'

Or Apollo in making peace with Poseidon (21.462–7)

ἐννοσίγαι', οὐκ ἄν με σαόφρονα μυθήσαιο
ἔμμεναι, εἰ δὴ σοί γε βροτῶν ἕνεκα πτολεμίξω
δειλῶν, οἳ φύλλοισιν ἐοικότες ἄλλοτε μέν τε
ζαφλεγέες τελέθουσιν, ἀρούρης καρπὸν ἔδοντες,
ἄλλοτε δὲ φθινύθουσιν ἀκήριοι. ἀλλὰ τάχιστα
παυώμεσθα μάχης· οἱ δ' αὐτοὶ δηριαάσθων.

'Earth-shaker, you should not call me sane if I do battle with you for the sake of men, those poor wretches who, like leaves, for a time shine brightly, when they eat the fruits of the earth, and then wither away lifeless. Let us stop fighting at once; let *them* have strife.'

If they pity at all the human condition as such, it is with the feelings of a detached observer. Thus when Zeus addresses the horses of Achilles,

---

[1] A valuable study of pity in Homer is W. Burkert, *Zum altgriechischen Mitleidsbegriff* (Diss. Erlangen 1955), which deserves to be better known than it seems to be.

the sympathy goes to them, who are immortal, rather than to mankind
(17.443-7)

> ἆ δειλώ, τί σφῶϊ δόμεν Πηλῆϊ ἄνακτι
> θνητῷ, ὑμεῖς δ' ἐστὸν ἀγήρω τ' ἀθανάτω τε;
> ἦ ἵνα δυστήνοισι μετ' ἀνδράσιν ἄλγε' ἔχητον;
> οὐ μὲν γάρ τί πού ἐστιν ὀϊζυρώτερον ἀνδρὸς
> πάντων ὅσσα τε γαῖαν ἔπι πνείει τε καὶ ἕρπει.

'Ah poor wretches, why did I give you to king Peleus, a mortal, when
you are ageless and immortal? To let you share the troubles of
unhappy mankind? For all the creatures that breathe and walk
upon the earth there is none more miserable than man.'

Moreover, the implacable hatred of Hera and Athena for Troy will be
allowed to run its course: the city and its inhabitants that Zeus loves
will be destroyed.[1]

None of this is in any way taken back in Book 24; and yet there the
gods briefly appear as what they are throughout the *Odyssey*, the
guarantors of justice and kindness among mortals. In the rest of the *Iliad*
when the gods come (more or less reluctantly) to an agreement, men
suffer. By imposing his will in Books 1 and 8 Zeus creates the 'ten
thousand woes for the Greeks'. Sarpedon in Book 16 and Hector in Book
22 are not spared, because the gods as a group disapprove of Zeus's
tinkering with fate, and he complies. But in Book 24, by agreeing, the
gods cause Priam's supplication to be accepted and show the favour
due to Hector for his piety after, if not before, his death. There is then,
it finally emerges, some measure of justice or kindness in Zeus and the
gods; but it remains true that they are also the heedless dispensers of
misfortune to men (525-48). If this is a contradiction, then Homer's
gods are no more nor less contradictory than human life, in which such
values and such facts are both alike real and present. And on the level
of human morality the two aspects of the gods' character are
complementary: whether it is the gods' will that men pity and respect
each other, or whether men live together in subjection to gods who deal
out good and evil at their inscrutable pleasure, in either case men cannot
afford to be cruel or indifferent among themselves.

(*b*) Several times in the *Iliad* a supplication is either made or

[1] Griffin, chs. 3, 5, 6, deals admirably with the Iliadic gods. My only reservation
is that he does not do justice to Book 24.

attempted on the battle-field.[1] It is always rejected or cut short, and the suppliant despatched to his death. Such mercilessness is a feature of war which Homer deliberately stresses (cf. 751–3 n.). In Book 24 a supplication is accepted. And this act is far more than the fulfilment of a conventional duty; for the values of humanity and fellow-feeling implicit in the convention are fully and profoundly represented in the scene between Achilles and Priam.[2]

(c) Loss of burial is one of the 'sufferings' singled out in the proem to the *Iliad*. In the course of the work, heroes again and again say in taunting their opponents, that they will not be lamented or buried;[3] and it is assumed that anyone who dies on the battlefield will be a prey for dogs and birds.[4] In this respect too, Homer designedly represents war as harsh and implacable. The truce in Book 7 in which both sides recover their corpses is an exceptional interlude, a foil for the bulk of the poem like Book 23 (see 3 (ii) and (iii)(a) below). In Book 24 Hector's body is recovered; and it concludes with a lament and burial. Once again, a brief interval in which the civilized rites of peace are performed.

Iliad 24 is not a happy ending. The conclusion of the poem is overshadowed by the coming death of Achilles and fall of Troy; and it constitutes only a slight break in the war. But the *Iliad* is great not least because it can speak authentically for pity or kindness or civilization without showing them victorious in life. Its humanity does not float on shallow optimism; it is firmly and deeply rooted in an awareness of human reality and suffering.

3. BOOK 24 IN THE STRUCTURE OF THE ILIAD[5]

Like the other parts of the *Iliad*, Book 24 has many significant connections with the rest of the poem. Some of these may be treated

[1] See 6.45ff.; 10.454ff.; 11.130ff.; 20.463ff.; 21.64ff., 115ff.; 22.338ff.

[2] See further 3 (i) (*b*) and (iii) (*d*) below. Cf. Deichgräber 98–9. On the meaning of supplication in Homer and tragedy, see Vickers, ch. 8.

[3] 4.237; 8.379–80; 11.395, 453–4; 13.831–2; 16.836; 22.335–6, 354.

[4] See 2.393; 11.818; 17.241, 558; 18.271, 283; 22.89, 509. Corpses are, of course, sometimes saved, e.g. Patroclus'; cf., besides Book 7, 13.194; 19.228.

[5] In this section I am much indebted to Beck 42–102, which is by far the best treatment of this matter. Note that I have pursued one or two minor points

under three headings: (i) Book 24 as the completion of the story, (ii) Books 23 and 24 as complementary conclusions to the *Iliad*, (iii) echoes of Books 1, 2 and 9 in Book 24.

(i) (*a*) In 23.184–91 Aphrodite and Apollo protect Hector's body. Aphrodite keeps away the dogs and anoints it 'so that he (Achilles) should not lacerate it as he dragged it about' (187); and Apollo covers the place where it lies with a cloud so that the sun should not shrivel up his flesh 'before' (πρίν 190).[1] Line 187, if it may stand, looks forward to the dragging in Book 24 and is echoed in 24.21. So explicit and yet so brief an anticipation is surprising; and the purpose of the anointing might more naturally be to clean the body (cf. 14.170–2) and preserve it from worms or insects (cf. 19.38–9; 24.414–15). But even if we delete 187, the 'before' of line 190 must imply 'before Hector was buried' and thus points forward to Book 24. Now 23.184–91 are closely linked to the threat of Achilles which precedes them:

> χαῖρέ μοι, ὦ Πάτροκλε, καὶ εἰν Ἀΐδαο δόμοισι·
> πάντα γὰρ ἤδη τοι τελέω τὰ πάροιθεν ὑπέστην.
> δώδεκα μὲν Τρώων μεγαθύμων υἱέας ἐσθλούς,
> τοὺς ἅμα σοὶ πάντας πῦρ ἐσθίει· Ἕκτορα δ' οὔ τι
> δώσω Πριαμίδην πυρὶ δαπτέμεν, ἀλλὰ κύνεσσιν. (179–83)

'Hail, Patroclus, though you are in the house of Hades. Now I am fulfilling all that I promised you before. As for the twelve brave sons of the great-hearted Trojans, the fire is consuming all of them with you. But Hector, son of Priam, I shall give not to the fire to devour, but to the dogs.'

These words are countered by 184–5:

> ὣς φάτ' ἀπειλήσας· τὸν δ' οὐ κύνες ἀμφεπένοντο,
> ἀλλὰ κύνας μὲν ἄλαλκε Διὸς θυγατὴρ Ἀφροδίτη...

further in the commentary on the relevant passages from Book 24. I have not always given references to these in order not to overload the reader with detail.

[1] On the elliptical use of πρίν, see 800 n. In general, cf. *Od.* 23.138–9 πρίν γ' ἡμέας ἐλθέμεν ἔξω | ἀγρὸν ἐς ἡμέτερον πολυδένδρεον. That passage, like *Il.* 23.190, prepares allusively at a late stage in the poem for its conclusion, the visit to Laertes and the settlement with the suitors' kinsmen.

Such were his threats; but the dogs did not do their work on Hector; Zeus's daughter Aphrodite kept them off...

Further, in 23.179–83 Achilles says he is fulfilling the promises he had made to his dead friend in 18.333–7 (cf. 21.27–8; 23.19–23). So the moment at which Achilles declares that he is paying his debt to Patroclus by leaving Hector to the dogs is so narrated that it looks ahead to Book 24 where Hector receives the funeral owing to him. It is also striking that the promises of Book 18 have in one respect been modified: there Achilles said he would bring back Hector's 'arms and head' (τεύχεα καὶ κεφαλήν), in other words threatens to cut off Hector's head as Hector had threatened to cut off Patroclus' (17.125–7; 18.175–7). That threat is dropped, and the poet's reason for dropping it is clearly that a decapitated body could not be given back for burial.[1]

The poetic force of this passage lies in the contrast between the burial accomplished and the burial withheld, which is the more intense because the disrespect for Hector is a kind of tribute to Patroclus. That contrast is announced in Achilles' words to his dying enemy (22.335–6):

... σὲ μὲν κύνες ἠδ' οἰωνοὶ
ἑλκήσουσ' ἀϊκῶς, τὸν δὲ κτεριοῦσιν 'Αχαιοί.

'...the dogs and birds will savage *you* vilely; but the Greeks will give *him* a funeral.'

It continues when Achilles' decision to return and bury Patroclus is immediately followed by his dragging Hector back to his tent (22.385–404), when in his lament for his friend he includes his evil intentions against his dead enemy (23.17–26), and when he drags Hector's body round Patroclus' tomb (24.14–18). But the contrast is due to be resolved, as it is in Book 24, above all when Achilles asks Patroclus to accept the release of Hector's body (592–5); and 23.184–91 hint at the coming resolution.

It might be asked why Apollo and Aphrodite do not act when Achilles first drags Hector in Book 22. That would have undone the powerful transition from the defilement of Hector's head to his mother's

---

[1] Cf. Schadewaldt, *HWW* 344 n. 1. Note also how much is made of the head in 22.401–5 (quoted below).

tearing her hair – the mourner's response imitates the death itself (401–9):[1]

> τοῦ δ' ἦν ἑλκομένοιο κονίσαλος, ἀμφὶ δὲ χαῖται
> κυάνεαι πίτναντο, κάρη δ' ἅπαν ἐν κονίῃσι
> κεῖτο πάρος χαρίεν· τότε δὲ Ζεὺς δυσμενέεσσι
> δῶκεν ἀεικίσσασθαι ἑῇ ἐν πατρίδι γαίῃ.
>
> Ὣς τοῦ μὲν κεκόνιτο κάρη ἅπαν· ἡ δέ νυ μήτηρ
> τίλλε κόμην, ἀπὸ δὲ λιπαρὴν ἔρριψε καλύπτρην
> τηλόσε, κώκυσεν δὲ μάλα μέγα παῖδ' ἐσιδοῦσα·
> ᾤμωξεν δ' ἐλεεινὰ πατὴρ φίλος, ἀμφὶ δὲ λαοὶ
> κωκυτῷ τ' εἴχοντο καὶ οἰμωγῇ κατὰ ἄστυ.

The dust rose as he was dragged; his dark hair was spread out and his whole head, once beautiful, lay in the dust; but now Zeus had given it to enemies to dishonour in his own homeland. Thus his whole head was covered in dust; and his mother tore her hair, and threw her veil away and wailed loudly as she saw her son. And his father groaned pitifully and the people around were seized by wailing and groaning in the city.

In time the gods will look after Hector's body, as they did Patroclus' (17.268–73) and Sarpedon's (16.666–83), whose deaths are parallel to Hector's in other respects too. But here the corpse is first degraded; and thus Zeus's aloofness is set against the violent grief of Hector's family and people. To begin with, the horror of the death is unmitigated. But Aphrodite and Apollo are appropriately introduced in Book 23 when their action counters Achilles' attempt to go on insulting Hector, and this prepares for Book 24 when all the gods agree to let the corpse be ransomed.

(b) 22.337–54 are also a kind of preparation for Book 24. There Hector begs Achilles to return his corpse, promising that his parents will give 'bronze and gold' as a ransom, and Achilles fiercely rejects the request. Then Hector prophesies Achilles' death:

> φράζεο νῦν, μή τοί τι θεῶν μήνιμα γένωμαι
> ἤματι τῷ ὅτε κέν σε Πάρις καὶ Φοῖβος Ἀπόλλων
> ἐσθλὸν ἐόντ' ὀλέσωσιν ἐνὶ Σκαίῃσι πύλῃσιν. (358–60)

'Mind I do not become a cause of the gods' wrath against you on

[1] Cf. 1, p. 4, n. 1 above on *Od.* 8.523–4.

the day when Paris and Phoebus Apollo kill you, great warrior
though you are, at the Scaean gates.'

This episode has some features which are unique in the battle-scenes
of the *Iliad*. A ransom is offered whenever someone begs to be taken
alive, and heroes often threaten their enemies with loss of burial (see
2 (ii) (*b*) and (*c*) above); but only here is it suggested that a dead body
might be ransomed,[1] and only here will the hero be seen to enact his
threat. Further, only here is there any question of the gods being
angered if a corpse is left as carrion.[2] Hector's unburied body is thus
thrust upon us as a narrative and a moral problem, a problem
heightened by the contrast with Patroclus'. As such, it awaits a solution.

The solution comes about through a reversal. Achilles threatens 'no
one will keep the dogs away (ἀπαλάλκοι) from your body' (22.348);
but someone does (23.185 ἄλαλκε... 'Αφροδίτη).[3] Achilles proclaims
that he will never let the body be buried in return for gifts; but he does.
Conversely, Hector's prophecy comes true in a way that he did not
mean. The gods' resentment is indeed aroused (24.113, 134; cf. 53-4),
but it is also placated. The reversal is prefigured in Book 9. The words
with which Achilles refuses Agamemnon's and Hector's offers are
designedly similar:

> οὐδ' εἴ μοι δεκάκις τε καὶ εἰκοσάκις τόσα δοίη
> ὅσσα τέ οἱ νῦν ἔστι, καὶ εἴ ποθεν ἄλλα γένοιτο,...
> οὐδ' εἴ μοι τόσα δοίη ὅσα ψάμαθός τε κόνις τε,

---

[1] The unusual motif is stressed by repetition: in 254-8 Hector offered a pact
by which the winner of the duel would return the body of the loser (cf. 7.76-91).

[2] See further 54 n. Similarly, heroes often despoil their enemies' corpses, but
only when Hector takes Patroclus' armour (17.200-6) is it suggested that there
was something amiss: that this represents civilized feeling is clear from 6.417
when Achilles is said not to have despoiled Eetion because religious scruples
restrained him. These are not anomalies or inconsistencies, since throughout
the poem what happens in battle is implicitly grim and disturbing; the
disturbance is only made explicit when what the victor does has important
consequences in the narrative.

[3] Cf. C. Segal, *The theme of the mutilation of the corpse in the Iliad* (Leiden 1971)
55. Hecuba's words in 22.88-9 ('the swift dogs will eat you, far from us, by
the Greek ships') and Andromache's in 22.508-9 ('... the worms will eat you,
far from your parents, by the beaked ships when the dogs have had their fill')
are thus also reversed. So is Andromache's assumption that Hector's body will
never lie in fine clothing (22.510-14).

οὐδέ κεν ὥς ἔτι θυμὸν ἐμὸν πείσει' Ἀγαμέμνων,
πρίν γ' ἀπὸ πᾶσαν ἐμοὶ δόμεναι θυμαλγέα λώβην. (9.379–87)

'Not if he offered me ten and twenty times as many goods as he now
has, and more, if he could find them...not if he offered me as many
as there are grains of sand or specks of dust, not even then would
Agamemnon persuade me – until he has paid back in full to me that
rankling insult.'

οὐδ' εἴ κεν δεκάκις τε καὶ εἰκοσινήριτ' ἄποινα
στήσωσ' ἐνθάδ' ἄγοντες, ὑπόσχωνται δὲ καὶ ἄλλα,
οὐδ' εἴ κέν σ' αὐτὸν χρυσῷ ἐρύσασθαι ἀνώγοι
Δαρδανίδης Πρίαμος· οὐδ' ὥς σέ γε πότνια μήτηρ
ἐνθεμένη λεχέεσσι γοήσεται, ὃν τέκεν αὐτή,
ἀλλὰ κύνες τε καὶ οἰωνοὶ κατὰ πάντα δάσονται. (22.349–54)

'Not if they came and put before me ten- and twenty-fold compensation and promised more, not if Priam ordered your body to be
weighed out in gold, not even then will your mother lay you on the
bier and give you a lament; but the dogs and birds will devour you
entirely.'

The rejection of Book 9 is withdrawn in Book 19, that of Book 22 in
Book 24. The theme of the wrath of Achilles is extended from the
quarrel with Agamemnon to the vengeance for Patroclus;[1] and as the
first wrath came to an end, so must the second. Nor would Hector's
death be enough to extinguish it. If it is to come to an end, then it
must first be represented as unyielding and horrifying; otherwise the
story would lack shape or point or grandeur. Hence the description of
how Achilles insulted, in words and in deed, his dead enemy goes well
beyond what we read elsewhere in the poem; and it begins where he
refuses to think of accepting a ransom.

(c) In 22.412–28[2] Priam, having seen the dead Hector, begs the
mourning Trojans to let him leave the city and go to supplicate Achilles.
There they hold him back; but in Book 24 Priam goes, scattering the

[1] For the word χόλος and cognates referring to Achilles' lust for revenge, see
15.68; 18.322; 18.337 = 23.23; 19.16. The Odyssey likewise extends the tale
of its hero's wiles and sufferings beyond his return home, with powerful effect:
cf. 1.18–19; 11.115–17.
[2] On this passage and on reversal ('Umkehr') as a typical pattern of events in
the Iliad, see Reinhardt, ID 468–9 and passim.

mourning citizens from his house (237–48); his speeches in the two contexts – the first pathetically begging, the second harshly authoritative – stand in vivid contrast. In Book 22 the thought of going alone (416) is merely a man's desperate impulse; in Book 24 Priam takes gifts, as Zeus commanded, he finds a divine escort, supplied by Zeus, and if he goes alone, that is Zeus's will (148, 177). The earlier passage thus supports in the narrative what Priam says in 24.198–9: 'my own heart's desires tell me to go there'.[1] Further, the argument of his appeal to Achilles, the comparison of himself and Peleus as the old fathers bereft of their only son, is prefigured in 22.420–6: the elaborate speech in Book 24 can thus be seen as a version of his immediate response to his son's death. And if Priam does not exactly follow Hermes' command to invoke Achilles' father and mother and son (467) but confines himself to Peleus, that too is prepared in Book 22: he has already conceived in his own mind the essential form of his appeal. In short, 22.412–28 prepare for Book 24 by setting the motive and the manner of his supplication in the first outburst of his grief.

Here too there is a reversal: the notion that Priam could go and supplicate Achilles, like the notion that Achilles could receive the suppliant, seems absurd in Book 22; it becomes a fact in Book 24. And other reversals go with this one. Like Hector, Priam first envisages a supplication which is never enacted (22.111–30, 414–28). Again like Hector, Priam leaves Troy to meet Achilles 'alone' (22.39; 24.148, 177, 203, 519), risking death; Hecuba tries to prevent both departures. Both men in fact supplicate their enemy. But Priam succeeds where Hector failed. In doing so, he becomes a new kind of hero[2] who shows endurance (24.505–6) and evokes wonder (480–4) not merely by facing death but by humbling himself and curbing his hatred before his greatest enemy. This, like the other reversals in Book 24 and the whole *Iliad*, also brings out the power of the gods. The outcome of things always lies with them; and so even if a man can prophesy truly, he can never foresee with certainty. But they tend to work on what they find in the human heart, impulses or plans or scruples. The poet's way of shaping, and then fulfilling or overturning, expectations reflects this theology.

---

[1] See further 181–7, 198 nn.

[2] On Priam as hero, see 181–7, 328, 629–32 nn. 'Endure' or 'suffer' is also what heroes do: cf. 3.157; 11.317; 14.85–7; 23.607; *Od.* 3.104; 4.243 – for war in Homer is suffering even more than it is action.

(d) If Priam's speech and action in Book 24 are carefully prepared in Book 22, Achilles' complete a development of character – or better, enlargement of experience and comprehension – which stretches through the whole poem. What characterizes him from the beginning is a ferocious pride. Insulted by Agamemnon, he has lost the honour which was to compensate for the brevity of his life (1.352–6 τιμήν...ἔτισεν...ἠτίμησεν), and so Thetis asks Zeus to give it him in a different form (1.503–10 τίμησον...ἠτίμησεν... τῖσον...τίσωσιν...τιμῇ) : what before Achilles won by helping his fellows he will now win through their suffering and death as they miss his presence on the battlefield. He has also the prospect of threefold recompense for the injury done to him (1.212–14). But in Book 9 when he has the chance to win honour from his companions by helping them once more (9.300–6 τίσουσι...κῦδος) and by accepting the gifts (602–5 τίσουσιν...τιμῆς), he refuses. He even questions the point of seeking honour in battle, if merit is not to be rewarded and death comes to everyone alike:

> ἐν δὲ ἰῇ τιμῇ ἠμὲν κακὸς ἠδὲ καὶ ἐσθλός.
> κάτθαν' ὁμῶς ὅ τ' ἀεργὸς ἀνὴρ ὅ τε πολλὰ ἐοργώς. (319–20)

'The coward and the brave get the same honour. The man who achieves nothing and the man who achieves much die alike.'[1]

If in Book 1 he was still in search of honour, here for a moment he turns his back on it altogether, and if there he accepted as a destiny that his life was to be short, here he chooses to live long at home without fame rather than die young at Troy with it (401–20). But it soon becomes clear that he was protesting too much: the rejection of glory was merely the extreme expression of wounded pride. After Phoenix' speech he retorts:

> ...οὔ τί με ταύτης
> χρεὼ τιμῆς· φρονέω δὲ τετιμῆσθαι Διὸς αἴσῃ,
> ἥ μ' ἕξει παρὰ νηυσὶ κορωνίσιν, εἰς ὅ κ' ἀϋτμὴ
> ἐν στήθεσσι μένῃ καί μοι φίλα γούνατ' ὀρώρῃ. (607–10)

---

[1] Contrast Sarpedon in 12.322–8 – a classic statement of the hero's code of honour; for him a warrior must seek glory precisely because life is short and precarious. Contrast also 6.488–9 (Hector to Andromache) 'all men, brave or cowardly, come to their destined end': this is given as a reason for *continuing* to fight.

'I have no need of this honour. I reckon myself honoured by the decree of Zeus,[1] which will keep me by my beaked ships so long as there is breath in my chest and movement in my knees.'

Originally the honour from Zeus was designed to bring increased honour from men, when Achilles returned to battle. Here it is an end in itself. Achilles will salve his self-esteem simply by watching the Greeks' discomfiture. Nonetheless, these words also mark a retreat: he will not abandon Troy altogether, as he had threatened; and when Ajax invokes the good will of his comrades (φιλότητος ἑταίρων) with which they honoured (ἐτίομεν) him more than anyone else (630–1; cf. 256–8) and urges that the compensation is adequate, Achilles admits that the arguments are satisfactory. So while re-affirming his resolve he retreats a step further: he will rejoin the battle, but only when Hector reaches the Myrmidon's camp and burns up the Greek ships (644–55). In Book 9, then, Achilles reinforces his resentment and insists on his own honour at his companions' expense; at the same time he comes to a point where his return to battle is more clearly envisaged than it had been in Book 1 (240–4).[2] In Book 16 he is again moved when Patroclus, like Ajax, begs him to use his valour on his comrades' behalf; again, though he seems almost ready to renounce it (60–1),[3] he clings to his anger.[4] The result of this mental conflict is that he lets his friend enter the battle to save the Greek ships from destruction. In order not to diminish his own honour (84–90 τιμήν...κῦδος...ἀτιμότερον) he tells Patroclus to do no more than that: this shows still more clearly that he is thinking of coming back to war himself; and his speech ends with the wild and wonderful fantasy of the two of them sacking Troy alone after all the

[1] This is a riposte to Agamemnon's words in 1.174–5: 'I have others who will honour me, above all Zeus.' In the meantime Agamemnon has had to recognize that it is Achilles whom Zeus is favouring (9.116–18), while he himself is the god's victim (2.375–6; 9.17–22).

[2] Cf. D. Motzkus, *Untersuchungen zum neunten Buch der Ilias unter besonderer Berücksichtigung der Phoenixgestalt* (Diss. Hamburg 1964) 116–19. This work also makes it very clear why Phoenix cannot be eliminated from Book 9. (See also Reinhardt, *ID* 212–42.)

[3] The same phrase he uses here, ἀλλὰ τὰ μὲν προτετύχθαι ἐάσομεν ('but let that be...'), recurs in 18.112 when he really does give up his quarrel.

[4] It has often been thought that this speech, like the one in 11.608–15, is incompatible with the Embassy of Book 9, because Achilles ignores it. For a lucid and thorough refutation of that view see Motzkus 120–33.

Greeks and Trojans have died.[1] Throughout this series of events, Achilles is motivated by pride: the dramatic tension and the moral problem lie in the struggle between an egoistic and damaging pride which means withholding help from the Achaeans and a more public-spirited one which would mean returning to war.

This conflict is resolved, abruptly and unexpectedly, in Book 18. As Thetis points out (74–7), he has got what he asked for in Book 1 (407–12): the Greeks are indeed in a desperate condition. But now he has let Patroclus and many others die: the loss of his dearest and most honoured comrade – Πάτροκλος, τὸν ἐγὼ περὶ πάντων τῖον ἑταίρων (18.81; cf. 17.655 etc.) – is the appropriate price to pay for the harm he brought his comrades as a whole. So if in Book 9 he had almost decided to prolong his life because it seemed pointless to seek renown in battle if he could not keep his own prize, here he is ready to throw away a life which seems pointless because he failed his companion:

> αὐτίκα τεθναίην, ἐπεὶ οὐκ ἄρ' ἔμελλον ἑταίρῳ
> κτεινομένῳ ἐπαμῦναι... (18.98–9)

'Let me die at once, since I could not save my friend from death...'

But this time his sense of futility is overcome in action: he must go and avenge Patroclus, although he knows he will die soon after killing Hector (115; cf. 96). And now that he has something to fight for, he is ready to win glory again as a fighter in the face of death:

> ὣς καὶ ἐγών, εἰ δή μοι ὁμοίη μοῖρα τέτυκται,
> κείσομ' ἐπεί κε θάνω· νῦν δὲ κλέος ἐσθλὸν ἀροίμην,
> καί τινα Τρωϊάδων καὶ Δαρδανίδων βαθυκόλπων
> ἀμφοτέρησιν χερσὶ παρειάων ἀπαλάων
> δάκρυ' ὀμορξαμένην ἁδινὸν στοναχῆσαι ἐφείην... (18.120–4)

'I too, since my fate is the same [as Heracles'], shall lie dead when

[1] This passage aroused a flurry of objections in antiquity (see the scholia). It is rightly vindicated by U. von Wilamowitz, *Die Ilias und Homer* (Berlin 1916) 121–3; J. Th. Kakridis, *Gymnasium* 78 (1971) 507–11. It is also paralleled in Diomede's words at 9.46–9 ('let all the Greeks go home; Sthenelus and I will fight till we make an end of Troy') – one of many ways in which Diomede corresponds to Achilles and stands in for him in the earlier part of the *Iliad*: cf. Andersen 10. And elsewhere too in the *Iliad* words which on their first appearance have no tragic consequences are later echoed with overtones of doom (e.g. 5.436–42 and 16.702–9; 11.362–7 and 20.449–54).

my time has come; but now let me win glory, and make the Trojan
women, wiping the tears from their soft cheeks with both hands, wail
loudly...'

At this point, then, Achilles rejoins the community of warriors as its
avenger,[1] and his pride is no longer a reason for isolation but for
participation.

In the following books Achilles' aim is revenge; he is bent on
destroying the enemy and deaf to all thoughts of mercy – Patroclus has
died, he himself must die, why should the Trojans live (21.99–113;
22.261–72)? But in Book 24 he has to outlive that purpose. This is partly
because of Zeus's command; but Achilles in accepting Priam's
supplication, like Priam in coming to make it, is not only obedient to
the god. The old man's speech awakens his grief for Patroclus (511–12),
and this is natural, since Achilles' love for his friend is compared to a
father's for his son (23.222–5) and since Patroclus is to him what Hector
is to Priam, closest to his heart and uppermost in his mind.[2] There is
still a danger that if Priam reacted to the sight of Hector's body Achilles'
savagery might be aroused (583–6); and he never mentions Patroclus
in front of Priam, just as he avoids being together with the old man
in the presence of the corpse. But Achilles' love for his friend is one
source of his sympathy for Priam, no longer just a cause for hatred and
rage against the Trojans. Thus his speech shows that he has in fact done
what Apollo blamed him for not doing (24.39–54): after weeping for
his friend, he has learned to live with his grief by seeing that it is not
unique and to set aside his lust for revenge.

More prominent than Patroclus in the actual words of the two men
is Peleus. Priam's speech makes Achilles think of his own father and
so enables him to feel pity for the Trojan father too. At the same time
the thought of Peleus puts his own life in a different light (538–42). If
in Book 18 he was eager to win renown by bringing death to the Trojans
and sorrow to their women, here he associates the suffering he causes
Priam and his sons with his failure to care for his father's old age; and
if in 18 he could overcome the sense that his life had been wasted by

[1] The vengeance is not only for Patroclus: cf. 19.203–5; 21.134; 22.272. Having
failed ἑταίρῳ | κτεινομένῳ ἐπαμῦναι (18.98–9) he goes τειρομένοις ἑτάροισιν
ἀμυνέμεν (129).
[2] That the two men's griefs are parallel is brought out in detail: see 160, 162–4,
637–42 nn.

going out to fight and kill, here he sees it as wasted because he is only fighting and killing. Again, if in Book 9 it had seemed futile to do battle because his own pride was unsatisfied, here it seems so because of the sorrow he brings to others; and if there and elsewhere he had delighted in the harm he did to his companions, here he is moved by the harm he does to his enemies.[1] Here, as throughout, he knows his own life is soon to end; this knowledge had made him all the more embittered over his injury (1.352 etc.) and all the more implacable before Lycaon and Hector (21.109–13; 22.365–6): here it is simply a part of his feeling for his father. In short, ambition, vindictiveness and resentment all give way to pity. The war will go on, with Achilles taking part; and even now his anger is not far away. But here Achilles is clinging to his kinder, not his fiercer self: contrast

μηκέτι νῦν μ' ἐρέθιζε, γέρον...
τῷ νῦν μή μοι μᾶλλον ἐν ἄλγεσι θυμὸν ὀρίνῃς (24.560, 568)

'Do not provoke me any more, old man...I am already grieving bitterly: do not stir up my heart still further'

with

μή μοι σύγχει θυμὸν ὀδυρόμενος καὶ ἀχεύων (9.612)

'Do not try to confuse my heart with your weeping and wailing'.

What this pity means is revealed by the whole of Achilles' speech. It is not only an emotion, but an insight: because he sees that suffering is unavoidable and common to all men, he can keep back, not without a struggle, his own pride, rage and grief. The result is that he acquires a new form of honour from Zeus (24.110),[2] through neither inaction nor violence, but restraint; not to the detriment of comrades or of enemies, but to the benefit of a fellow-man; and not by persuading or almost coercing, but by obeying the supreme god.

One could imagine an epic like the *Iliad* which ended with the sack of Troy or the death of Achilles.[3] Both events are often foretold in the

[1] Like Odysseus in *Od.* 8.521–31 (discussed in 1 above).
[2] κυδαίνειν is what Zeus does to Achilles in giving the Trojans victory (13.348–50). 'Zeus gave κῦδος to so-and-so' is regularly used (e.g. 8.216; 15.612) when a hero shines in battle. So this is an exceptional form of κῦδος.
[3] C. M. Bowra, *Tradition and design in the Iliad* (Oxford 1930) 103–9 usefully contrasts the end of the *Iliad* with what 'the saga' told.

work as we have it; and in Book 22 the narrative for a while even seems
to be moving towards them. Hector prophesies how Achilles will be
killed, and that episode, in this and other ways, resembles the death
of Patroclus, whose prophecy of Hector's death is not only true but told
in the poem; and Achilles is all ready to mount an attack on Troy. But
instead of more death and war we are given two burials. This is no doubt
a planned surprise: the forecast of Zeus in Book 15 had said simply that
Achilles would slay Hector and that the Trojans would be driven back
until their city fell (68–71);[1] and the events of Book 24 are not foreseen
or foreshadowed – and then only dimly – until Book 23. But Book 22,
and indeed the whole poem, in a larger sense tends towards the
conclusion as we have it; and there the theme of Achilles' wrath is
brought to an end in such a way as to deepen both the protagonists'
and the audience's understanding of the life of men, of the working of
the gods, and of the morality which can still exist despite human
violence and divine indifference. If the *Iliad* had moved in a straight
line from Hector's death to Achilles', it would have stopped; as it is,
it is completed.

(ii) Book 23 falls naturally into two parts, the first concerning the
funeral of Patroclus, the second the funeral-games. In the funeral
Achilles fulfils the promises he had made to the dead Patroclus
(18.333–7; cf. 23.19–23, 179–83), and he has constantly had it in mind
to bury him (19.23–33; 22.336, 385–90). Before, the ghost of Patroclus
appears urging him to accomplish the burial.[2] This is not a necessity for
the workings of the plot since there is no doubt that Achilles will bury
his friend. The function of the episode is rather to effect a separation
between the two. When Patroclus has been buried, his shade will visit

---

[1] Divine forecasts in the *Iliad* are only outlines of what is to come: cf. 119 n.,
and Schadewaldt, *IS* 110–13. This is both artistic and realistic: the detail of
what actually happens is not dully pre-empted, and that also faithfully
represents the interplay of destiny and decision in human affairs.

[2] Only here in the *Iliad* do we meet the notion that a soul cannot 'pass the gates
of Hades' (71) if it is not buried – just as only with Hector's corpse it is
suggested that the gods will be angry if there is no burial (see p. 20, n. 2 above).
When burial becomes the central theme, it is natural that beliefs concerning
it emerge more fully.

When Patroclus says he is a wandering ἀν' εὐρυπυλὲς Ἀΐδος δῶ (74) we must
take the preposition to mean either 'towards', 'up to' (cf. 19.212; 22.452) or
'along' (cf. 10.339; 18.546; *IG* 14.645 ii 32), rather than 'through'.

Achilles no more; and when Achilles moves to embrace the ghost which had told him to give his hand (75), it escapes his grasp. Patroclus cannot be forgotten: at the beginning of Book 24 Achilles' grief and rage are what they were before; and even after he accepts Priam's supplication, he is still concerned to placate his dead friend (592–6). Moreover, the farewell to Patroclus includes the prospect of an ultimate reunion: the shade tells Achilles to bury their bones together (82–92) and Achilles has the mound made in such a way as to allow this (243–8). But in the funeral he pays what is owing to the dead man and sends him to his rest: on the level of outward form or social convention he has done his duty by Patroclus, whatever feelings remain in his heart. Thus in the games Achilles is ready tactfully to hold back those feelings before the Greeks, as he does again in Book 24 before Priam.[1]

The place of the games in the *Iliad* as a whole[2] may be indicated by quoting the simile in Book 22 which describes how Achilles pursued Hector round the walls of Troy (158–66):

πρόσθε μὲν ἐσθλὸς ἔφευγε, δίωκε δέ μιν μέγ' ἀμείνων
καρπαλίμως, ἐπεὶ οὐχ ἱερήϊον οὐδὲ βοείην
ἀρνύσθην, ἅ τε ποσσὶν ἀέθλια γίγνεται ἀνδρῶν,
ἀλλὰ περὶ ψυχῆς θέον Ἕκτορος ἱπποδάμοιο.
ὡς δ' ὅτ' ἀεθλοφόροι περὶ τέρματα μώνυχες ἵπποι
ῥίμφα μάλα τρωχῶσι· τὸ δὲ μέγα κεῖται ἄεθλον,
ἢ τρίπος ἠὲ γυνή, ἀνδρὸς κατατεθνηῶτος·
ὡς τὼ τρὶς Πριάμοιο πόλιν πέρι δινηθήτην
καρπαλίμοισι πόδεσσι...

It was a great warrior who fled, and a far greater one who pursued him, swiftly; for they were not trying to win a sacrificial animal or an ox-hide, prizes for which men run in races: they were running for the life of Hector the horse-tamer. As when race-horses run swiftly

---

[1] He mentions Patroclus in neutral tones at 619. More richly expressive of this tact is the speech in lines 272–86. There he is implicitly asserting his supremacy, as in Book 1, and referring to his grief over Patroclus: what he explicitly says is that he would win first prize because his *horses* are the best, but he will not take part, because his *horses* are grieving for their lost groom. (For the horses' grief cf. 17.426–40; 19.404–17; for the close connection between the ἀρετή of man and horse, 2.761–2; 16.833–5; 23.571.)

[2] For this view of the games cf. Stawell 84–90; J. Redfield, *Nature and culture in the Iliad* (Chicago and London 1975) 206–12.

round a course for a fine prize, a tripod or a woman, which is
offered after a man has died, so they circled three times around
Priam's city...

The games, like the battle, are a combat in which men strive for victory,
helped or hindered by the gods:[1] but in the games, which take place
at a funeral when a man has died, what is at stake is a prize, whereas
in the battle it is the life of the participants themselves. And the games,
like the funeral, represent a relief from war. Thus Book 23, like Book
24, is a counterweight to the bulk of the poem.

Again like Book 24, the latter part of 23 renews themes which go back
to the beginning of the poem. Achilles does not take part in the games,
just as he stays out of the fighting after the quarrel; but here he is the
ἀγωνοθέτης and arbitrator, courteous and dispassionate, not the
injured party, bitter and egoistic; and it is others' honour, not his own,
which is his concern. The aim in the contests is to prove merit or
superiority,[2] just as the quarrel in Book 1 had become a question of who
was 'best' (1.91, 244, 412 etc.); and the result is not always
unquestioned. There is a dispute over a prize in Book 23 as there is over
booty in Book 1:[3] Antilochus objects to Achilles' intention of giving the
second prize to Eumelus, because though 'good' or 'best', he had failed
to pray to the gods; and Menelaus objects in his turn to its going to
Antilochus because his opponent used trickery. Antilochus' threatened
anger (543) is at once appeased by Achilles. But then, Menelaus, like
Achilles in Book 1, considers himself 'cheated' by an inferior man
(23.571–2, 577–8, 605; 1.132, 225–32; 9.375). Angry, like the Achilles
of Book 1, he stands with the staff in his hand; and as Achilles invoked
'the staff...which is carried by the sons of the Achaeans who give law
and to whom Zeus has given judgements' (1.234–9) – an implicit
appeal to his audience's sense of justice – so Menelaus first demands a
judgement from the Greeks and then tries to engineer one himself by

[1] For divine influence or intervention in the games (as in the fighting) see 23.383,
388, 771, 865. For the participants' recognition of it, 546–7, 660, 724, 872.

[2] For ἄριστος and the like see 276, 357, 536, 546, 571, 578, 659, 669, 802, 891.
Note that both Eumelus and Diomede seem to be 'best' (357, 536), but this
leads to no trouble.

[3] For χόλος, ἔρις and the like, see 482, 489–90, 543, 567, 603. Reinhardt, *ID*
60, 81 and Schadewaldt, *HWW* 347 note the relation of this theme to Book
1.

challenging Antilochus to swear he had not used foul means. If
Antilochus had made the oath, there would have been a settlement like
the one in Book 19 when Agamemnon swears he never touched
Briseis. But this quarrel does not develop that far; Antilochus soothes
his opponent, and Menelaus generously returns the prize he had
claimed. Unlike Achilles, who had had no regard for Agamemnon's
status as a king and as his senior (1.277–81; 9.160–6), Antilochus
respects the seniority and superiority of Menelaus (23.587–8); and
unlike Agamemnon, who did not properly reward Achilles' labours on
his behalf (1.149–71; 9.314–45), Menelaus recognizes what Antilochus
has done for him (23.607–11). Nestor, whom Achilles ignored in Book
1, is given the honour due to him (647–50); and he responds by
speaking in praise of Achilles, as Antilochus does later on: Achilles and
his valour are not, as they were before, a cause of resentment and
distress (αἰναρέτη Patroclus calls him, with an expressive coinage, in
16.31).[1] The book ends with Achilles' recognizing what he had so
fiercely questioned in Book 1, that Agamemnon is 'best in power and
in years' (891); and if in Book 1 he attacked the king as a poor fighter
(225–8), here he graciously exempts him from the competition
altogether.

Thus Book 23 winds up the theme of the quarrel. It adds something
to Book 19, because there, even when the quarrel is formally concluded,
Achilles remains the outsider: at first he is unwilling to go through the
ceremony of accepting the gifts; then he refuses to take food before
fighting, as Odysseus insists the army must do; and when the elders
beseech him (303–4 γέροντες...λισσόμενοι) to eat, as the elders had
beseeched him to relent in Book 9 (cf. 18.448 τὸν δὲ λίσσοντο γέροντες,
referring to that episode), he still refuses as he did there, though his
motive is now grief, not pride (209–14). But in Book 23, for the duration
of the games at least, Achilles is master of ceremonies and a
magnanimous ruler among his peers. The festive atmosphere of ease
and good will, in which merit is recognized and rewarded all round,
so that competition never becomes conflict, is epitomized in one of
Homer's most wonderful similes (597–600):

$$\text{τοῖο δὲ θυμὸς}$$
$$\text{ἰάνθη ὡς εἴ τε περὶ σταχύεσσιν ἐέρση}$$

---

[1] Cf. e.g., 1.176–80; 11.762–4.

ληΐου ἀλδήσκοντος, ὅτε φρίσσουσιν ἄρουραι·
ὡς ἄρα σοί, Μενέλαε, μετὰ φρεσὶ θυμὸς ἰάνθη.

His heart was gladdened as [the corn is] by the dew on the ears when
the crop is growing and the fields bristle: so Menelaus' heart was
gladdened...

It remains for Achilles to overcome his rage and grief and to show pity
to an enemy – a process far less joyful but also far more profound than
the mollification of Menelaus.[1]

(iii) (a) 24.31 = 1.493. The eleven days of Achilles' anger in Book
1 and the eleven days of the pro-Greek gods' resistance – both of which
lead to divine assemblies – correspond. Likewise the nine days of the
plague in Book 1 (53) and the nine days of lamentation for Hector in
Book 24 (664, 784). The phrase for the appearance of dawn which
occurs twenty times in the *Odyssey*, ἦμος δ' ἠριγένεια φάνη ῥοδοδάκτυλος
Ἠώς, is used only twice in the *Iliad*, in 1.477 and 24.788, at the end of
the events concerning two figures who have roused such damaging
passions in Achilles, Chryseis and the dead Hector. If 24.790 is genuine,
then again a line commoner in the *Odyssey* (three times) is reserved for
the first and last book of the *Iliad* (cf. 1.57): it thus contrasts the fateful
first assembly with the peaceful gathering which lays Hector to rest.
Thus Books 1 and 24 with their long and analogous lapses of time
'frame' the whole *Iliad*, whose main action occupies only three days.
This is not a purely formal or numerical matter since the events linked
to these time-markers are in significant contrast. There is a similar
correspondence between Books 7 and 23, which directly enclose the

[1] Further parallels or contrasts between the great quarrel and the quarrel of
Book 23: 23.602. 'I shall yield (ὑποείξομαι) of my own accord' ~ 1.293–4 'I
should be called a coward indeed if I yielded (ὑπείξομαι)'; 23.603–4 'Your wits
never went astray before' ~ 1.177 'You always did love strife and war', 1.225–8
'You never did show courage'; 23.606 'No one could have persuaded me but
you' ~ 9.345, 386 'He will never persuade me'; 23.609 'I will give in to
your request (λισσομένῳ)' ~ 18.448 50 'The elders besought him (λίσσοντο cf.
9.698 etc.)...but he refused'; 23.611 'My heart is not proud and harsh
(ὑπερφίαλος καὶ ἀπηνής)' ~ 9.698–700 'I wish you had not besought Achilles;
he is arrogant (ἀγήνωρ) anyway, and you have made him more so' (cf. 16.35
etc.). One by one, these could hardly be called 'echoes', but together they
indicate how the overall pattern of the episode in 23 can remind us of the initial
quarrel.

central three days of the poem. In both books two days are spent on burial-rites; and in both there is remission from war, in 7 after the duel with Ajax from which Hector unexpectedly returns alive (306–10), in 23 after the death of Hector.

(b) At the end of Book 1 Thetis comes in secret to Zeus with Achilles' request and prevails on him to favour her son by giving the Trojans the upper hand in war. A divine assembly follows, begun by a speech of protest from a truculent Hera, in which Zeus imposes his will; and a quarrel among the gods is averted by the thought that human beings are not worth such trouble. In Book 24 there is another divine assembly, also begun by a speech of protest, this time from Apollo: there Zeus brings the gods, including a truculent Hera, to agree in showing concern for humanity, by letting Hector be buried; he then openly summons Thetis before them – Hera welcomes her warmly – and sends her to Achilles; she persuades him to accept Zeus's will. Whereas in Book 1 the gods' exchanges are an almost comic equivalent to the grim quarrel on earth, and leave the strife among men and Zeus's destructive plan untouched, in Book 24 they are more serious and lead to a fresh decision by Zeus which brings a measure of reconciliation among men. And whereas in Book 1 Zeus respects an obligation to Thetis (393–406) by giving Achilles a form of honour which comes from the death of his companions, in Book 24 Zeus puts Thetis in his debt (111) by giving Achilles a form of honour which comes from his showing mercy to an enemy.

(c) In Book 2 Zeus sends a false dream to Agamemnon which leads him to prepare the Greeks for battle in the belief that Troy is now to fall: this begins the 'ten thousand sorrows for the Achaeans'. The god's expression of concern and pity for the man is deceptive. In Book 24 Zeus, whose pity and concern are now real, sends Iris, a true messenger, to Priam and leads him to go and supplicate Achilles: this brings the poem to its peaceful conclusion. The parallel is stressed by repetition and echo: $24.173b–4 = 2.26b–7$, $63b–4$; $24.220–2$ correspond to $2.80–1$ (Nestor to Agamemnon): εἰ μέν τις τὸν ὄνειρον Ἀχαιῶν ἄλλος ἔνισπε, | ψεῦδός κεν φαῖμεν καὶ νοσφιζοίμεθα μᾶλλον... ('If another of the Greeks had told us the dream, we would call it false and reject it...').

(d) In Book 1 the old Chryses comes as a supplicant to Agamemnon, bringing gifts and begging for the return of his daughter; Agamemnon

turns him away harshly, with a threat of violence if Chryses should
return; Chryses is afraid and yields. In Book 24 the old Priam comes
as a supplicant to Achilles, bringing gifts and begging for the return
of his son's body: Achilles accepts the supplication – though not before
he has spoken harshly to Priam, and a frightened Priam has yielded to
his threat. Finally, he sends off the old man with a promise of an
eleven-day treaty. There are a number of verbal echoes:

24.501–2 ～ 1.12–13

　　　ὁ γὰρ ἦλθε θοὰς ἐπὶ νῆας Ἀχαιῶν
　　　λυσόμενός τε θύγατρα φέρων τ' ἀπερείσι' ἄποινα

24.555–7 ～ 1.18–20

　　　ὑμῖν μὲν θεοὶ δοῖεν Ὀλύμπια δώματ' ἔχοντες
　　　ἐκπέρσαι Πριάμοιο πόλιν, εὖ δ' οἴκαδ' ἱκέσθαι·
　　　παῖδα δ' ἐμὴν λύσαιτε φίλην, τὰ δ' ἄποινα δέχεσθαι

24.560   ～ 1.32

　　　μή μ' ἐρέθιζε...

24.569–70 ～ 1.26, 28

　　　μή σε, γέρον, κοίλῃσιν ἐγὼ παρὰ νηυσὶ κιχείω...
　　　μή νύ τοι οὐ χραισμῇ σκῆπτρον καὶ στέμμα θεοῖο

24.571   = 1.33

　　　ὡς ἔφατ', ἔδεισεν δ' ὁ γέρων καὶ ἐπείθετο μύθῳ

24.780–1   ～ 1.25

　　　ἀλλὰ κακῶς ἀφίει, κρατερὸν δ' ἐπὶ μῦθον ἔτελλε

(e) In Book 9 an embassy comes by night to Achilles' tent. Achilles
leaps up in surprise (193) and greets the envoys, and he gives them
a meal. They then beg him to relent and offer gifts (cf. 18.448 λίσσοντο
γέροντες). Phoenix' speech in particular has a suppliant character,
because it contains the description of the Λιταί and the story of
Meleager whose friends and relatives begged (585 ἐλλίσσοντο) him to
return to battle.[1] Phoenix, whom Peleus had treated as a son, represents
himself as in his turn like a father to Achilles (480–95). Achilles rejects
the appeal and the gifts, but has a bed made for Phoenix in his tent.
In Book 24 Priam comes by night to Achilles' tent, causing a far deeper
surprise (480–4), and supplicates him as he sits, comparing himself to
Achilles' father. Achilles accepts the supplication and gifts; and if in
9 he rejected Phoenix' admonitions, in 24 he himself admonishes Priam,
whom he persuades first to accept his suffering, and then to eat. At the
end of their conversation, he has a bed prepared for his visitor on his

---

[1] The story of Meleager points forward in other ways too: see 614–17 n.

porch. In both 9 (663–5) and 24 (675–6) the scene concludes by describing how Achilles slept with his concubine beside him; in Book 24 the concubine is Briseis, whose loss caused all the trouble.[1]

Another link is between 9.628–38 and 24.39–52. Apollo and Ajax both criticize Achilles for his savagery. Apollo argues: 'Men have lost dearer ones, brothers or sons, before now, and they had to learn to live with it; but he goes on dragging Hector round his friend's tomb.' Ajax argues: 'Men have accepted compensation before now for the murder of a brother or son, and restrained their anger; but you go on harbouring resentment over one single girl.' It is striking too that Ajax' example is the reality of Book 24; the man Achilles treated like a son has been killed and his anger is apparently beyond appeasement. In Book 24 Achilles, as he did not in Book 9, in the end does what his critic demands.

These correspondences confirm what is already clear for other reasons: the grand design of the *Iliad*, which culminates in the reversal of Book 24, is prepared with subtlety and in detail from the beginning of the poem.[2]

4. LANGUAGE AND STYLE[3]

(i) Homer's Greek could never have been spoken. This is partly because it includes forms which belong to different *periods* of the language. Thus we find

Early	Later
Genitives in -οιο: eg. 2 δόρποιο	Genitives in -ου: e.g. 3 ὕπνου
Aorists and imperfects without augment: e.g. 4 κλαῖε	Aorists and imperfects with augment: e.g. 5 ἐστρέφετο

---

[1] Some details in these two scenes may belong to the stock of epic poetry: see 623–8, 673–6 nn., and for 9.193 ταφὼν δ' ἀνόρουσε, cf. 11.776; *Od.* 16.12. But in the narrative of the *Iliad* they occur only here: formulae, here and elsewhere in Homer (see 4 ii (a)–(d) below), are selected and used, not merely trotted out.

[2] For some other important links with earlier books see 69–70, 123–5, 131–2, 283–320, 723–76 nn.

[3] For a helpful and stimulating account written in English from the philological point of view see L. R. Palmer, 'The language of Homer' in *CH* 75–178, which includes a Homeric grammar. The standard work on Homeric grammar and morphology is Chantraine, *GH*.

'Tmesis' (i.e. prepositions stand-   Preposition and verb fused: e.g.
ing apart from the verb to   136 ἀπέλυσας
which they belong):[1] e.g. 185
ἀπό...ἐρύξει

Digamma[2] respected: e.g. 85 ὅς   Digamma ignored: e.g. 72 ἢ γάρ
(ϝ)οἱ, 213 ἄντιτα (ϝ)ἔργα   οἱ, 354 νόου ἔργα

Uncontracted forms: e.g. 522   Contracted forms: e.g. 7 ἄλγεα,
ἄλγεα, 287 εὔχεο, 129 ἔδεαι   290 εὔχεο, 434 κέλῃ

It also combines different *dialects*. The predominant dialect in Homer is Ionic; but there is also a wealth of elements foreign to Ionic, above all Aeolic ones. (Ionic and Aeolic were neighbours in the eastern Aegean.) Thus we find both Ionic and Aeolic forms of some of the commonest words and terminations: e.g. ἄν (Ionic) and κε/κεν (Aeolic); εἰ (Ionic) and αἰ (Aeolic); ἡμεῖς, ἡμέας (Ionic) and ἄμμες, ἄμμε (Aeolic); infinitives in -ειν, -ναι (Ionic) and in -μεν, -μεναι (Aeolic). Sometimes these are blended in such a way as to produce artificial forms: e.g. ἷῆς (496), in which the η is Ionic but the form of the root ἵ- (= μί-) is Aeolic, or νήεσσιν (408), in which the η and the final ν before a vowel are Ionic, but the termination -εσσι for the dative plural is Aeolic. Exactly how this linguistic amalgam was formed we cannot know. It may be that poetic traditions belonging to different dialects converge in Homer; but deliberate archaism and borrowing by him and his forerunners must also play a part and could well have characterized Greek epic diction from its beginnings. What is clear is that Homer's language is both conservative and composite.

One important factor which shapes Homeric language is its metre. Where there are variant forms of words these are regularly metrical alternatives. Thus for the infinitive of the verb 'to be' there are no fewer than five metrical variants (εἶναι, ἔμεν, ἔμμεν, ἔμεναι, ἔμμεναι) and for

---

[1] This phenomenon reflects their original status as adverbs; cf. 38, 61 nn. There are still a few mild examples of tmesis in Attic comedy and prose: see Kühner–Gerth II §445.

[2] The digamma (ϝ = English *w*) is known from inscriptions and from ancient grammarians; cf. LSJ s.v. δίγαμμα; Dion. Hal. *Ant. Rom.* 1.20. It is lost very early in Ionic, but its presence is often felt in Homer. Thus the word (ϝ)ἄστυ in all its fourteen occurrences in Book 24 is treated as beginning with a consonant. For the neglect of the digamma in the word οἱ, cf. 53 and West on Hes. *W.D.* 526.

the third person singular of the future, no fewer than four (ἔσται, ἔσεται, ἔσσεται, ἐσσεῖται). Metrical convenience also helps to cause some artificial word-formations: e.g. ἦμαρ as a plural (73 n.), εὐρύοπα as a nominative (296 n.), χέρνιβον (304 n.), φραδέος (354 n.) and ἐάων (528 n.); cf pp. 57–8. Sometimes artificialities arise from a kind of compromise with the spoken language: this seems to be the case with what the ancient grammarians called diectasis ('stretching apart'), e.g. ἀντιάασθε (62), εἰσορόων (632) or ἀστυβοώτην (701). The contracted forms (ἀντιᾶσθε, εἰσορῶν, *ἀστυβώτης) of ordinary speech do not fit into the hexameter. There must have been uncontracted forms in the tradition (as it were *ἀντιάεσθε, *εἰσοράων, *ἀστυβοήτης); and when contraction set in, the poets adapted the obsolete form in such a way as to preserve its metrical shape, which contraction had altered.

The work of Milman Parry did much to illuminate Homer's Greek as a language of traditional verse.[1] Beginning with the use of names for gods and men and their ornamental epithets, he showed how the choice of epithet was tightly related to metre. Thus Achilles (in the nominative) is ὠκύς or δῖος or πόδας ὠκύς or ποδάρκης δῖος Ἀχιλλεύς, Menelaus ξανθός or βοὴν ἀγαθὸς Μενέλαος, according to metrical convenience; and the meaning of epithets of this kind is 'loose' in so far as it is not tied to individual contexts. Further, ornamental epithets tend to form systems characterized by extension and economy: i.e. for each name (in its various forms or cases) there are a number of different epithets, each of which fits a different slot in the line; and as a rule there is only one epithet for each metrical need.[2] Parry observed first that diction of this kind implied a tradition of some antiquity, and then that its origins must lie in oral composition, since such fixed patterns supply a basis for improvisation.[3] He also showed that the formulaic element

[1] See *MHV*; the introduction by Adam Parry well defines the scope, the value and the limitations of his father's work. For other brief accounts of Parry's work, see J. B. Hainsworth, *The flexibility of the Homeric formula* (Oxford 1968) ch. 1; C. M. Bowra in *CH* 26–37. Bowra's is also on the whole a sensitive account of Homeric style in its formulaic aspect.

[2] There are, of course, exceptions to this rule, since Homer is not a computer: e.g. Ἕκτορος ἀνδροφόνοιο and Ἕκτορος ἱπποδάμοιο. See in general A. Hoekstra, *Homeric modifications of formulaic prototypes* (Amsterdam and London 1965) 13; B. Alexanderson, *Eranos* 68 (1970) 1–46. And often such exceptions reflect a distinct poetic intent: see 4 (ii) (a) below.

[3] It is unlikely that Homer used writing; but our understanding of his work does not depend in the least on deciding whether he did or not. In what

spreads well beyond noun–epithet combinations: e.g. when, as often
happens, lines are repeated verbatim without there being any significant relation between them (e.g. 372 = 386 = 405; 378 = 389 =
410 = 432) or when, as again often happens, set verbal patterns recur
in standard situations, as before a speech:

$$
\left.\begin{matrix} \tau \grave{o} \nu \\ \tau \grave{\eta} \nu \end{matrix}\right\}
\left.\begin{matrix} \delta(\grave{\epsilon}) \\ \delta' \, \mathring{\alpha} \rho \end{matrix}\right\}
\left.\begin{matrix} \chi o \lambda \omega \sigma \alpha \mu \acute{\epsilon} \nu \eta \\ \mathring{\alpha} \pi \alpha \mu \epsilon \iota \beta \acute{o} \mu \epsilon \nu o \varsigma \\ \acute{\upsilon} \pi \acute{o} \delta \rho \alpha \, \mathring{\iota} \delta \grave{\omega} \nu \\ \mathring{\epsilon} \pi \iota \kappa \epsilon \rho \tau o \mu \acute{\epsilon} \omega \nu \\ \text{etc.} \end{matrix}\right\}
\quad \pi \rho o \sigma \acute{\epsilon} \varphi \eta \qquad \text{noun} + \text{epithet}
$$

$$
\left.\begin{matrix} \tau \grave{o} \nu \, \delta' \\ \tau \grave{\eta} \nu \, \delta' \end{matrix}\right\}
\left.\begin{matrix} \alpha \mathring{\upsilon} \tau \epsilon \, \pi \rho o \sigma \acute{\epsilon} \epsilon \iota \pi \epsilon \\ \mathring{\eta} \mu \epsilon \acute{\iota} \beta \epsilon \tau' \, \acute{\epsilon} \pi \epsilon \iota \tau \alpha \end{matrix}\right\}
\quad \text{noun} + \text{epithet}
$$

and so forth; it is striking and obvious how these formulae dovetail with
the noun–epithet formulae. On a larger scale stereotypes can be felt
behind certain recurrent scenes,[1] of arming, visiting, eating, going to
bed etc., where phrases and patterns are freely repeated.

If Homer's language is in certain respects traditional and artificial,
and if his technique shows some features peculiar to oral composition,
it does not follow that Homer's style is either hackneyed or primitive.
As in all verse, what is technically convenient can also be poetically
effective; and poetic effect, in its most elementary form, is produced
by difference from ordinary language. Thus the ornamental epithets,
whose use is so closely bound up with metrical needs, have nonetheless
a definite meaning[2] and a general purpose – indeed, they are one of the
splendours of Homeric art. 'Rosy-fingered' or 'horse-tamer' convey an
idea, whether or not that idea is operative within a particular context;
and this use of adjectives helps to make the world of Homer's epic what
it is: mean or humdrum objects and persons and animals do not trail

follows, by 'oral' I mean simply 'exhibiting some features characteristic of a
certain kind of oral poetry'.
[1] These were helpfully studied by W. Arend, *Die typischen Scenen bei Homer* (Berlin
1933); the book was well reviewed by Milman Parry (see *MHV* 404–7), though
he failed to see what it said or suggested about Homer's poetic use of typical
scenes, as opposed to their technical usefulness.
[2] A few decorative epithets seem to be archaic survivals which may well have
conveyed no definite meaning to the poet or his audience: e.g. διάκτορος (339),
ἐριούνιος (360), ἀμιχθαλόεσσαν (753). But they are an interesting and curious
minority.

such clouds of verbal glory behind them. So traditional diction has its poetic purpose: it is only necessary to appreciate what that purpose is. Further, if oral composition suggests some degree of improvisation – i.e. the poem *need* not have been worked out to the last verbal detail in the poet's mind before recitation – it by no means excludes premeditation, artistry or profundity, of every sort. If the *Iliad* is more than a rag-bag or bundle of rag-bags, then it is necessarily the product of thought, though how far that thought was conscious or unconscious, prolonged or immediate, eludes us, as it does whenever a poet does not tell us the story of his work's composition. And there are differences of quality in oral as in written poetry. Homer is a great oral poet; and greatness in poetry is manifested not only in grandeur of design, but in power and propriety of language. It is intuitively clear that Homer does use language in that way; and an understanding of the poet's technique should and can be applied to illustrating, not obscuring, that intuition.

In some lectures published in 1861[1] Matthew Arnold gave a brilliant account of Homer whom he characterized as 'rapid in his movement ...plain in his words and style...simple in his ideas...noble in his manner'. His concern was to define the 'general effect' of the poet, something he was right to distinguish from the 'quaintness' which the translator he was criticizing, F. W. Newman, found in certain elements of the epic vocabulary. What Newman was observing was what many have observed in a more scholarly fashion since, that Homer's was an artificial language; but Arnold saw, with the acumen of the critic, that what is artificial in origin need not be artificial in effect ('rapid... plain...') and that judgements of poetic quality are vacuous if they take no account of moral quality ('simple...noble...'),[2] of what can be learned from the poet's words about life and living. Arnold's work is as fresh and enlightening now as it ever was; and anyone who wants to see why Homer's is the style of a great poet, as such comparable to

---

[1] *On translating Homer*, followed by *Last words on translating Homer*, a reply to F. W. Newman's *Homeric translation in theory and practice*. All these can be found together in the New Universal Library edition (1905).

[2] Note also Arnold's definition of the 'grand style' in *Last words*: 'I think it will be found that the grand style arises in poetry, when a noble nature, poetically gifted, *treats with simplicity or with severity a serious subject*' (his italics). From antiquity, compare above all the treatise *On the sublime* and D. A. Russell in the introduction to his commentary on it, p. xlii.

Dante's or Milton's, cannot do better than read his lectures. A commentator, for his part, should use what Parry and others discovered about Homer's technique to bring down to precise detail Arnold's comprehensive insight, and illustrate not only what the poet's means are but to what effect he uses them. So in what follows I consider a selection – only a selection – of stylistic features which occur in Book 24, together with parallels from other books, on a larger scale than would be appropriate in the commentary itself.[1]

(ii) (a) MODIFICATIONS OF STANDARD PHRASING

In 24.88, 141–2, 236, 416, 483, Homer can be seen to adopt a more forceful or emotive expression in place of a metrically equivalent alternative. Such heightening of conventional diction can often be found. Thus in *Il.* 1.122 Achilles addresses Agamemnon as 'Ατρείδη κύδιστε, φιλοκτεανώτατε πάντων. Eight times in the *Iliad* the words 'Ατρείδη κύδιστε are followed by ἄναξ ἀνδρῶν 'Αγάμεμνον. Achilles' phrasing here, in which the second superlative sounds like a sarcastic echo of the first, brings out his disrespect and his resentment; he uses the conventional line-ending again in 19.146, 199, when he and Agamemnon patch up their quarrel.[2] In *Il.* 6.255 Hecuba says to Hector ἦ μάλα δὴ τείρουσι δυσώνυμοι υἷες 'Αχαιῶν. We find four times in the *Iliad* and once in the *Odyssey* the line-ending ἀρήιοι υἷες 'Αχαιῶν. This was available here; but an epithet which brings out Hecuba's anxiety and hostility is preferred. In *Il.* 23.10 and 98 Achilles uses the words ὀλοοῖο τεταρπώμεσθα γόοιο. Four times in the *Iliad* the phrase ἁδινοῦ ἐξῆρχε γόοιο occurs; we also read once each in the *Iliad* ἁδινὸν στοναχῆσαι, ἁδινὰ στενάχουσι, ἁδινὰ στεναχίζων, κλαῖ' ἁδινά, and in the *Odyssey* ἁδινὸν γοόωσα, ἁδινὰ στεναχίζων, ἁδινὰ στενάχοντα, κλαῖον...ἁδινώτερον. ἁδινοῖο would have been an obvious epithet in *Il.* 23.10 and 98; but one is chosen which conveys more of the mourner's feelings (cf. στυγερῆ...δαιτί in Achilles' mouth in 23.48). A powerful oxymoron also results: wailing is 'grim', but for a mourner it is a kind

---

[1] In the following sections I have not made continual cross-references to the commentary; but further comment on the passages from Book 24 will generally be found there.

[2] Cf. W. Whallon, *Y.C.S.* 17 (1961) 104–5.

of 'pleasure', the only pleasure he has.[1] In *Od.* 19.208–9 Penelope, unaware that it is Odysseus she is speaking with, weeps for him: …κλαιούσης ἑὸν ἄνδρα παρήμενον. Four times in the *Odyssey* it is said of Penelope (κλαῖεν ἔπειτ') Ὀδυσῆα φίλον πόσιν (a phrase itself more subjective than Ὀδυσῆα δίφιλον which occurs twice in the *Iliad*).[2] But with 'her own husband sitting beside her', fresh wording is invented to stress the irony and the pathos of the situation.[3]

Another such modification occurs in 24.380–8. There Hermes asks a two-pronged question of a kind frequent in Homer: 'Is it that *x*, or is it that *y*?', to which the customary answer is 'It is not *x* nor *y*, but…'[4] Priam, however, replies at once with a counter-question: 'Who are you?' He is eager to discover who Hermes is, to see if he can tell him more about Hector's body (cf. 406–9); and the god, who already of course knows the answer to his own question, does not need to have it answered. The other place in the *Iliad* where this pattern is modified is likewise expressive. In 16.7–19 Achilles asks Patroclus 'Why are you weeping? Have you had bad news from home, or is it out of pity for the Greeks?' This pair of alternatives is unusual because only one is false, rather than both. Achilles, like Hermes in Book 24, clearly knows the answer to his question; he poses it all the same in order to evoke from Patroclus what he feels. This is a sign of compassion (cf. 5 ᾤκτιρε); at the same time there is a touch of mockery or contempt. He shows the same mixture of attitudes when he compares his friend to a little girl who tugs tearfully at her mother's dress, asking to be picked up (7–10). Patroclus, ignoring the question in the urgency of his concern, breaks straight into an impassioned appeal on the Greeks' behalf.

Homer's tact – avoidance of a standard phrase where it would be burdensome or inept – has unfortunately seemed less worthy of atten-

---

[1] For similar oxymoric phrases, see, e.g., 4.104, 16.842 τῷ δὲ φρένας ἄφρονι πεῖθεν; *Od.* 15.399 κήδεσι…τερπώμεθα λευγαλέοισι (cf. p. 7 n. 4 above); 16.29 ἐσορᾶν ἄϊδηλον ὅμιλον. In general, see Fehling, *WF* 286–93; also 262, 796 nn.

[2] Cf. *Il.* 15.91 ἤ μάλα δή σ' ἐφόβησε Κρόνου πάϊς, ὅς τοι ἀκοίτης (addressed to Hera), rather than Κ. π. ἀγκυλομήτεω. The speaker, Themis, thus expresses her sympathy for the humiliated wife.

[3] For more examples of expressively modified epithets, see Parry, *MHV* 156–61.

[4] Cf. J. T. Kakridis, *Homeric researches* (Lund 1949) 108–20 together with good remarks on the lines from Book 16. The relevant passages are: *Il.* 1.62–7 with 93–4; 6.377–86; 16.36–52; *Od.* 2.28–45, 11.170–9 with 198–203, 397–410; 16.95–116; 24.109–24. In the last case the reply does not take the exact form 'it is not *x* nor *y*, but…'; but the question is directly and fully answered.

tion than places where such phrases appeared ill-fitted to their context.[1]
Examples of such tact dictated by formal considerations can be found
in 24.474, 760, 776, 791–800; more substantial ones are 477 where the
reaction to Priam's entry, which would normally come at once, comes
only after he has taken hold of Achilles' knees and hands, and 486,
where the opening of Priam's supplication cuts short the phraseology
typical of such contexts. Two more examples may be added here. In
Il. 6.476–81 Hector utters a prayer for his son Astyanax: 'May he rule
Troy and be a great warrior, like me.' Prayers in Homer are regularly
followed by a sentence indicating how the god responded or did not
respond;[2] here there is no such phrase. Hector and Andromache both
know that Troy will fall, but how soon is not plain; and the death of
Astyanax is only forecast when the sack of the city is imminent, after
Hector's death (24.734–9). Thus while the characters have only a
foreboding, the hearer is not given foresight. This enables him to feel
more completely with them; and a statement of Zeus's intentions would
fall too heavily into the delicate and responsive exchange between
husband and wife. Just after this, in 6.494, Hector picks up his helmet;
line 495 begins with the epithet ἵππουριν. In four places in the *Iliad*
where a hero puts on his helmet the next line runs ἵππουριν· δεινὸν δὲ
λόφος καθύπερθεν ἔνευεν. The normal continuation is suppressed here
because the horse-tail crest has already figured when its movement
frightens Astyanax (470 δεινὸν...νεύοντα): the standard phrase has in
fact helped to shape a uniquely striking and moving episode.[3] To
mention the helmet again as 'nodding fearfully' in a general way would
impair what the poet has just achieved.

[1] See, e.g., Bowra in *CH* 29–30. But if, for example, beached ships are 'swift'
or the sky 'starry' by day, there is no ineptitude. Such epithets of their very
nature are independent of particular contexts: they indicate what is typically
so, not what is always actually or visibly so. So in everyday English we speak
of 'a fast car' whether or not it is moving.

[2] Cf. *Il.* 1.43, 357, 457; 3.302; 5.121; 6.311; 10.295; 15.377; 16.249, 527;
23.198–9, 771; 24.314. *Od.* 2.267; 3.385; 4.767; 5.451; 6.328; 20.102. There
is no reference to the god's response or failure to respond after *Il.* 3.324, 355
and 7.205. The main aim there seems to be to avoid anticipating the result
of the duel; such anticipation is employed for the great deaths of the poem,
not for minor and indecisive combats.

[3] The ornamental epithet κορυθαίολος, which is reserved for Hector, seems also
to have played its part: cf. Whallon (p. 40 n. 2) 111.

(b) REPEATED LINES AND PATTERNS

It is typical of Homer, by contrast with literary epic, to repeat lines word-for-word, or almost word-for-word, and to describe recurrent events in more or less stereotyped patterns. Such repetitions are of course technically convenient. But foreshadowing and echo in Homer, as in all literature, are also an indispensable way of giving shape and significance to a narrative; and Homer naturally employs for that purpose the kinds of repetition which his technique afforded him. Thus Priam in trying to evoke Achilles' pity uses the same words he uttered in hectoring his sons (255–6 = 493–4): the two passages show how his sorrow and his rage are a reaction to one and the same tragedy. Achilles in responding to Priam uses the same words Hecuba spoke in trying to dissuade him from going (203–5 = 519–21): his tone is one of compassion, hers of horror. The two passages are complementary, and together bring out the tragic quality of Priam's enterprise. In 748 and 762 Hecuba and Helen begin their laments with an exactly corresponding form of address: for both women he was uniquely precious.[1] Of many parallels outside Book 24 I mention only 4.163–5 = 6.447–9, where Agamemnon says to Menelaus, and Hector to Andromache: 'This I know full well in my heart: the day will come when the sacred city of Troy will be destroyed, and Priam and the people of Priam of the fine ashen spear.' The repetition of these impressive lines allows us to view the fall of the city through both Greek and Trojan eyes, as a just punishment for wrongdoing, and as unquestioned but inexplicable suffering: both viewpoints are essential to the whole poem.

Similarly, we find three messenger-scenes in quick succession in Book 24: Iris' visit to Thetis, Thetis' to Achilles and Iris' to Priam.[2] In all these a stock pattern is repeated: the messenger goes swiftly (77 ὦρτο...ἀελλόπος, 121 βῆ...ἀΐξασα, 159 ὦρτο...ἀελλόπος) and finds (83 εὖρε, 123 εὖρε, 160 κίχεν) a mourner surrounded (83, 123, 161 ἀμφί) by companions or family. These three episodes prepare not only the plot, but also the themes and feelings of the poem for the meeting of Achilles and Priam. What the messenger finds is foreknowledge of

---

[1] For further examples in Book 24 see 131–2, 224, 258–9, 283–320 nn.

[2] On the typical pattern of messenger- and visiting-scenes, see Arend (p. 38 n. 1) 28–53; on these ones, Deichgräber 47–8. Particularly close to the scenes in 24 are 15.150–7, 237–43; *Od.* 3.29–33.

Achilles' death, grief for Patroclus and for Hector: all these come
together to be absorbed and mastered in that encounter. In contrast
to these scenes stands a fourth, Thetis' visit with Iris to Olympus (95–9
βῆ δ' ἴεναι...ἀϊχθήτην, | εὗρον δ'...περὶ δ' ἄλλοι...): here the
mourner finds the 'blessed, immortal gods', remote from men's suffering
even where they are concerned to limit or alleviate it. This creates one
of those contrasts between divine and human life which are essential
to the whole poem. A similarly artistic chain of repeated visits is
4.250–421, where Agamemnon goes from one Greek hero to another,
exhorting them to fight: here too, together with much variation, there
is repetition (255, 283, 311; 336, 368; 272, 326; 292, 364), as well
as obviously similar patterns of narrative and themes in speech (338–40,
370–1; 257–64, 341–8). This introduces us from the Greek point of view,
rather as 3.161–244 had done from the Trojan point of view, to some
of the main Achaean heroes and their different characters; the episode
also shows Agamemnon, in contrast to the fiasco of his speech in Book
2 which feigned despair, as the effective and authoritative general who
directly encourages or rebukes his men. The result of his words here
is that the Achaeans are stirred to battle as the sea is by the wind (422–7):
this contrasts with the way they were stirred to flight, again as the sea
is by the wind, after the speech of Book 2 (142–9).

Such repetitions also contribute to the structure of the whole poem.
Thus the words with which Thetis admonishes Achilles (24.131–2) are
the same as those with which Patroclus prophesies Hector's death. This
is part of a pattern which connects the fates of Hector and Achilles. Both
are honoured by Zeus before their short lives end (see especially 1.505–6,
15.611–14); both triumph over their enemy, Hector over Patroclus,
Achilles over Hector, in scenes where the dying man foresees the death
of his killer (16.851–4, 22.356–60), who has previously mocked his
victim for his hopes of success (16.837–42, 22.331–6); and in both those
scenes the lines which describe the departure of the soul to Hades are
the same and found only there in the *Iliad* (16.855–7 = 22.361–3). This
kind of repetition, then, is a means towards embodying the tragic design
of the whole poem, in which victory includes the sure promise of death
for the greatest victors. Repetition often figures too in other forms of
ironic foreshadowing. Thus the words Agamemnon uses in Book 2 as
part of a ruse to stiffen his troops' resolve (110–18, 139–41) are spoken
in bitter earnest in Book 9 (17–28): the man who hoped to achieve a

4 LANGUAGE AND STYLE

rapid victory by simulating despair is then plunged into real despair.
Again: the simile which prefaces that speech in Book 9 recurs in Book
16, and only there, when Patroclus is standing before Achilles (3–4):
'he wept like a dark spring that pours its murky water down a steep
rock'. In both places the Greeks are in dire distress. In Book 9 an
embassy follows which fails to satisfy Achilles' resentment, in Book 16
there follows an appeal which succeeds – but by bringing death to
Patroclus both ends Achilles' first wrath and begins his second. Book
24 is characterized by happy reversal more than by grim fulfilment;
but the echoes of Books 1, 2 and 9 discussed above (3 (iii)) are another
example of such significant repetition, both of lines or phrases and of
patterns.[1]

(c) RITUAL ACTIONS

A feature of Homeric narrative is the scene which describes, serially and
in some detail, a 'ritual' action, i.e. something done in a correct and
customary fashion (Latin *rite*). This in Book 24 we have the preparation
of the gifts and the waggon, the libation, the meal, the bed-making and
the funeral.[2] These episodes have a distinct purpose or effect, which is
enhanced rather than diminished if they seem conventional. The *Iliad*'s
concern is with human passion, violence and suffering; but the world
of the poem is one in which order and ceremony are also upheld and
in which men or animals or objects have an uncommon excellence and
beauty. This contrast is essential to the quality and meaning of the
poem: it makes the *Iliad* tragic rather than merely gory or horrifying.
The ritual actions of Book 24 belong to the peaceful part of life, and
the vocabulary which describes them tends to stress that things are
well done or well made: περικαλλέας...περικαλλές (229, 234);
εὔτροχον...καλήν...εὖ οἰήκεσσιν ἀρηρός...εὖ...ἐϋξέστῳ...ἐϋξέστης
(266–75); εὖ κατὰ κόσμον...ἐπισταμένως...περιφραδέως...καλοῖς

---

[1] For more examples of such repetition, see above 3 (i) (including p. 25 n. 1).
The whole topic is treated with great finesse and penetration by Reinhardt,
ID.
[2] The libation, the meal and the bed-making may be typical scenes, traditionally
worded: at all events, they occur elsewhere in Homer in similar form (see
notes). This is not likely to be true of the others: the funeral is strikingly
different in wording from that of Book 23, the preparation of the waggon and
the gifts are unique.

(622–6); καλά (644); εὖ (802) etc.; so does the bit-by-bit description of the action and the objects concerned. The fetching of the gifts has pathos in itself, because Priam is not sparing his wealth to save his son's body (235–7); and the placing of all these episodes gives them meaning. The preparation of gifts and waggon and the libation stand in contrast to the horror, anxiety and anger voiced in the speeches of Hecuba and Priam: this is a journey to be made with careful preparation and under good auguries; but it also expresses extreme grief and evokes extreme fear. The meal and the bedding-down are the sign that Priam has learned to live with his sorrow (635–42); and Achilles' hospitality is the proper sequel to his pity and consolation. The funeral ends the whole poem: it represents civilization maintained in the midst of war, as the ransom represented it maintained against rage and revenge. The placing of ritual actions in Book 1 is closely comparable. A formal account of how Chryseis was put on board ship and how the army purified itself makes an interlude in the story of the wrath and its consequences: 'After fighting thus with violent words, they rose (304–5)...Nor did Agamemnon desist from the quarrel (318–9).' Likewise the journey to and from Chryse, the return of Chryseis and the prayer, sacrifice and meal that went with it: 'She left him there angry (428–9)...But he raged, sitting beside his swift ships (488–9).' The human anger is less easily placated than Apollo's; but the rituals are still performed in the midst of it.

(d) EVERYDAY FORMULAE AND THEIR MODIFICATIONS

The artificiality of Homer's language at various levels has attracted much attention in modern times. But also noteworthy are places where colloquial speech can be felt through the consistent elevation of epic diction. Sometimes, as quite often in Attic tragedy (e.g. Soph. *O.T.* 430 and Jebb ad loc.), a colloquial turn of phrase serves to give sharp expression to powerful feelings (e.g. 205, 212–13, 239); but perhaps more prominent in Book 24 are 'everyday formulae', i.e. correct responses to standard situations in life, phrases of request, assent, acceptance, welcome etc. Examples of these are 104, 105, 139(?), 197, 300, 373, 379, 660–1, 669. Many more can be found elsewhere in the poem, naturally enough since the *Iliad* represents what it must also have sprung from, a highly civilized environment. Thus in 18.386 and 425

Charis and Hephaestus in greeting Thetis use the words πάρος γε μὲν οὔ τι θαμίζεις, 'you're not a frequent visitor' (cf. *Od.* 5.88). Virtually the same phrase accompanies a greeting in Plato, *Republic* 328c (with the word θαμίζεις); such a remark is clearly, whether true or not as a statement of fact, part of a natural convention of welcoming.[1] Or in *Il.* 23.306–9 Nestor begins a long lecture to his son Antilochus on racing tactics by saying that 'there is no need to instruct' him on the subject. We can recognize here a polite convention which veils the often distasteful business of giving advice: similarly Hephaestus admonishes Hera in 1.577 'though she knows it herself', and comparable phrases can be found in later Greek and in Latin.[2] Sometimes, like accounts of ritual actions, these everyday formulae introduce a note of calm and courtesy in pointed contrast to passions which have swept aside ceremony, as in 300, 660–1, 669. Sometimes they can be twisted so as to express indignation or disgust: so apparently at 56–7. Compare 3.428 where Helen greets Paris in the normal way (cf. 24.104) 'you have come from the war', and then goes on 'how I wish you'd died there!'; or *Od.* 6.324–7 when Odysseus prays to Athene 'Hear me now, since you did *not* hear me before', which reverses the usual formula of prayer or request (cf., e.g., *Il.* 1.451–6; 5.115–20; 14.233–5; 16.233–8).

(e) DESCRIPTIONS OF DAWN

These occur in both *Iliad* and Odyssey in a rich variety of forms.[3] In the *Odyssey*, where they are much more frequent, they are more like mere time-markers; but in the *Iliad* they are regularly used with a more specific purpose. It was noted above (3 (iii) (a)) how the phrase so common in the *Odyssey*, ἦμος δ' ἠριγένεια φάνη ῥοδοδάκτυλος Ἠώς, was reserved for Books 1 and 24 in the *Iliad*; and others are also used purposefully. Thus in 24.694–6 we read: 'Hermes went off to Olympus: Dawn was scattered over the whole earth; they drove into the city,

---

[1] Cf. Plato, *Hipp. Maj.* 281a ὡς διὰ χρόνου ἡμῖν κατῆρας εἰς τὰς Ἀθήνας (answered by the words οὐ θαμίζω εἰς τούσδε τοὺς τόπους); Theoc. 14.2; 15.1. Also our jocular 'Long time no see.'

[2] Cf. Thuc. 4.17.3; Hor. *Ep.* 1.17.1–2 and Kiessling–Heinze ad loc.; note also Hes. *W.D.* 202 and West ad loc. Closely related is Isoc. 9.78–80 'I am only encouraging you to do what you seek to do of your own accord'; cf. St Paul, Romans 15:14; Galatians 5:10; also Hebrews 6:9; Ov. *Tr.* 5.14.43–6.

[3] Cf. Bowra in *CH* 30.

moaning and groaning...' The god leaves for the home of the gods;
dawn illumines the earth where there is suffering and sorrow. The
contrast of the divine and human worlds, being a major theme of the
whole poem, naturally finds expression in a multitude of details (see,
e.g., 58–61, 67, 258–9, 460–4, 534–8); and it figures in the descriptions
of dawn. Thus in a more formal way in 8.1–3 (cf. *Od.* 5.1–2): 'Dawn
was *scattered* over the *whole earth*: Zeus made a *gathering* of the gods on
the *peak of Olympus*' or 23.226–8 'When the morning-star went to show
light to the earth... then the pyre *faded* and the flame *failed*.' Or more
significantly in 2.48–51 'Dawn went to Olympus to show light to Zeus
and the other gods: Agamemnon told the heralds to summon the Greeks
to the assembly' – an assembly which is to be an all-too-human affair;
11.1–4 'Dawn *rose* from her bed to bring *light* to men and gods: Zeus
sent down (προΐαλλε) grim *Strife* to the Greek ships'; or 18.616–19.5
'Thetis *leapt down* from Olympus like a hawk, *bringing the arms* from
Hephaestus: Dawn *rose* from Ocean to *bring light* to gods and men:
Thetis came to the ships bringing the god's gifts and found her son
mourning.' The special favour from the god is set against the general
blessing of light; but this favour is given to a sorrowing man, and is
to bring sorrow to other men (cf., e.g., 18.122–4), those whom Achilles
is to slaughter and the Trojans as a whole.

The phrases for daybreak, then, illustrate both Homer's art of
variation and his ability to use such variation for a deeper purpose.

(*f*) SIMILES

Book 24 contains only three extended similes (41–4, 80–2, 480–4); but
they well represent Homer's use of this device. All exhibit a pattern of
comparison-with-contrast (particularly the last), by which a normal
event is set in detail against the actual event. The similes in the *Iliad*
very often contain an implicit contrast with narrative, when they put
something from the everyday world or the world of peace beside the
grand and terrible happenings of war.[1] E.g. 12.433–5 'They held on
as an honest labouring-woman holds the scales; with the weight and
the wool she makes it equal on either plate, to earn a miserable wage
for her children'; or 16.641–3 'They kept gathering round the corpse
as when flies in a farmyard buzz about the milky pails in spring-time...'

[1] Cf. O. Taplin, *G. & R.* 27 (1980) 15.

Sometimes too the contrast is delicately pointed. One example is 22.158–66 (discussed in 3 (ii) above); another is 21.255–62. There Achilles is running away (φεῦγε) and the river, flowing with a great roar (μεγάλῳ ὀρυμαγδῷ), is catching him up: this is compared to a man leading along (ὀχετηγός...ἡγεμονεύῃ) an irrigation-channel which gurgles (κελαρύζει) as it catches him up. The pebbles which the channel sweeps along (260–1) correspond to the corpses which the river is sweeping along (235–6). The passage concludes grimly 'the gods are stronger than men'; and the simile with its sharp contrasts illustrates that statement. In the *Odyssey*, compare 5.432–5 (of Odysseus ship-wrecked in the sea): 'As when many pebbles stick to the suckers of a polyp when it is dragged out of its lair, so the skin was stripped off his hands against the rocks.' The sea-beast, in its own element, comes out with stones sticking to it: the human being, out of his element, leaves his skin on the rock. Or 16.216–18 'They wept shrilly, more loudly than...vultures whose young ones the country folk have snatched before they are fledged.' The subjects here are Odysseus and Telemachus who have just been re-united; the suitors have in fact failed to kill Telemachus; and he has now come to maturity. The simile intensifies the joy of the moment by pointing to what might have been instead.[1]

All the similes in Book 24 are implicitly connected in a number of ways with the narrative: the explicit connection does not exhaust their significance. This again is characteristic of Homer.[2] Compare, for example, 17.53–60: 'As a man raises a flourishing shoot of olive in a lonely place where water gushes up abundantly; it is beautiful, it flourishes, and the breaths of all the winds shake it, and it burgeons with a white flower. But suddenly a wind comes with a great storm, uproots it from its trench and outstretches it on the earth: such was the son of Panthus, Euphorbus, whom Menelaus killed and despoiled.' The simile is of a common type: the fall of a warrior is compared to the fall of a tree. Here the simile expresses, beyond that, not only the beauty of the young man, but also the care of the parents, whose bereavement

---

[1] Note that in 16.17–21 Eumaeus, the swine-herd, greets and kisses Telemachus as a father embraces his only son who has returned after ten years: the two similes are complementary. For 'linked' similes, cf., e.g., *Il.* 16.756–61 and 823–28; 22.21–4 and 162–7; C. Moulton, *Similes in the Homeric poems* (Göttingen 1977) esp. 80, 133–9.

[2] Cf. H. Fränkel, *Die homerischen Gleichnisse* (Göttingen 1921).

is so often mentioned in Homeric descriptions of deaths;[1] and the winds which the sapling resists and the wind which finally flattens it are like the combats Euphorbus has come through before and the one in which he has just succumbed.[2] Or 18.316–23: 'Achilles began the loud lament, laying his murderous hands on the breast of his companion, groaning constantly like a well-bearded lion whose cubs a huntsman has snatched from the dense wood: he is grieved when he comes too late; and he goes after the man, tracking his footsteps to see if he can find him, for sharp anger seizes him: groaning thus deeply he (Achilles) spoke...' Here the warrior is, as so often, like the fierce and noble lion. The loss of the cubs is like Achilles' loss of Patroclus; Achilles, like the lion, is too late; and, like the lion, he searches in anger for the killer.[3]

Sometimes it is striking how the simile is in one way or another stretched to fit the context.[4] Examples in Book 24 are the personification of line 42 or the ambiguity of line 480. Comparable is the bold personification of 14.17: the sea 'spies out' the winds, because Nestor is considering whether to join the battle; or the physically impossible picture of 13.200: two lions walk carrying their prey 'high' in their paws, because the two Ajaxes hold the man they have killed aloft. So although the similes have a life and interest of their own, they are consistently shaped to enhance the narrative.

(g) ASSONANCE, WORD-PLAY, ETC.[5]

A great many figures of style may be seen as a form of repetition, either cumulative or antithetical. Thus we find reduplication through synonyms, e.g. 337 μήτ' ἄρ τις ἴδῃ μήτ' ἄρ τε νοήσῃ or 365 δυσμενέες καὶ ἀνάρσιοι; this is strengthened by 'rhyme' (homoeoteleuton) in 245 ἀλαπαζομένην...κεραϊζομένην τε or by 'alliteration' (homoearchon) in 157 οὔτε...ἄφρων οὔτ' ἄσκοπος οὔτ' ἀλιτήμων. Emphasis is also produced by taut anaphora (e.g. 229–34, 516, 688) or by looser

[1] Cf. Griffin 124–7, 135. Fränkel (p. 49 n. 2) 40 aptly compares 18.56.
[2] Cf., e.g., 11.297; 12.40; 13.39, 795.
[3] The simile thus anticipates what is to come: cf. 16.751–3; 18.207–14; 21.522–5.
[4] See further Fränkel (p. 49 n. 2) 105.
[5] In this section I have been greatly helped by Fehling, *WF* and by L. P. Rank, *Etymologiseering en verwante verschijnselen bij Homerus* (Assen 1951); they also illustrate more abundantly some of the phenomena noted here, and many other related ones.

repetition of a key-word or leading idea (e.g. 'bring' and 'escort' in 182–4, 437–9). Other forms of emphatic accumulation may be found in, e.g., 36–7, 261–2. Stylistic heightening of this kind can be used with considerable refinement and suggestiveness. See, e.g., 608–9, 771–2; or 57–61, 258–9, 464, 534–8 where the reiterated antithesis 'god/gods' ~ 'man/men' (cf., e.g., 5.442; 22.9) points up the subject of the whole poem: god-like men who have to endure what the gods give to every man, suffering and death.

Assonance is likewise a calculated form of heightening: see, e.g., 58, 390, 433. It seems particularly frequent in speeches, where it reinforces the dominant tone, benign irony (23.604 νόον νίκησε νεοίη), grim sarcasm (6.143 = 20.429 ἆσσον...θᾶσσον; 17.41–2 οὐ μὰν ἔτι δηρὸν ἀπείρητος...οὐδ᾽ ἔτ᾽ ἀδήριτος; 22.373 μάλα...μαλακώτερος) or earnest concern (Od. 1.48 δαΐφρονι δαίεται; 4.765–2 μνῆσαι... μνηστῆρας), though there are also striking examples in narrative, e.g. 11.215–16 ἐκαρτύναντο...ἀρτύνθη; 461–2 αὖε...ἤϋσεν.

Assonance borders on word-play, as in some of the examples just quoted, or in 1.290–1 (Agamemnon attacking Achilles): εἰ δέ μιν αἰχμητὴν ἔθεσαν θεοὶ αἰὲν ἐόντες, | τοὔνεκά οἱ προθέουσιν ὀνείδεα μυθήσασθαι; ('If the immortal gods made him a warrior – is that why insults run out from his mouth?'). The Greeks themselves sometimes connected θεός with τίθημι (Hdt. 2.52.1); and προθέειν is a word Homer uses of bold warriors in battle (22.459 = Od. 11.515). Agamemnon caustically implies that Achilles' divinely-given valour serves above all for *verbal* combat. In 24.730 and 611 too, there is word-play with an implicit etymology. This kind of punning is common in Homer. Almost humorous examples are 2.758 Πρόθοος θοὸς ἡγεμόνευεν or Od. 24. 465–6 Εὐπείθει | πείθοντο; but the device can also play a part in very serious contexts. E.g. 21.599–601 αὐτὰρ ὁ (Apollo) Πηλεΐωνα δόλῳ ἀποέργαθε λαοῦ. | αὐτῷ γὰρ ἑκάεργος Ἀγήνορι πάντα ἐοικώς | ...ἔστη πρόσθε ποδῶν: the pun here is reminiscent of a type common in invocations where the god is asked to do, or seen to have done, what his name implies.[1] Or 16.141–3 = 19.388–90 τὸ μὲν οὐ δύνατ᾽ ἄλλος Ἀχαιῶν | πάλλειν, ἀλλά μιν οἶος ἐπίστατο πῆλαι Ἀχιλλεύς, | Πηλιάδα μελίην: this is the spear with which Achilles is to kill Hector and without which Patroclus is to be killed by him. Or 19.328–30 'before, I hoped

---

[1] E.g. Hes. *W.D.* 3 and West ad loc.; Aesch. *Ag.* 973–4, 1080–2, *S.c.T.* 145–6; Men. *Epitr.* 907.

that οἷον ἐμὲ φθίσεσθαι ἀπ' Ἄργεος ἱπποβότοιο | αὐτοῦ ἐνὶ Τροίῃ, σὲ δέ τε Φθίη νδε νέεσθαι': the echo here stresses the tragic irony – both Achilles and Patroclus in fact die and fail to return to Phthia. Similarly, in the *Odyssey* the hero's name is linked with the verb ὀδύσσομαι because the gods are or seem to be angry with him (1.60–2; 5.340, 423).[1]

A subtler form of word-play is the use of the same language in both literal and metaphorical applications: see 129–30, 522–3, 553–4, 617. This helps to bring out the sense of significant actions in the narrative: eating is connected with 'digesting' sorrows or contrasted with 'eating out' one's heart, sitting associated with letting grief 'lie' or a corpse 'lie unburied'. One could compare the Attic dramatists' art of making action and speech, including metaphor, lend each other meaning:[2] e.g. Soph. *O.C.* 149–236. There Oedipus first moves from forbidden to open ground and sits down; then, in response to the chorus' questions, he moves in words to the fearful revelation of his identity (211 πέρα ματεύων; 217 λέγ', ἐπείπερ ἐπ' ἔσχατα βαίνεις; 219 τάχυνε); as a result, the chorus try to make him move out of the country altogether. Simple words like 'go', 'hurry', 'further', and the actions they designate, acquire a particular depth in this context. Again, the play on 'father' and 'son' in the exchange between Hermes and Priam is essential to the significance of the episode (362 n.).

Such word-play sometimes forms an important part of the intercourse between speakers: see 371–3, 551–4. Here the beginning of one speech echoes with some variation of sense the end of the one before it. This is a feature of other Homeric exchanges: e.g. 6.519–22 (Paris) 'Have I not come ἐναίσιμον ὡς ἐκέλευες?' – (Hector) 'No one who was ἐναίσιμος would call you a coward'; 8.352–60 (Hera) 'The Greeks will be destroyed (ὀλλυμένων...ὄλωνται), since Hector μαίνεται οὐκέτ' ἀνεκτῶς' – (Athena) 'I hope he will lose (ὀλέσειε) his valour, destroyed (φθίμενος) by the Greeks; but my father φρεσὶ μαίνεται οὐκ ἀγαθῇσι.' Here the effect is one of sympathetic response; it may equally be one of impassioned or sarcastic retort: e.g. 18.96–8 (Thetis) 'For your death will come immediately (αὐτίκα) after Hector's' – (Achilles) 'Let me die immediately (αὐτίκα *tout court*)!'; *Od.* 17.444–6 (Odysseus) 'I have come here πήματα πάσχων' – (Antinous) 'What god brought this

[1] Note, in a different way, 19.407–9.
[2] In general on this topic, see O. Taplin *G.R.B.S.* 12 (1971) 25–44, *The stagecraft of Aeschylus* (Oxford 1977) and *Greek tragedy in action* (London 1978).

πῆμα here?' This device is part of the skill which Homer shows in constructing complementary speeches, well illustrated in the debate on Olympus, the meeting of Achilles and Priam and the laments of the Trojan women in Book 24.[1] What Thucydides or Sophocles, for example, achieved in this art was learnt not only from contemporary rhetoric but from the father of Greek literature.

5. METRE AND PROSODY

(i) METRE[2]

The metre of Homer is the hexameter. Like all Greek metres, it is quantitative, i.e. it is a pattern of long and short syllables (whereas English verse is a pattern of stressed and unstressed syllables). Its scheme is:

$$
\begin{array}{cccccc}
1 & 2 & 3 & 4 & 5 & 6 \\
-\smile\smile & -\smile\smile & -\smile\smile & -\smile\smile & -\smile\smile & -\smile
\end{array}
$$

($\smile$ denotes a short, $-$ a long syllable; the numbers mark the feet). The end of the line, as in several Greek verse-forms, is marked by a truncated foot and, as in all Greek verse-forms, by an *anceps*, i.e. a syllable which can be long or short indifferently. Lines consisting entirely of long syllables hardly ever occur: *Il.* 2.544; 23.221; *Od.* 15.334; 21.15; 22.175 seem to be the only examples.

The internal articulation of the line is subject to certain rules, above all the caesura. This means that there must be word-end in the third foot after the initial $-$ or $-\smile$; occasionally the caesura is displaced to the fourth foot, in which case it always comes after the initial long: e.g. 251, 449, 623–4, 665. It is clear that its purpose is to stop the line falling over-neatly into two or three exactly equal sections. Two other rules, whose purpose is less clear, concern the fourth foot. (*a*) There should not be word-end after $-\smile$ there: exceptions are very rare: in Book 24,

---

[1] Particularly fine examples outside Book 24 are the quarrel of Book 1 or the exchange between Hector and Andromache in Book 6, too complex to be discussed here. For some helpful remarks on them, see D. Lohmann, *Die Komposition in den Reden der Ilias* (Berlin 1970) 96–100, 131–8; he deals with the topic as a whole, 96–156.

[2] For a more detailed exposition of Homeric metre see P. Maas, *Greek metre* (Oxford 1962) §§82–9; Bowra, *CH* 19–25.

54 INTRODUCTION

only 60, 526, 753. Lines 35 and 423 are not exceptions because νέκυν-περ-ἐόντα and ἐπεί-σφι-φίλος make a single word from a metrical point of view.[1] (b) If the end of the fourth foot coincides with the end of a word, and if it scans – –, then the second long syllable should contain a long vowel (see below on 'Prosody').[2] Exceptions are very rare: in Book 24, only 557, 617, 743 (all monosyllables). Lines 80, 467, 485, 682 and 694 are not exceptions, because the syllable treated as long is a preposition which fuses with the following word.

Together, (a) and (b) seem to show that an effect of tailing-off had to be avoided in the fourth foot.

Breaks or pauses in sense tend to be avoided at certain points in the line: (a) at the end of the second foot, (b) at the end of the third foot, and (c) after the end of the fourth foot. In Book 24 there are no exceptions to (a),[3] (b) or (c).[4] (a) and (b), like the caesura, seem designed to prevent too 'pat' a division of the line, and (c) to ensure that its impetus, as it approaches its expected and necessary end, is not interrupted. However they should be interpreted, these restrictions make it clear that in Homer metre and syntax are sensitively related: the verse cannot simply impose itself on the sentence.

To illustrate briefly the interplay of regularity and variety and the marriage of syntax and metre in Homer's verse, here are samples first of some patterns of lines, and then of groups and lines, with a modicum of comment. The comment is subjective; but where one is writing about poetry, it is less unfaithful to the object to make subjective comments than to abstain from comment altogether.

(1) Lines which fall naturally into two parts:

79   ἔνθορε μείλανι πόντῳ· | ἐπεστονάχησε δὲ λίμνη

772   σῇ τ' ἀγανοφροσύνῃ | καὶ σοῖς ἀγανοῖς ἐπέεσσιν

cf., e.g., 97, 112, 156, 222, 260, 354, 688. In all these places the second part of the line complements and reinforces the first; parallelism of phrasing and meaning in the two parts heightens this effect.

(2) Lines which fall naturally into three parts:

(a) 36 ἥ τ' ἀλόχῳ ἰδέειν | καὶ μητέρι | καὶ τέκεϊ ᾧ

cf., e.g., 157.

[1] See further H. Fränkel, Wege und Formen frühgriechischen Denkens (Munich 1955) 122 n. 3, 142–6; Maas §§ 135–40.
[2] See further Leaf, Appendix N.
[3] Exceptions (after only a light pause) found elsewhere are 7.238, 9.106, 21.63.
[4] Exceptions are collected by Fränkel (above, n. 1) 108. Nowhere in Homer is there a pause in sense later than the first long of the fifth foot.

(b) 479 δεινὰς | ἀνδροφόνους, | αἵ οἱ πολέας κτάνον υἷας
cf., e.g., 192, 261, 269, 753.
 (c) 216 ἑσταότ', | οὔτε φόβου μεμνημένον | οὔτ' ἀλεωρῆς
cf., e.g., 308, 424, 571, 704, 725.

In all these cases there is an effect of emphatic cumulation; in 479 this is particularly fine, because the second and third limbs of the phrase are each more precise, more pointed and more poignant than the preceding one.

(3) Lines which have a marked pause in the first foot:

224 εἶμι, | καὶ οὐχ ἅλιον ἔπος ἔσσεται. εἰ δέ μοι αἶσα
τεθνάμεναι παρὰ νηυσὶν 'Αχαιῶν χαλκοχιτώνων,
βούλομαι· | αὐτίκα γάρ με κατακτείνειεν 'Αχιλλεύς...
728 ...πρὶν γὰρ πόλις ἥδε κατ' ἄκρης
πέρσεται· | ἢ γὰρ ὄλωλας ἐπίσκοπος, ὅς τέ μιν αὐτὴν
ῥύσκευ, | ἔχες δ' ἀλόχους κεδνὰς καὶ νήπια τέκνα...

cf., e.g., 52, 148, 216, 376, 385, 407, 501, 619, 706, 752.

In all these cases, the words emphasized in this way carry a weighty charge of meaning, and often, as in the quoted examples, of grandeur and pathos too.

(4) Variety: e.g. 358–61

ὡς φάτο, | σὺν δὲ γέροντι νόος χύτο, | δείδιε δ' αἰνῶς,
ὀρθαὶ δὲ τρίχες ἔσταν | ἐνὶ γναμπτοῖσι μέλεσσι,
στῆ δὲ ταφών· | αὐτὸς δ' ἐριούνιος ἐγγύθεν ἐλθών,
χεῖρα γέροντος ἑλὼν | ἐξείρετο καὶ προσέειπε...

In this highly dramatic moment, the lively variety of metrical pattern from line to line is expressive; but such variety is found throughout Homer, and it is necessary to prevent monotony, especially for a reciting poet. It is often particularly striking in speeches: e.g. 725–45, where it adds considerably to the pathos.

(5) Regularity: e.g. 602–9

καὶ γάρ τ' ἠΰκομος Νιόβη ἐμνήσατο σίτου,
τῇ περ δώδεκα παῖδες ἐνὶ μεγάροισιν ὄλοντο,
ἓξ μὲν θυγατέρες, | ἓξ δ' υἱέες ἡβώοντες.
τοὺς μὲν 'Απόλλων πέφνεν | ἀπ' ἀργυρέοιο βιοῖο
χωόμενος Νιόβῃ, | τὰς δ' "Αρτεμις ἰοχέαιρα,
οὕνεκ' ἄρα Λητοῖ ἰσάσκετο καλλιπαρήῳ·
φῆ δοιὼ τεκέειν, | ἢ δ' αὐτὴ γείνατο πολλούς·
τὼ δ' ἄρα καὶ δοιώ περ ἐόντ' ἀπὸ πάντας ὄλεσσαν
cf. 397–400 (Hermes' account of his 'origins').

At times a marked regularity can have its value. In these passages of rapid exposition, it neatly parcels up the information, and in the quoted example, the brief and symmetrical manner is also pointed and tragic (cf., e.g., 21.106–13, where it hammers in Achilles' stern message to Lycaon): the mere two children of Leto (one son, one daughter), whom Niobe compared unfavourably to herself, the mother of twelve, were the death of all her twelve (six sons, six daughters).

The wealth and beauty of the Homeric hexameter comes out the more strongly if it is compared with its treatment in Hellenistic writers, e.g. Callimachus, *Hymns*.[1] The hexameter as forged by Callimachus is a form of considerable finesse, but it tends to be monotonous and precious, whereas Homer is flexible without any loss of power and dignity.

(ii) PROSODY[2]

In Greek verse syllables are treated as either long or short. (This is no doubt a simplification of normal speech, since some long syllables must have taken more time to utter than others, and some short syllables less time than others, depending on whether, or what, consonants accompany them.) In the Greek language some vowels are naturally long (i.e. always η, ω and sometimes α, ι, υ), others are naturally short (i.e. always ε, ο and sometimes α, ι, υ). Long vowels make a long syllable; short vowels make a short syllable, unless they are followed by two or more consonants. In that case the syllable is long. It *may*, however, be treated as short before certain combinations of plosive (π, τ, κ; φ, θ, χ; β, δ, γ) and liquid or nasal (λ, ρ; μ, ν): e.g. 324 τἔτράκυκλον, 517 πτερόεντᾰ προσηύδα, 795 τά γἔ χρυσείην. This is because such pairs of consonants can be treated not as *t-r/p-r/ch-r* etc. but as *tr/pr/chr* etc. In Homer this is a metrical licence (whereas in Attic it reflects everyday speech); and it usually serves to get into the

---

[1] On this matter, see Maas §§ 90–100.

[2] For more detail see Maas §§ 123–34. An illuminating treatment from a phonetic point of view is W. S. Allen, *Vox graeca* (Cambridge 1968) 97–105. He uses the words 'heavy' and 'light' to distinguish the *quantity* of a syllable from the *length* of vowels. The distinction is useful; but I have stuck to the traditional terminology ('long' and 'short' applied to syllables as well as vowels), because English readers would naturally confuse 'heavy' and 'light' with 'stressed' and 'unstressed'.

hexameter words which would not otherwise fit it: thus τετρᾰκῡκλὸν or (-)πρŏσηῡδᾱ are impossible. ψ, ξ and ζ are double consonants (ps, ks, sd); so is initial ῥ (a rolled r): thus, e.g., 370 σὲ ῥέξω. Some combinations of vowels are normally fused or slurred, so as to form one long syllable: αι, αυ, ει, ευ, ηυ, οι, ου, υι. These are called diphthongs. When they remain separate, this is marked in the text by a double dot: e.g., εὔσκοπον. The other combinations of vowels do not normally form a diphthong; when they do, this is marked in the text by a loop: e.g. εὔχε͜ο.

When there is a vowel or diphthong at the end of one word and another vowel at the beginning of the next, one of three things may happen:

(a) Elision (Latin elidere = 'squeeze out'). If the first vowel is short, it is normally eliminated, and this is marked by an apostrophe in the text: e.g. 2 ἐσκίδναντ(ο) ἰέναι. Final αι is also sometimes elided when it terminates a middle/passive form of the verb: e.g. 91 μίσγεσθ(αι) ἀθανάτοισιν.

(b) Correption (Latin corripere = 'tighten up'). If the first vowel is long, it is normally shortened: e.g. 59 ἐγὼ αὐτή, 398 γέρων δὲ δὴ ὡς. With diphthongs correption is only apparent because the final vowel becomes semi-consonantal (like English y or w) before the following vowel: e.g. 82 ἔρχετᾰι ὠμηστῇσιν, 730 ῥύσκε͜υ, ἔχες.

(c) Hiatus (Latin hiare = 'gape'). The first vowel or diphthong may be neither elided nor correpted: e.g. 52 ἕλκεῑ· οὐ, 207 ὅ γε̆, οὐ, 318 ἀφνειοῖο, ἐΰ.

'Epic lengthening.'[1] Syllables are sometimes treated as long for metrical convenience: e.g. 47 κασίγνητον ὁμογάστριον, 88 Θέτῑ· καλέει. This can happen even where there is hiatus: e.g. 285 δέπαῑ, ὄφρα.[2] It also happens within words: e.g. 32 ἀθανάτοισι,[3] 330 ἀπονέοντο, 604 θῡγάτερες. This is sometimes done by changing the form of the word: e.g. 13 ὑπείρ (for ὑπέρ), 79 μείλανι (for μέλανι), 425 διδοῦναι (for διδόναι), 593 εἰν (for ἐν). Apparent 'epic lengthening' and hiatus are

---

[1] When this happens, it is almost always on the first syllable of the foot, clearly a weightier position than the second.

[2] See further N. J. Richardson on H.H.Dem. 99.

[3] This word keeps its artificial long syllable in all the rest of Greek verse – a striking illustration of Homer's powerful influence on later poetry, in small things as in great.

58

sometimes due to the presence of the digamma: e.g. 364 ἔδϝεισας, 36 ἦ τ' ἀλόχῳ ϝιδέειν...καὶ τέκεῖ ϝϝῷ, 75 ὄφρα τι ϝοι ϝείπω πυκινὸν ϝέπος. But the digamma is quite often ignored: e.g. 53 νεμεσσηθῶμέν οἱ (cf. 72), 354 νόου ἔργα, 452 ποίησάν ἄνακτι.

Homeric prosody is highly elastic, much more so than that of any other Greek verse-form. Like the artificialities of his word-formation, this lends a stylized and elevated character to his diction. It also indicates that the Homeric hexameter is markedly traditional and markedly oral: such prosodic freedom can hardly be invented by one man or a few men, and it serves a poet who at the strictly technical level composes like an improviser.

BIBLIOGRAPHICAL NOTE

The oldest commentary on Homer, the scholia (i.e. the notes, derived from a variety of sources, which stand in the margins of some of the manuscripts), still have a good deal to teach us, as we have recently been reminded by J. Griffin, *C.Q.* n.s. 26 (1976) 161–85 and N. J. Richardson, *C.Q.* n.s. 30 (1980) 265–87; and where Homer is concerned, a classical scholar must be more than ever aware that he is trying to clamber on to the shoulders of the Alexandrian critics. The edition of the older *Iliad* scholia by H. Erbse (Berlin 1969–77) is truly magisterial: I only wish I had spent more time learning from it than I already have. The commentary of Eustathius, who wrote in the twelfth century A.D. but drew heavily on earlier sources, is infuriatingly verbose, but contains some good remarks. Of modern commentaries on the whole *Iliad*, W. Leaf's (London 1900–2: reprinted Amsterdam 1971) is the most consistently helpful; and although it tends, like all nineteenth-century 'analysis' of Homer, to find fault at any cost, it does so much less than it might have, given the time in which it was written. J. van Leeuwen's (Leiden 1912–13) is dull and sketchy, but not worthless; and it usefully registers in the margin repeated lines and phrases. The modest commentaries of J. U. Fäsi–F. R. Franke (fifth edition, Berlin 1871), D. B. Monro (Oxford 1884: frequently reprinted) and K. F. Ameis– C. Hentze–P. Cauer (fourth edition of Books 22–4, Leipzig and Berlin 1906: reprinted Amsterdam 1965), which were designed mainly for schools, are not contemptible; and once or twice they raise questions or offer solutions that I have not seen elsewhere. Monro's introductions to each book guide the reader soberly through the thickets and quicksands of contemporary criticism; the long appendix to Ameis–Hentze (third edition, Leipzig 1896) is an exhaustive compendium of that criticism: it is sometimes instructive, though highly indigestible. Much the same goes for P. von der Mühll, *Kritisches Hypomnema zur Ilias* (Basel 1952). M. M. Willcock's *A companion to the Iliad* (Chicago and London 1976), which gives notes on Richmond Lattimore's translation, is lucid and thoughtful on a number of points.

Of commentaries on Book 24 alone, R. Peppmueller's (Berlin 1876) is a monument of philistinism, but also of accumulative industry: its massive collection of Homeric parallels is sometimes of use. F. Martinazzoli's (Turin 1948) – another school edition – is much less bulky, but more tactful and sensitive.

The list which follows is not a guide to writings on *Iliad* 24; it simply gives details of books which I have referred to by the author's surname and/or abridged title. One or two which I have referred to in this way in only one context, where the full title is also mentioned, do not appear here. Its aim is thus to record those works which for one reason or another I have found particularly helpful; but it does not include standard commentaries on ancient texts (e.g. Fraenkel on Aeschylus, *Agamemnon* or West on Hesiod, *Theogony*) or Liddell and Scott's lexicon (LSJ).

Andersen, Ø. *Die Diomedesgestalt in der Ilias* (*Symbolae Osloenses* Supp. 25: Oslo 1978)

Archaeologia Homerica: Die Denkmäler und das frühgriechische Epos, ed. F. Matz and H.-G. Buchholz (Göttingen 1967). [*AH*]

Beck, G. *Die Stellung des 24 Buches der Ilias in der alten Epentradition* (Diss. Tübingen 1964)

Chantraine, P. *Grammaire homérique* (Paris 1948–53)

A Companion to Homer, ed. A. J. B. Wace and F. H. Stubbings (London 1962). [*CH*]

Deichgräber, K. 'Der letzte Gesang der Ilias', *Abhandlungen der Mainzer Akademie der Wissenschaften und Literatur*, Geistes-und sozialwiss. Klasse, 1972, No. 5

Denniston, J. D. *The Greek Particles*[2] (Oxford 1954)

Fehling, D. *Die Wiederholungsfiguren und ihr Gebrauch bei den Griechen vor Gorgias* (Berlin 1969). [*WF*]

Fraenkel, Ed. *Beobachtungen zu Aristophanes* (Rome 1962). [*BA*]

Griffin, J. *Homer on life and death* (Oxford 1980)

Johansen, K. F. *The Iliad in early Greek art* (Copenhagen 1967)

Kassel, R. *Untersuchungen zur griechischen und römischen Konsolationsliteratur* (*Zetemata* 18: Munich 1958)

Kühner, R. and Gerth, B. *Ausführliche Grammatik der griechischen Sprache*[3] (Hanover and Leipzig 1890–1904)

Kullmann, W. *Die Quellen der Ilias* (*Hermes* Einzelschr. 14: Wiesbaden 1960)

Kurtz, D. and Boardman, J. *Greek burial customs* (London 1971)

Neumann, G. *Gesten und Gebärden in der griechischen Kunst* (Berlin 1965)

Parry, M. *The making of Homeric verse* (Oxford 1971). [*MHV*]

Reinhardt, K. *Die Ilias und ihr Dichter* (Göttingen 1961). [*ID*]

Schadewaldt, W. 'Iliasstudien', *Abhandlungen der sächsischen Akademie der Wissenschaften*, Phil.-hist. Klasse, 43 (1938) no. 6 (reprinted Darmstadt 1966). [*IS*]

Schadewaldt, W. *Von Homers Welt und Werk*[3] (Stuttgart 1959). [*HWW*]

Stawell, F. M. *Homer and the Iliad* (London 1909)

van der Valk, M. *Researches on the text and scholia of the Iliad* (Leiden 1963–4)

Vickers, B. *Towards Greek tragedy* (London 1973)

Wackernagel, J. *Vorlesungen über Syntax* (Basel 1926–8)

NOTE ON THE TEXT AND APPARATUS

The text is my own, though it does not differ much from any current ones. The apparatus is highly selective and drastically simplified. I use the letters **a** and **b** to indicate variant readings, including those contained in papyri (there are no Ptolemaic papyri of *Iliad* 24) and mentioned in the scholia. So **a** and **b** do not stand for any definite body of manuscripts; some further particulars will usually be found in the note on the line concerned. Where a variant occurs only in a papyrus I use the letter **p**. Where I record readings preserved in quotations I give the author's name; references will be found in the notes. For fuller details the reader should consult T. W. Allen's *editio maior* of the *Iliad* (Oxford 1931) or his Oxford Classical Text (third edition, 1920: constantly reprinted).

ΙΛΙΑΔΟΣ Ω

ΙΛΙΑΔΟΣ Ω

Λῦτο δ᾽ ἀγών, λαοὶ δὲ θοὰς ἐπὶ νῆας ἕκαστοι
ἐσκίδναντ᾽ ἰέναι. τοὶ μὲν δόρποιο μέδοντο
ὕπνου τε γλυκεροῦ ταρπήμεναι· αὐτὰρ Ἀχιλλεὺς
κλαῖε φίλου ἑτάρου μεμνημένος, οὐδέ μιν ὕπνος
ᾕρει πανδαμάτωρ, ἀλλ᾽ ἐστρέφετ᾽ ἔνθα καὶ ἔνθα,   5
Πατρόκλου ποθέων ἀδροτῆτά τε καὶ μένος ἠΰ,
ἠδ᾽ ὁπόσα τολύπευσε σὺν αὐτῷ καὶ πάθεν ἄλγεα,
ἀνδρῶν τε πτολέμους ἀλεγεινά τε κύματα πείρων·
τῶν μιμνησκόμενος θαλερὸν κατὰ δάκρυον εἶβεν,
ἄλλοτ᾽ ἐπὶ πλευρὰς κατακείμενος, ἄλλοτε δ᾽ αὖτε   10
ὕπτιος, ἄλλοτε δὲ πρηνής· τοτὲ δ᾽ ὀρθὸς ἀναστὰς
δινεύεσκ᾽ ἀλύων παρὰ θῖν᾽ ἁλός· οὐδέ μιν ἠὼς
φαινομένη λήθεσκεν ὑπεὶρ ἅλα τ᾽ ἠϊόνας τε.
ἀλλ᾽ ὅ γ᾽ ἐπεὶ ζεύξειεν ὑφ᾽ ἅρμασιν ὠκέας ἵππους,
Ἕκτορα δ᾽ ἕλκεσθαι δησάσκετο δίφρου ὄπισθεν,   15
τρὶς δ᾽ ἐρύσας περὶ σῆμα Μενοιτιάδαο θανόντος
αὖτις ἐνὶ κλισίῃ παυέσκετο, τόνδε δ᾽ ἔασκεν
ἐν κόνι ἐκτανύσας προπρηνέα· τοῖο δ᾽ Ἀπόλλων
πᾶσαν ἀεικείην ἄπεχε χροῒ φῶτ᾽ ἐλεαίρων
καὶ τεθνηότα περ· περὶ δ᾽ αἰγίδι πάντα κάλυπτε   20
χρυσείῃ, ἵνα μή μιν ἀποδρύφοι ἑλκυστάζων.
Ὣς ὁ μὲν Ἕκτορα δῖον ἀείκιζεν μενεαίνων·
τὸν δ᾽ ἐλεαίρεσκον μάκαρες θεοὶ εἰσορόωντες,
κλέψαι δ᾽ ὀτρύνεσκον ἐΰσκοπον Ἀργειφόντην.
ἔνθ᾽ ἄλλοις μὲν πᾶσιν ἑήνδανεν, οὐδέ ποθ᾽ Ἥρῃ   25
οὐδὲ Ποσειδάων᾽ οὐδὲ γλαυκώπιδι κούρῃ,
ἀλλ᾽ ἔχον ὥς σφιν πρῶτον ἀπήχθετο Ἴλιος ἱρὴ
καὶ Πρίαμος καὶ λαὸς Ἀλεξάνδρου ἕνεκ᾽ ἄτης,
ὃς νείκεσσε θεάς, ὅτε οἱ μέσσαυλον ἵκοντο,
τὴν δ᾽ ᾔνησ᾽ ἥ οἱ πόρε μαχλοσύνην ἀλεγεινήν.   30
ἀλλ᾽ ὅτε δή ῥ᾽ ἐκ τοῖο δυωδεκάτη γένετ᾽ ἠώς,

6–9 suspecti   6 ἀνδροτῆτα codd. fere omnes   28 ἀρχῆς a

καὶ τότ' ἄρ' ἀθανάτοισι μετηύδα Φοῖβος Ἀπόλλων·
"σχέτλιοί ἐστε, θεοί, δηλήμονες· οὔ νύ ποθ' ὑμῖν
Ἕκτωρ μηρί' ἔκηε βοῶν αἰγῶν τε τελείων;
τὸν νῦν οὐκ ἔτλητε νέκυν περ ἐόντα σαῶσαι,   35
ᾗ τ' ἀλόχῳ ἰδέειν καὶ μητέρι καὶ τέκεϊ ᾧ
καὶ πατέρι Πριάμῳ λαοῖσί τε, τοί κέ μιν ὦκα
ἐν πυρὶ κήαιεν καὶ ἐπὶ κτέρεα κτερίσαιεν.
ἀλλ' ὀλοῷ Ἀχιλῆϊ, θεοί, βούλεσθ' ἐπαρήγειν,
ᾧ οὔτ' ἄρ φρένες εἰσὶν ἐναίσιμοι οὔτε νόημα   40
γναμπτὸν ἐνὶ στήθεσσι, λέων δ' ὡς ἄγρια οἶδεν,
ὅς τ' ἐπεὶ ἄρ μεγάλῃ τε βίῃ καὶ ἀγήνορι θυμῷ
εἴξας εἶσ' ἐπὶ μῆλα βροτῶν, ἵνα δαῖτα λάβῃσιν·
ὡς Ἀχιλεὺς ἔλεον μὲν ἀπώλεσεν, οὐδέ οἱ αἰδὼς
γίγνεται, ἥ τ' ἄνδρας μέγα σίνεται ἠδ' ὀνίνησι.   45
μέλλει μέν πού τις καὶ φίλτερον ἄλλον ὀλέσσαι,
ἠὲ κασίγνητον ὁμογάστριον ἠὲ καὶ υἱόν·
ἀλλ' ἤτοι κλαύσας καὶ ὀδυράμενος μεθέηκε·
τλητὸν γὰρ Μοῖραι θυμὸν θέσαν ἀνθρώποισιν.
αὐτὰρ ὅ γ' Ἕκτορα δῖον, ἐπεὶ φίλον ἦτορ ἀπηύρα,   50
ἵππων ἐξάπτων περὶ σῆμ' ἑτάροιο φίλοιο
ἕλκει· οὐ μήν οἱ τό γε κάλλιον οὐδέ τ' ἄμεινον.
μή, ἀγαθῷ περ ἐόντι, νεμεσσηθῶμέν οἱ ἡμεῖς·
κωφὴν γὰρ δὴ γαῖαν ἀεικίζει μενεαίνων."
    Τὸν δὲ χολωσαμένη προσέφη λευκώλενος Ἥρη·   55
"εἴη κεν καὶ τοῦτο τεὸν ἔπος, ἀργυρότοξε,
εἰ δὴ ὁμὴν Ἀχιλῆϊ καὶ Ἕκτορι θήσετε τιμήν.
Ἕκτωρ μὲν θνητός τε γυναῖκά τε θήσατο μαζόν·
αὐτὰρ Ἀχιλλεύς ἐστι θεᾶς γόνος, ἣν ἐγὼ αὐτὴ
θρέψα τε καὶ ἀτίτηλα καὶ ἀνδρὶ πόρον παράκοιτιν,   60
Πηλέϊ, ὃς περὶ κῆρι φίλος γένετ' ἀθανάτοισι.
πάντες δ' ἀντιάασθε, θεοί, γάμου· ἐν δὲ σὺ τοῖσι
δαίνυ' ἔχων φόρμιγγα, κακῶν ἔταρ', αἰὲν ἄπιστε."
    Τὴν δ' ἀπαμειβόμενος προσέφη νεφεληγερέτα Ζεύς·
"Ἥρη, μὴ δὴ πάμπαν ἀποσκύδμαινε θεοῖσιν·   65
38 κτερίσειαν a   45 iniuria, nisi fallor, damnatus

οὐ μὲν γὰρ τιμή γε μί᾽ ἔσσεται· ἀλλὰ καὶ Ἕκτωρ
φίλτατος ἔσκε θεοῖσι βροτῶν οἳ ἐν Ἰλίῳ εἰσίν·
ὣς γὰρ ἔμοιγ᾽, ἐπεὶ οὔ τι φίλων ἡμάρτανε δώρων.
οὐ γάρ μοί ποτε βωμὸς ἐδεύετο δαιτὸς ἐΐσης,
λοιβῆς τε κνίσης τε· τὸ γὰρ λάχομεν γέρας ἡμεῖς.   70
ἀλλ᾽ ἤτοι κλέψαι μὲν ἐάσομεν – οὐδέ πῃ ἔστι –
λάθρῃ Ἀχιλλῆος θρασὺν Ἕκτορα· ἦ γάρ οἱ αἰεὶ
μήτηρ παρμέμβλωκεν ὁμῶς νύκτας τε καὶ ἦμαρ.
ἀλλ᾽ εἴ τις καλέσειε θεῶν Θέτιν ἆσσον ἐμεῖο,
ὄφρα τί οἱ εἴπω πυκινὸν ἔπος, ὥς κεν Ἀχιλλεὺς   75
δώρων ἐκ Πριάμοιο λάχῃ ἀπό θ᾽ Ἕκτορα λύσῃ.᾽᾽
   Ὣς ἔφατ᾽, ὦρτο δὲ Ἶρις ἀελλόπος ἀγγελέουσα,
μεσσηγὺς δὲ Σάμου τε καὶ Ἴμβρου παιπαλοέσσης
ἔνθορε μείλανι πόντῳ· ἐπεστονάχησε δὲ λίμνη.
ἡ δὲ μολυβδαίνῃ ἰκέλη ἐς βυσσὸν ὄρουσεν,   80
ἥ τε κατ᾽ ἀγραύλοιο βοὸς κέρας ἐμβεβαυῖα
ἔρχεται ὠμηστῇσιν ἐπ᾽ ἰχθύσι κῆρα φέρουσα.
εὗρε δ᾽ ἐνὶ σπῆϊ γλαφυρῷ Θέτιν, ἀμφὶ δ᾽ ἄρ᾽ ἄλλαι
εἵαθ᾽ ὁμηγερέες ἅλιαι θεαί· ἡ δ᾽ ἐνὶ μέσσῃς
κλαῖε μόρον οὗ παιδὸς ἀμύμονος, ὅς οἱ ἔμελλε   85
φθίσεσθ᾽ ἐν Τροίῃ ἐριβώλακι, τηλόθι πάτρης.
ἀγχοῦ δ᾽ ἱσταμένη προσέφη πόδας ὠκέα Ἶρις·
᾽᾽ὄρσο, Θέτι· καλέει Ζεὺς ἄφθιτα μήδεα εἰδώς.᾽᾽
τὴν δ᾽ ἠμείβετ᾽ ἔπειτα θεὰ Θέτις ἀργυρόπεζα·
᾽᾽τίπτε με κεῖνος ἄνωγε μέγας θεός; αἰδέομαι δὲ   90
μίσγεσθ᾽ ἀθανάτοισιν, ἔχω δ᾽ ἄχε᾽ ἄκριτα θυμῷ.
εἶμι μέν, οὐδ᾽ ἅλιον ἔπος ἔσσεται, ὅττι κεν εἴπῃ.᾽᾽
   Ὣς ἄρα φωνήσασα κάλυμμ᾽ ἕλε δῖα θεάων
κυάνεον, τοῦ δ᾽ οὔ τι μελάντερον ἔπλετο ἔσθος.
βῆ δ᾽ ἰέναι, πρόσθεν δὲ ποδήνεμος ὠκέα Ἶρις   95
ἡγεῖτ᾽· ἀμφὶ δ᾽ ἄρα σφι λιάζετο κῦμα θαλάσσης.
ἀκτὴν δ᾽ ἐξαναβᾶσαι ἐς οὐρανὸν ἀϊχθήτην,
εὗρον δ᾽ εὐρύοπα Κρονίδην, περὶ δ᾽ ἄλλοι ἅπαντες

80 ὄρουσεν] ἵκανεν Plato   81 ἐμμεμαυῖα Plato a   82 ἐπ᾽] μετ᾽
Plato   κῆρα] πῆμα Plato a

εἶαθ᾽ ὁμηγερέες μάκαρες θεοὶ αἰὲν ἐόντες.
ἡ δ᾽ ἄρα πὰρ Διὶ πατρὶ καθέζετο, εἶξε δ᾽ ᾽Αθήνη.   100
῞Ηρη δὲ χρύσεον καλὸν δέπας ἐν χερὶ θῆκε
καί ῥ᾽ εὔφρην᾽ ἐπέεσσι· Θέτις δ᾽ ὤρεξε πιοῦσα.
τοῖσι δὲ μύθων ἦρχε πατὴρ ἀνδρῶν τε θεῶν τε·
"ἤλυθες Οὔλυμπόνδε, θεὰ Θέτι, κηδομένη περ,
πένθος ἄλαστον ἔχουσα μετὰ φρεσίν· οἶδα καὶ αὐτός·   105
ἀλλὰ καὶ ὧς ἐρέω τοῦ σ᾽ εἵνεκα δεῦρο κάλεσσα.
ἐννῆμαρ δὴ νεῖκος ἐν ἀθανάτοισιν ὄρωρεν
῞Εκτορος ἀμφὶ νέκυι καὶ ᾽Αχιλλῆϊ πτολιπόρθῳ·
κλέψαι δ᾽ ὀτρύνεσκον ἐΰσκοπον ᾽Αργειφόντην·
αὐτὰρ ἐγὼ τόδε κῦδος ᾽Αχιλλῆϊ προτιάπτω,   110
αἰδῶ καὶ φιλότητα τεὴν μετόπισθε φυλάσσων.
αἶψα μάλ᾽ ἐς στρατὸν ἐλθὲ καὶ υἱέϊ σῷ ἐπίτειλον·
σκύζεσθαί οἱ εἰπὲ θεούς, ἐμὲ δ᾽ ἔξοχα πάντων
ἀθανάτων κεχολῶσθαι, ὅτι φρεσὶ μαινομένῃσιν
῞Εκτορ᾽ ἔχει παρὰ νηυσὶ κορωνίσιν οὐδ᾽ ἀπέλυσεν,   115
αἴ κέν πως ἐμέ τε δείσῃ ἀπό θ᾽ ῞Εκτορα λύσῃ.
αὐτὰρ ἐγὼ Πριάμῳ μεγαλήτορι ῏Ιριν ἐφήσω
λύσασθαι φίλον υἱόν, ἰόντ᾽ ἐπὶ νῆας ᾽Αχαιῶν,
δῶρα δ᾽ ᾽Αχιλλῆϊ φερέμεν, τά κε θυμὸν ἰήνῃ."
῝Ως ἔφατ᾽, οὐδ᾽ ἀπίθησε θεὰ Θέτις ἀργυρόπεζα,   120
βῆ δὲ κατ᾽ Οὐλύμποιο καρήνων ἀΐξασα,
ἷξεν δ᾽ ἐς κλισίην οὗ υἱέος· ἔνθ᾽ ἄρα τόν γε
εὗρ᾽ ἁδινὰ στενάχοντα· φίλοι δ᾽ ἀμφ᾽ αὐτὸν ἑταῖροι
ἐσσυμένως ἐπένοντο καὶ ἐντύνοντ᾽ ἄριστον·
τοῖσι δ᾽ ὄϊς λάσιος μέγας ἐν κλισίῃ ἱέρευτο.   125
ἡ δὲ μάλ᾽ ἄγχ᾽ αὐτοῖο καθέζετο πότνια μήτηρ,
χειρί τέ μιν κατέρεξεν ἔπος τ᾽ ἔφατ᾽ ἔκ τ᾽ ὀνόμαζε·
"τέκνον ἐμόν, τέο μέχρις ὀδυρόμενος καὶ ἀχεύων
σὴν ἔδεαι κραδίην, μεμνημένος οὔτε τι σίτου
οὔτ᾽ εὐνῆς; ἀγαθὸν δὲ γυναικί περ ἐν φιλότητι   130
μίσγεσθ᾽· οὐ γάρ μοι δηρὸν βέῃ, ἀλλά τοι ἤδη
ἄγχι παρέστηκεν θάνατος καὶ μοῖρα κραταιή.

109 ὀτρύνουσιν a

ἀλλ᾽ ἐμέθεν ξύνες ὦκα, Διὸς δέ τοι ἄγγελός εἰμι·
σκύζεσθαι σοί φησι θεούς, ἐξ δ᾽ ἔξοχα πάντων
ἀθανάτων κεχολῶσθαι, ὅτι φρεσὶ μαινομένῃσιν   135
Ἕκτορ᾽ ἔχεις παρὰ νηυσὶ κορωνίσιν οὐδ᾽ ἀπέλυσας.
ἀλλ᾽ ἄγε δὴ λῦσον, νεκροῖο δὲ δέξαι ἄποινα."
  Τὴν δ᾽ ἀπαμειβόμενος προσέφη πόδας ὠκὺς Ἀχιλλεύς·
"τῇδ᾽ εἴη ὃς ἄποινα φέροι καὶ νεκρὸν ἄγοιτο,
εἰ δὴ πρόφρονι θυμῷ Ὀλύμπιος αὐτὸς ἀνώγει."   140
  Ὣς οἵ γ᾽ ἐν νηῶν ἀγύρει μήτηρ τε καὶ υἱὸς
πολλὰ πρὸς ἀλλήλους ἔπεα πτερόεντ᾽ ἀγόρευον.
Ἶριν δ᾽ ὄτρυνε Κρονίδης εἰς Ἴλιον ἱρήν·
"βάσκ᾽ ἴθι, Ἶρι ταχεῖα, λιποῦσ᾽ ἕδος Οὐλύμποιο
ἄγγειλον Πριάμῳ μεγαλήτορι Ἴλιον εἴσω   145
λύσασθαι φίλον υἱὸν ἰόντ᾽ ἐπὶ νῆας Ἀχαιῶν,
δῶρα δ᾽ Ἀχιλλῆϊ φερέμεν, τά κε θυμὸν ἰήνῃ,
οἶον, μηδέ τις ἄλλος ἅμα Τρώων ἴτω ἀνήρ.
κῆρύξ τίς οἱ ἔποιτο γεραίτερος, ὅς κ᾽ ἰθύνοι
ἡμιόνους καὶ ἄμαξαν ἐΰτροχον, ἠδὲ καὶ αὖτις   150
νεκρὸν ἄγοι προτὶ ἄστυ, τὸν ἔκτανε δῖος Ἀχιλλεύς.
μηδέ τί οἱ θάνατος μελέτω φρεσὶ μηδέ τι τάρβος·
τοῖον γάρ οἱ πομπὸν ὀπάσσομεν Ἀργειφόντην,
ὃς ἄξει ἧός κεν ἄγων Ἀχιλῆϊ πελάσσῃ.
αὐτὰρ ἐπὴν ἀγάγῃσιν ἔσω κλισίην Ἀχιλῆος,   155
οὔτ᾽ αὐτὸς κτενέει ἀπό τ᾽ ἄλλους πάντας ἐρύξει·
οὔτε γάρ ἐστ᾽ ἄφρων οὔτ᾽ ἄσκοπος οὔτ᾽ ἀλιτήμων,
ἀλλὰ μάλ᾽ ἐνδυκέως ἱκέτεω πεφιδήσεται ἀνδρός."
  Ὣς ἔφατ᾽, ὦρτο δὲ Ἶρις ἀελλόπος ἀγγελέουσα.
ἷξεν δ᾽ ἐς Πριάμοιο, κίχεν δ᾽ ἐνοπήν τε γόον τε.   160
παῖδες μὲν πατέρ᾽ ἀμφὶ καθήμενοι ἔνδοθεν αὐλῆς
δάκρυσιν εἵματ᾽ ἔφυρον, ὁ δ᾽ ἐν μέσσοισι γεραιὸς
ἐντυπὰς ἐν χλαίνῃ κεκαλυμμένος· ἀμφὶ δὲ πολλὴ
κόπρος ἔην κεφαλῇ τε καὶ αὐχένι τοῖο γέροντος,
τήν ῥα κυλινδόμενος καταμήσατο χερσὶν ἑῇσι.   165
θυγατέρες δ᾽ ἀνὰ δώματ᾽ ἰδὲ νυοὶ ὠδύροντο,

148, 177 οἷος a

τῶν μιμνησκόμεναι οἳ δὴ πολέες τε καὶ ἐσθλοὶ
χερσὶν ὑπ' 'Αργείων κέατο ψυχὰς ὀλέσαντες.
στῆ δὲ παρὰ Πρίαμον Διὸς ἄγγελος, ἠδὲ προσηύδα
τυτθὸν φθεγξαμένη· τὸν δὲ τρόμος ἔλλαβε γυῖα·   170
"θάρσει, Δαρδανίδη Πρίαμε, φρεσί, μηδέ τι τάρβει·
οὐ μὲν γάρ τοι ἐγὼ κακὸν ὀσσομένη τόδ' ἱκάνω,
ἀλλ' ἀγαθὰ φρονέουσα· Διὸς δέ τοι ἄγγελός εἰμι,
ὅς σευ ἄνευθεν ἐὼν μέγα κήδεται ἠδ' ἐλεαίρει.
λύσασθαί σε κέλευσεν 'Ολύμπιος "Εκτορα δῖον,   175
δῶρα δ' 'Αχιλλῆϊ φερέμεν, τά κε θυμὸν ἰήνῃ,
οἶον, μηδέ τις ἄλλος ἅμα Τρώων ἴτω ἀνήρ.
κῆρύξ τίς τοι ἔποιτο γεραίτερος, ὅς κ' ἰθύνοι
ἡμιόνους καὶ ἄμαξαν ἐΰτροχον, ἠδὲ καὶ αὖτις
νεκρὸν ἄγοι προτὶ ἄστυ, τὸν ἔκτανε δῖος 'Αχιλλεύς.   180
μηδέ τί τοι θάνατος μελέτω φρεσὶ μηδέ τι τάρβος·
τοῖος γάρ τοι πομπὸς ἅμ' ἕψεται 'Αργειφόντης,
ὅς σ' ἄξει ἧός κεν ἄγων 'Αχιλῆϊ πελάσσῃ.
αὐτὰρ ἐπὴν ἀγάγῃσιν ἔσω κλισίην 'Αχιλῆος,
οὔτ' αὐτὸς κτενέει ἀπό τ' ἄλλους πάντας ἐρύξει·   185
οὔτε γάρ ἐστ' ἄφρων οὔτ' ἄσκοπος οὔτ' ἀλιτήμων,
ἀλλὰ μάλ' ἐνδυκέως ἱκέτεω πεφιδήσεται ἀνδρός."
'Η μὲν ἄρ' ὣς εἰποῦσ' ἀπέβη πόδας ὠκέα ῏Ιρις,
αὐτὰρ ὅ γ' υἷας ἄμαξαν ἐΰτροχον ἡμιονείην
ὁπλίσαι ἠνώγει, πείρινθα δὲ δῆσαι ἐπ' αὐτῆς.   190
αὐτὸς δ' ἐς θάλαμον κατεβήσετο κηώεντα
κέδρινον ὑψόροφον, ὃς γλήνεα πολλὰ κεχάνδει·
ἐς δ' ἄλοχον 'Εκάβην ἐκαλέσσατο φώνησέν τε·
"δαιμονίη, Διόθεν μοι 'Ολύμπιος ἄγγελος ἦλθε
λύσασθαι φίλον υἱὸν ἰόντ' ἐπὶ νῆας 'Αχαιῶν,   195
δῶρα δ' 'Αχιλλῆϊ φερέμεν, τά κε θυμὸν ἰήνῃ.
ἀλλ' ἄγε μοι τόδε εἰπέ, τί τοι φρεσὶν εἴδεται εἶναι;
αἰνῶς γάρ μ' αὐτόν γε μένος καὶ θυμὸς ἄνωγε
κεῖσ' ἰέναι ἐπὶ νῆας ἔσω στρατὸν εὐρὺν 'Αχαιῶν."
῍Ως φάτο, κώκυσεν δὲ γυνὴ καὶ ἀμείβετο μύθῳ·   200

192 κεχάνδει]]ονδει p

"ὤ μοι, πῇ δή τοι φρένες οἴχονθ᾽, ᾗς τὸ πάρος περ
ἔκλε᾽ ἐπ᾽ ἀνθρώπους ξείνους ἠδ᾽ οἷσιν ἀνάσσεις;
πῶς ἐθέλεις ἐπὶ νῆας ᾿Αχαιῶν ἐλθέμεν οἶος,
ἀνδρὸς ἐς ὀφθαλμοὺς ὅς τοι πολέας τε καὶ ἐσθλοὺς
υἱέας ἐξενάριξε; σιδήρειόν νύ τοι ἦτορ.   205
εἰ γάρ σ᾽ αἱρήσει καὶ ἐσόψεται ὀφθαλμοῖσιν,
ὠμηστὴς καὶ ἄπιστος ἀνὴρ ὅ γε, οὔ σ᾽ ἐλεήσει,
οὐδέ τί σ᾽ αἰδέσεται. νῦν δὲ κλαίωμεν ἄνευθεν
ἥμενοι ἐν μεγάρῳ· τῷ δ᾽ ὥς ποθι Μοῖρα κραταιὴ
γιγνομένῳ ἐπένησε λίνῳ, ὅτε μιν τέκον αὐτή,   210
ἀργίποδας κύνας ἆσαι ἑῶν ἀπάνευθε τοκήων,
ἀνδρὶ πάρα κρατερῷ – τοῦ ἐγὼ μέσον ἧπαρ ἔχοιμι
ἐσθέμεναι προσφῦσα· τότ᾽ ἄντιτα ἔργα γένοιτο
παιδὸς ἐμοῦ, ἐπεὶ οὔ ἑ κακιζόμενόν γε κατέκτα,
ἀλλὰ πρὸ Τρώων καὶ Τρωϊάδων βαθυκόλπων   215
ἑσταότ᾽, οὔτε φόβου μεμνημένον οὔτ᾽ ἀλεωρῆς."
    Τὴν δ᾽ αὖτε προσέειπε γέρων Πρίαμος θεοειδής·
"μή μ᾽ ἐθέλοντ᾽ ἰέναι κατερύκανε, μηδέ μοι αὐτὴ
ὄρνις ἐνὶ μεγάροισι κακὸς πέλευ· οὐδέ με πείσεις.
εἰ μὲν γάρ τίς μ᾽ ἄλλος ἐπιχθονίων ἐκέλευεν,   220
ἢ οἳ μάντιές εἰσι θυοσκόοι ἢ ἱερῆες,
ψεῦδός κεν φαῖμεν καὶ νοσφιζοίμεθα μᾶλλον·
νῦν δ᾽ αὐτὸς γὰρ ἄκουσα θεοῦ καὶ ἐσέδρακον ἄντην,
εἶμι, καὶ οὐχ ἅλιον ἔπος ἔσσεται. εἰ δέ μοι αἶσα
τεθνάμεναι παρὰ νηυσὶν ᾿Αχαιῶν χαλκοχιτώνων,   225
βούλομαι· αὐτίκα γάρ με κατακτείνειεν ᾿Αχιλλεὺς
ἀγκὰς ἑλόντ᾽ ἐμὸν υἱόν, ἐπὴν γόου ἐξ ἔρον εἵην."
    ῏Η, καὶ φωριαμῶν ἐπιθήματα κάλ᾽ ἀνέῳγεν·
ἔνθεν δώδεκα μὲν περικαλλέας ἔξελε πέπλους,
δώδεκα δ᾽ ἁπλοΐδας χλαίνας, τόσσους δὲ τάπητας,   230
τόσσα δὲ φάρεα λευκά, τόσους δ᾽ ἐπὶ τοῖσι χιτῶνας,
[χρυσοῦ δὲ στήσας ἔφερεν δέκα πάντα τάλαντα]
ἐκ δὲ δύ᾽ αἴθωνας τρίποδας, πίσυρας δὲ λέβητας,
ἐκ δὲ δέπας περικαλλές, ὅ οἱ Θρῇκες πόρον ἄνδρες
231 λευκά] καλά **a**   232 del. Christ

ἐξεσίην ἐλθόντι, μέγα κτέρας· οὐδέ νυ τοῦ περ   235
φείσατ' ἐνὶ μεγάροις ὁ γέρων, περὶ δ' ἤθελε θυμῷ
λύσασθαι φίλον υἱόν. ὁ δὲ Τρῶας μὲν ἅπαντας
αἰθούσης ἀπέεργεν ἔπεσσ' αἰσχροῖσιν ἐνίσσων·
"ἔρρετε, λωβητῆρες ἐλεγχέες· οὔ νυ καὶ ὑμῖν
οἴκοι ἔνεστι γόος, ὅτι μ' ἤλθετε κηδήσοντες;   240
ἦ οὔνεσθ' ὅτι μοι Κρονίδης Ζεὺς ἄλγε' ἔδωκε,
παῖδ' ὀλέσαι τὸν ἄριστον; ἀτὰρ γνώσεσθε καὶ ὔμμες·
ῥηΐτεροι γὰρ μᾶλλον Ἀχαιοῖσιν δὴ ἔσεσθε
κείνου τεθνηῶτος ἐναιρέμεν. αὐτὰρ ἔγωγε
πρὶν ἀλαπαζομένην τε πόλιν κεραϊζομένην τε   245
ὀφθαλμοῖσιν ἰδεῖν, βαίην δόμον Ἄϊδος εἴσω."
    Ἦ, καὶ σκηπανίῳ δίεπ' ἀνέρας· οἱ δ' ἴσαν ἔξω
σπερχομένοιο γέροντος· ὁ δ' υἱάσιν οἷσιν ὁμόκλα,
νεικείων Ἕλενόν τε Πάριν τ' Ἀγάθωνά τε δῖον
Πάμμονά τ' Ἀντίφονόν τε βοὴν ἀγαθόν τε Πολίτην   250
Δηΐφοβόν τε καὶ Ἱππόθοον καὶ δῖον ἀγαυόν·
ἐννέα τοῖς ὁ γεραιὸς ὁμοκλήσας ἐκέλευε·
"σπεύσατέ μοι, κακὰ τέκνα, κατηφόνες· αἴθ' ἅμα πάντες
Ἕκτορος ὠφέλετ' ἀντὶ θοῆς ἐπὶ νηυσὶ πεφάσθαι.
ὤ μοι ἐγὼ πανάποτμος, ἐπεὶ τέκον υἷας ἀρίστους   255
Τροίῃ ἐν εὐρείῃ, τῶν δ' οὔ τινά φημι λελεῖφθαι,
Μήστορά τ' ἀντίθεον καὶ Τρωΐλον ἱππιοχάρμην
Ἕκτορά θ', ὃς θεὸς ἔσκε μετ' ἀνδράσιν, οὐδὲ ἐῴκει
ἀνδρός γε θνητοῦ πάϊς ἔμμεναι, ἀλλὰ θεοῖο.
τοὺς μὲν ἀπώλεσ' Ἄρης, τὰ δ' ἐλέγχεα πάντα λέλειπται,   260
ψεῦσταί τ' ὀρχησταί τε, χοροιτυπίῃσιν ἄριστοι,
ἀρνῶν ἠδ' ἐρίφων ἐπιδήμιοι ἁρπακτῆρες.
οὐκ ἂν δή μοι ἄμαξαν ἐφοπλίσσαιτε τάχιστα,
ταῦτά τε πάντ' ἐπιθεῖτε, ἵνα πρήσσωμεν ὁδοῖο;"
    Ὣς ἔφαθ', οἱ δ' ἄρα πατρὸς ὑποδείσαντες ὁμοκλὴν   265
ἐκ μὲν ἄμαξαν ἄειραν ἐΰτροχον ἡμιονείην
καλὴν πρωτοπαγέα, πείρινθα δὲ δῆσαν ἐπ' αὐτῆς,
κὰδ δ' ἀπὸ πασσαλόφι ζυγὸν ᾕρεον ἡμιόνειον

241 οὔνεσθ']]ούνο[**p**: ὀνόσασθ' **a**

πύξινον ὀμφαλόεν, εὖ οἰήκεσσιν ἀρηρός·
ἐκ δ᾽ ἔφερον ζυγόδεσμον ἅμα ζυγῷ ἐννεάπηχυ.　　　　270
καὶ τὸ μὲν εὖ κατέθηκαν ἐϋξέστῳ ἐπὶ ῥυμῷ,
πέζῃ ἔπι πρώτῃ, ἐπὶ δὲ κρίκον ἕστορι βάλλον,
τρὶς δ᾽ ἑκάτερθεν ἔδησαν ἐπ᾽ ὀμφαλόν, αὐτὰρ ἔπειτα
ἑξείης κατέδησαν, ὑπὸ γλωχῖνα δ᾽ ἔκαμψαν.
ἐκ θαλάμου δὲ φέροντες ἐϋξέστης ἐπ᾽ ἀπήνης　　　　275
νήεον Ἑκτορέης κεφαλῆς ἀπερείσι᾽ ἄποινα,
ζεῦξαν δ᾽ ἡμιόνους κρατερώνυχας ἐντεσιεργούς,
τούς ῥά ποτε Πριάμῳ Μυσοὶ δόσαν ἀγλαὰ δῶρα.
ἵππους δὲ Πριάμῳ ὕπαγον ζυγόν, οὓς ὁ γεραιὸς
αὐτὸς ἔχων ἀτίταλλεν ἐϋξέστῃ ἐπὶ φάτνῃ.　　　　280
　Τὼ μὲν ζευγνύσθην ἐν δώμασιν ὑψηλοῖσι
κῆρυξ καὶ Πρίαμος, πυκινὰ φρεσὶ μήδε᾽ ἔχοντες·
ἀγχίμολον δέ σφ᾽ ἦλθ᾽ Ἑκάβη τετιηότι θυμῷ,
οἶνον ἔχουσ᾽ ἐν χειρὶ μελίφρονα δεξιτερῆφι,
χρυσέῳ ἐν δέπαϊ, ὄφρα λείψαντε κιοίτην·　　　　285
στῆ δ᾽ ἵππων προπάροιθεν ἔπος τ᾽ ἔφατ᾽ ἔκ τ᾽ ὀνόμαζε·
"τῆ, σπεῖσον Διὶ πατρί, καὶ εὔχεο οἴκαδ᾽ ἱκέσθαι
ἂψ ἐκ δυσμενέων ἀνδρῶν, ἐπεὶ ἄρ σέ γε θυμὸς
ὀτρύνει ἐπὶ νῆας, ἐμεῖο μὲν οὐκ ἐθελούσης.
ἀλλ᾽ εὔχεο σύ γ᾽ ἔπειτα κελαινεφέϊ Κρονίωνι　　　　290
Ἰδαίῳ, ὅς τε Τροίην κατὰ πᾶσαν ὁρᾶται,
αἴτει δ᾽ οἰωνόν, ταχὺν ἄγγελον, ὅς τέ οἱ αὐτῷ
φίλτατος οἰωνῶν, καί εὑ κράτος ἐστὶ μέγιστον,
δεξιόν, ὄφρα μιν αὐτὸς ἐν ὀφθαλμοῖσι νοήσας
τῷ πίσυνος ἐπὶ νῆας ἴῃς Δαναῶν ταχυπώλων.　　　　295
εἰ δέ τοι οὐ δώσει ἑὸν ἄγγελον εὐρύοπα Ζεύς,
οὐκ ἂν ἔγωγέ σ᾽ ἔπειτα ἐποτρύνουσα κελοίμην
νῆας ἐπ᾽ Ἀργείων ἰέναι μάλα περ μεμαῶτα."
　Τὴν δ᾽ ἀπαμειβόμενος προσέφη Πρίαμος θεοειδής·
"ὦ γύναι, οὐ μέν τοι τόδ᾽ ἐφιεμένη ἀπιθήσω·　　　　300
ἐσθλὸν γὰρ Διὶ χεῖρας ἀνασχέμεν, αἴ κ᾽ ἐλεήσῃ."
　Ἦ ῥα, καὶ ἀμφίπολον ταμίην ὄτρυν᾽ ὁ γεραιὸς
292 ταχύν] ἑὸν a

χερσὶν ὕδωρ ἐπιχεῦαι ἀκήρατον· ἡ δὲ παρέστη
χέρνιβον ἀμφίπολος πρόχοόν θ᾿ ἅμα χερσὶν ἔχουσα.
νιψάμενος δὲ κύπελλον ἐδέξατο ἧς ἀλόχοιο·   305
εὔχετ᾿ ἔπειτα στὰς μέσῳ ἔρκεϊ, λεῖβε δὲ οἶνον
οὐρανὸν εἰσανιδών, καὶ φωνήσας ἔπος ηὔδα·
"Ζεῦ πάτερ, Ἴδηθεν μεδέων, κύδιστε μέγιστε,
δός μ᾿ ἐς Ἀχιλλῆος φίλον ἐλθεῖν ἠδ᾿ ἐλεεινόν,
πέμψον δ᾿ οἰωνόν, ταχὺν ἄγγελον, ὅς τε σοὶ αὐτῷ   310
φίλτατος οἰωνῶν, καί εὗ κράτος ἐστὶ μέγιστον,
δεξιόν, ὄφρα μιν αὐτὸς ἐν ὀφθαλμοῖσι νοήσας
τῷ πίσυνος ἐπὶ νῆας ἴω Δαναῶν ταχυπώλων."
    Ὣς ἔφατ᾿ εὐχόμενος, τοῦ δ᾿ ἔκλυε μητίετα Ζεύς,
αὐτίκα δ᾿ αἰετὸν ἧκε, τελειότατον πετεηνῶν,   315
μόρφνον θηρητῆρ᾿, ὃν καὶ περκνὸν καλέουσιν.
ὅσση δ᾿ ὑψορόφοιο θύρη θαλάμοιο τέτυκται
ἀνέρος ἀφνειοῖο, ἐΰ κληῖσ᾿ ἀραρυῖα,
τόσσ᾿ ἄρα τοῦ ἑκάτερθεν ἔσαν πτερά· εἴσατο δέ σφι
δεξιὸς ἀΐξας διὰ ἄστεος· οἱ δὲ ἰδόντες   320
γήθησαν, καὶ πᾶσιν ἐνὶ φρεσὶ θυμὸς ἰάνθη.
    Σπερχόμενος δ᾿ ὁ γεραιὸς ἑοῦ ἐπεβήσετο δίφρου,
ἐκ δ᾿ ἔλασε προθύροιο καὶ αἰθούσης ἐριδούπου.
πρόσθε μὲν ἡμίονοι ἕλκον τετράκυκλον ἀπήνην,
τὰς Ἰδαῖος ἔλαυνε δαΐφρων· αὐτὰρ ὄπισθεν   325
ἵπποι, τοὺς ὁ γέρων ἐφέπων μάστιγι κέλευε
καρπαλίμως κατὰ ἄστυ· φίλοι δ᾿ ἅμα πάντες ἕποντο
πόλλ᾿ ὀλοφυρόμενοι ὡς εἰ θάνατόνδε κιόντα.
οἱ δ᾿ ἐπεὶ οὖν πόλιος κατέβαν, πεδίον δ᾿ ἀφίκοντο,
οἱ μὲν ἄρ᾿ ἄψορροι προτὶ Ἴλιον ἀπονέοντο,   330
παῖδες καὶ γαμβροί, τὼ δ᾿ οὐ λάθον εὐρύοπα Ζῆν
ἐς πεδίον προφανέντε· ἰδὼν δ᾿ ἐλέησε γέροντα,
αἶψα δ᾿ ἄρ᾿ Ἑρμείαν, υἱὸν φίλον, ἀντίον ηὔδα·
"Ἑρμεία, σοὶ γάρ τε μάλιστά γε φίλτατόν ἐστιν
ἀνδρὶ ἑταιρίσσαι, καί τ᾿ ἔκλυες ᾧ κ᾿ ἐθέλησθα,   335

310 ταχὺν] ἐὸν a   322 γεραιὸς ἑοῦ] γέρων ξεστοῦ a

βάσκ' ἴθι, καὶ Πρίαμον κοίλας ἐπὶ νῆας Ἀχαιῶν
ὣς ἄγαγ', ὡς μήτ' ἄρ τις ἴδῃ μήτ' ἄρ τε νοήσῃ
τῶν ἄλλων Δαναῶν, πρὶν Πηλεΐωνάδ' ἱκέσθαι.''
    Ὣς ἔφατ', οὐδ' ἀπίθησε διάκτορος Ἀργειφόντης.
αὐτίκ' ἔπειθ' ὑπὸ ποσσὶν ἐδήσατο καλὰ πέδιλα   340
ἀμβρόσια χρύσεια, τά μιν φέρον ἠμὲν ἐφ' ὑγρὴν
ἠδ' ἐπ' ἀπείρονα γαῖαν ἅμα πνοιῇς ἀνέμοιο·
εἵλετο δὲ ῥάβδον, τῇ τ' ἀνδρῶν ὄμματα θέλγει
ὧν ἐθέλει, τοὺς δ' αὖτε καὶ ὑπνώοντας ἐγείρει·
τὴν μετὰ χερσὶν ἔχων πέτετο κρατὺς Ἀργειφόντης.   345
αἶψα δ' ἄρα Τροίην τε καὶ Ἑλλήσποντον ἵκανε,
βῆ δ' ἰέναι κούρῳ αἰσυμνητῆρι ἐοικώς,
πρῶτον ὑπηνήτῃ, τοῦ περ χαριεστάτη ἥβη.
    Οἱ δ' ἐπεὶ οὖν μέγα σῆμα παρὲξ Ἴλοιο ἔλασσαν,
στῆσαν ἄρ' ἡμιόνους τε καὶ ἵππους, ὄφρα πίοιεν,   350
ἐν ποταμῷ· δὴ γὰρ καὶ ἐπὶ κνέφας ἤλυθε γαῖαν.
τὸν δ' ἐξ ἀγχιμόλοιο ἰδὼν ἐφράσσατο κῆρυξ
Ἑρμείαν, ποτὶ δὲ Πρίαμον φάτο φώνησέν τε·
''φράζεο, Δαρδανίδη· φραδέος νόου ἔργα τέτυκται.
ἄνδρ' ὁρόω, τάχα δ' ἄμμε διαρραίσεσθαι ὀΐω.   355
ἀλλ' ἄγε δὴ φεύγωμεν ἐφ' ἵππων, ἤ μιν ἔπειτα
γούνων ἁψάμενοι λιτανεύσομεν, αἴ κ' ἐλεήσῃ.''
    Ὣς φάτο, σὺν δὲ γέροντι νόος χύτο, δείδιε δ' αἰνῶς,
ὀρθαὶ δὲ τρίχες ἔσταν ἐνὶ γναμπτοῖσι μέλεσσι,
στῆ δὲ ταφών· αὐτὸς δ' ἐριούνιος ἐγγύθεν ἐλθών,   360
χεῖρα γέροντος ἑλὼν ἐξείρετο καὶ προσέειπε·
''πῇ, πάτερ, ὧδ' ἵππους τε καὶ ἡμιόνους ἰθύνεις
νύκτα δι' ἀμβροσίην, ὅτε θ' εὕδουσι βροτοὶ ἄλλοι;
οὐδὲ σύ γ' ἔδεισας μένεα πνείοντας Ἀχαιούς,
οἵ τοι δυσμενέες καὶ ἀνάρσιοι ἐγγὺς ἔασι;   365
τῶν εἴ τίς σε ἴδοιτο θοὴν διὰ νύκτα μέλαιναν
τοσσάδ' ὀνείατ' ἄγοντα, τίς ἂν δή τοι νόος εἴη;
οὔτ' αὐτὸς νέος ἐσσί, γέρων δέ τοι οὗτος ὀπηδεῖ
347 αἰσυητῆρι **a**

ἀνδρ᾿ ἀπαμύνασθαι, ὅτε τις πρότερος χαλεπήνῃ.
ἀλλ᾿ ἐγὼ οὐδέν σε ῥέξω κακά, καὶ δέ κεν ἄλλον   370
σεῦ ἀπαλεξήσαιμι· φίλῳ δέ σε πατρὶ ἐΐσκω."
Τὸν δ᾿ ἠμείβετ᾿ ἔπειτα γέρων Πρίαμος θεοειδής·
"οὕτω πῃ τάδε γ᾿ ἐστί, φίλον τέκος, ὡς ἀγορεύεις.
ἀλλ᾿ ἔτι τις καὶ ἐμεῖο θεῶν ὑπερέσχεθε χεῖρα,
ὅς μοι τοιόνδ᾿ ἧκεν ὁδοιπόρον ἀντιβολῆσαι,   375
αἴσιον, οἷος δὴ σὺ δέμας καὶ εἶδος ἀγητός,
πέπνυσαί τε νόῳ, μακάρων δ᾿ ἔξ ἐσσι τοκήων."
Τὸν δ᾿ αὖτε προσέειπε διάκτορος Ἀργειφόντης·
"ναὶ δὴ ταῦτά γε πάντα, γέρον, κατὰ μοῖραν ἔειπες.
ἀλλ᾿ ἄγε μοι τόδε εἰπὲ καὶ ἀτρεκέως κατάλεξον,   380
ἠέ πῃ ἐκπέμπεις κειμήλια πολλὰ καὶ ἐσθλὰ
ἄνδρας ἐς ἀλλοδαπούς, ἵνα περ τάδε τοι σόα μίμνῃ,
ἦ ἤδη πάντες καταλείπετε Ἴλιον ἱρὴν
δειδιότες· τοῖος γὰρ ἀνὴρ ὤριστος ὄλωλε
σὸς πάϊς· οὐ μὲν γάρ τι μάχης ἐπιδεύετ᾿ Ἀχαιῶν."   385
Τὸν δ᾿ ἠμείβετ᾿ ἔπειτα γέρων Πρίαμος θεοειδής·
"τίς δὲ σύ ἐσσι, φέριστε, τέων δ᾿ ἔξ ἐσσι τοκήων,
ὅς μοι καλὰ τὸν οἶτον ἀπότμου παιδὸς ἔνισπες; "
Τὸν δ᾿ αὖτε προσέειπε διάκτορος Ἀργειφόντης·
"πειρᾷ ἐμεῖο, γεραιέ, καὶ εἴρεαι Ἕκτορα δῖον.   390
τὸν μὲν ἐγὼ μάλα πολλὰ μάχῃ ἔνι κυδιανείρῃ
ὀφθαλμοῖσιν ὄπωπα, καὶ εὖτ᾿ ἐπὶ νηυσὶν ἐλάσσας
Ἀργείους κτείνεσκε, δαΐζων ὀξέϊ χαλκῷ·
ἡμεῖς δ᾿ ἑσταότες θαυμάζομεν· οὐ γὰρ Ἀχιλλεὺς
εἴα μάρνασθαι, κεχολωμένος Ἀτρεΐωνι.   395
τοῦ γὰρ ἐγὼ θεράπων, μία δ᾿ ἤγαγε νηῦς εὐεργής·
Μυρμιδόνων δ᾿ ἔξ εἰμι, πατὴρ δέ μοί ἐστι Πολύκτωρ.
ἀφνειὸς μὲν ὅ γ᾿ ἐστί, γέρων δὲ δὴ ὡς σύ περ ὧδε,
ἓξ δέ οἱ υἷες ἔασιν, ἐγὼ δέ οἱ ἕβδομός εἰμι·
τῶν μέτα παλλόμενος κλήρῳ λάχον ἐνθάδ᾿ ἕπεσθαι.   400
νῦν δ᾿ ἦλθον πεδίονδ᾿ ἀπὸ νηῶν· ἠῶθεν γὰρ
θήσονται περὶ ἄστυ μάχην ἑλίκωπες Ἀχαιοί.

388 ὅς] ὡς a

ἀσχαλόωσι γὰρ οἵδε καθήμενοι, οὐδὲ δύνανται
ἴσχειν ἐσσυμένους πολέμου βασιλῆες ᾿Αχαιῶν.᾿᾿
Τὸν δ᾿ ἠμείβετ᾿ ἔπειτα γέρων Πρίαμος θεοειδής·   405
᾿᾿εἰ μὲν δὴ θεράπων Πηληϊάδεω ᾿Αχιλῆος
εἶς, ἄγε δή μοι πᾶσαν ἀληθείην κατάλεξον,
ἢ ἔτι πὰρ νήεσσιν ἐμὸς πάϊς, ἦέ μιν ἤδη
ᾖσι κυσὶν μελεϊστὶ ταμὼν προὔθηκεν ᾿Αχιλλεύς.᾿᾿
Τὸν δ᾿ αὖτε προσέειπε διάκτορος ᾿Αργειφόντης·   410
᾿᾿ὦ γέρον, οὔ πω τόν γε κύνες φάγον οὐδ᾿ οἰωνοί,
ἀλλ᾿ ἔτι κεῖνος κεῖται ᾿Αχιλλῆος παρὰ νηῒ
αὔτως ἐν κλισίῃσι· δυωδεκάτη δέ οἱ ἤδε
κειμένῳ, οὐδέ τί οἱ χρὼς σήπεται, οὐδέ μιν εὐλαὶ
ἔσθουσ᾿, αἵ ῥά τε φῶτας ἀρηϊφάτους κατέδουσιν.   415
ἦ μέν μιν περὶ σῆμα ἑοῦ ἑτάροιο φίλοιο
ἕλκει ἀκηδέστως, ἠὼς ὅτε δῖα φανήῃ,
οὐδέ μιν αἰσχύνει· θηοῖό κεν αὐτὸς ἐπελθὼν
οἷον ἐερσήεις κεῖται, περὶ δ᾿ αἷμα νένιπται,
οὐδέ ποθι μιαρός· σὺν δ᾿ ἕλκεα πάντα μέμυκεν,   420
ὅσσ᾿ ἐτύπη· πολέες γὰρ ἐν αὐτῷ χαλκὸν ἔλασσαν.
ὥς τοι κήδονται μάκαρες θεοὶ υἷος ἑῆος
καὶ νέκυός περ ἐόντος, ἐπεί σφι φίλος περὶ κῆρι.᾿᾿
῝Ως φάτο, γήθησεν δ᾿ ὁ γέρων, καὶ ἀμείβετο μύθῳ·
᾿᾿ὦ τέκος, ἦ ῥ᾿ ἀγαθὸν καὶ ἐναίσιμα δῶρα διδοῦναι   425
ἀθανάτοις, ἐπεὶ οὔ ποτ᾿ ἐμὸς πάϊς, εἴ ποτ᾿ ἔην γε,
λήθετ᾿ ἐνὶ μεγάροισι θεῶν, οἳ ῎Ολυμπον ἔχουσι·
τῶ οἱ ἀπομνήσαντο καὶ ἐν θανάτοιό περ αἴσῃ.
ἀλλ᾿ ἄγε δὴ τόδε δέξαι ἐμεῦ πάρα καλὸν ἄλεισον,
αὐτόν τε ῥῦσαι, πέμψον δέ με σύν γε θεοῖσιν,   430
ὄφρα κεν ἐς κλισίην Πηληϊάδεω ἀφίκωμαι.᾿᾿
Τὸν δ᾿ αὖτε προσέειπε διάκτορος ᾿Αργειφόντης·
᾿᾿πειρᾷ ἐμεῖο, γεραιέ, νεωτέρου, οὐδέ με πείσεις,
ὅς με κέλῃ σέο δῶρα παρὲξ ᾿Αχιλῆα δέχεσθαι.
τὸν μὲν ἐγὼ δείδοικα καὶ αἰδέομαι περὶ κῆρι   435
συλεύειν, μή μοί τι κακὸν μετόπισθε γένηται.᾿᾿

413 ἤδε] ἠώς a

σοὶ δ' ἂν ἐγὼ πομπὸς καί κε κλυτὸν Ἄργος ἱκοίμην,
ἐνδυκέως ἐν νηΐ θοῇ ἢ πεζὸς ὁμαρτέων·
οὐκ ἄν τίς τοι πομπὸν ὀνοσσάμενος μαχέσαιτο."

Ἦ, καὶ ἐπαΐξας ἐριούνιος ἅρμα καὶ ἵππους   440
καρπαλίμως μάστιγα καὶ ἡνία λάζετο χερσίν,
ἐν δ' ἔπνευσ' ἵπποισι καὶ ἡμιόνοις μένος ἠΰ.
ἀλλ' ὅτε δὴ πύργους τε νεῶν καὶ τάφρον ἵκοντο,
οἱ δὲ νέον περὶ δόρπα φυλακτῆρες πονέοντο,
τοῖσι δ' ἐφ' ὕπνον ἔχευε διάκτορος Ἀργειφόντης   445
πᾶσιν, ἄφαρ δ' ὤϊξε πύλας καὶ ἀπῶσεν ὀχῆας,
ἐς δ' ἄγαγε Πρίαμόν τε καὶ ἀγλαὰ δῶρ' ἐπ' ἀπήνης.
ἀλλ' ὅτε δὴ κλισίην Πηληϊάδεω ἀφίκοντο
ὑψηλήν, τὴν Μυρμιδόνες ποίησαν ἄνακτι
δοῦρ' ἐλάτης κέρσαντες· ἀτὰρ καθύπερθεν ἔρεψαν   450
λαχνήεντ' ὄροφον, λειμωνόθεν ἀμήσαντες·
ἀμφὶ δέ οἱ μεγάλην αὐλὴν ποίησαν ἄνακτι
σταυροῖσιν πυκινοῖσι· θύρην δ' ἔχε μοῦνος ἐπιβλὴς
εἰλάτινος, τὸν τρεῖς μὲν ἐπιρρήσσεσκον Ἀχαιοί,
τρεῖς δ' ἀναοίγεσκον μεγάλην κληῗδα θυράων,   455
τῶν ἄλλων· Ἀχιλεὺς δ' ἄρ' ἐπιρρήσσεσκε καὶ οἶος·
δή ῥα τόθ' Ἑρμείας ἐριούνιος ᾦξε γέροντι,
ἐς δ' ἄγαγε κλυτὰ δῶρα ποδώκεϊ Πηλεΐωνι,
ἐξ ἵππων δ' ἀπέβαινεν ἐπὶ χθόνα φώνησέν τε·
"ὦ γέρον, ἤτοι ἐγὼ θεὸς ἄμβροτος εἰλήλουθα,   460
Ἑρμείας· σοὶ γάρ με πατὴρ ἅμα πομπὸν ὄπασσεν.
ἀλλ' ἤτοι μὲν ἐγὼ πάλιν εἴσομαι, οὐδ' Ἀχιλῆος
ὀφθαλμοὺς εἴσειμι· νεμεσσητὸν δέ κεν εἴη
ἀθάνατον θεὸν ὧδε βροτοὺς ἀγαπαζέμεν ἄντην·
τύνη δ' εἰσελθὼν λαβὲ γούνατα Πηλεΐωνος,   465
καί μιν ὑπὲρ πατρὸς καὶ μητέρος ἠϋκόμοιο
λίσσεο καὶ τέκεος, ἵνα οἱ σὺν θυμὸν ὀρίνῃς."

Ὣς ἄρα φωνήσας ἀπέβη πρὸς μακρὸν Ὄλυμπον
Ἑρμείας· Πρίαμος δ' ἐξ ἵππων ἆλτο χαμᾶζε,
Ἰδαῖον δὲ κατ' αὖθι λίπεν· ὁ δὲ μίμνεν ἐρύκων   470

440 ἀναΐξας a

ἵππους ἡμιόνους τε· γέρων δ᾽ ἰθὺς κίεν οἴκου,
τῇ ῥ᾽ Ἀχιλεὺς ἵζεσκε Διῒ φίλος· ἐν δέ μιν αὐτὸν
εὗρ᾽, ἕταροι δ᾽ ἀπάνευθε καθήατο· τὼ δὲ δύ᾽ οἴω,
ἥρως Αὐτομέδων τε καὶ Ἄλκιμος, ὄζος Ἄρηος,
ποίπνυον παρεόντε· νέον δ᾽ ἀπέληγεν ἐδωδῆς   475
ἔσθων καὶ πίνων· ἔτι καὶ παρέκειτο τράπεζα.
τοὺς δ᾽ ἔλαθ᾽ εἰσελθὼν Πρίαμος μέγας, ἄγχι δ᾽ ἄρα στὰς
χερσὶν Ἀχιλλῆος λάβε γούνατα καὶ κύσε χεῖρας
δεινὰς ἀνδροφόνους, αἵ οἱ πολέας κτάνον υἷας.
ὡς δ᾽ ὅτ᾽ ἂν ἄνδρ᾽ ἄτη πυκινὴ λάβῃ, ὅς τ᾽ ἐνὶ πάτρῃ   480
φῶτα κατακτείνας ἄλλων ἐξίκετο δῆμον,
ἀνδρὸς ἐς ἀφνειοῦ, θάμβος δ᾽ ἔχει εἰσορόωντας,
ὡς Ἀχιλεὺς θάμβησεν ἰδὼν Πρίαμον θεοειδέα·
θάμβησαν δὲ καὶ ἄλλοι, ἐς ἀλλήλους δὲ ἴδοντο.
τὸν καὶ λισσόμενος Πρίαμος πρὸς μῦθον ἔειπε·   485
"μνῆσαι πατρὸς σοῖο, θεοῖς ἐπιείκελ᾽ Ἀχιλλεῦ,
τηλίκου ὥς περ ἐγών, ὀλοῷ ἐπὶ γήραος οὐδῷ·
καὶ μέν που κεῖνον περιναιέται ἀμφὶς ἐόντες
τείρουσ᾽, οὐδέ τίς ἐστιν ἀρὴν καὶ λοιγὸν ἀμῦναι.
ἀλλ᾽ ἤτοι κεῖνός γε σέθεν ζώοντος ἀκούων   490
χαίρει τ᾽ ἐν θυμῷ, ἐπί τ᾽ ἔλπεται ἤματα πάντα
ὄψεσθαι φίλον υἱὸν ἀπὸ Τροίηθεν ἰόντα·
αὐτὰρ ἐγὼ πανάποτμος, ἐπεὶ τέκον υἷας ἀρίστους
Τροίῃ ἐν εὐρείῃ, τῶν δ᾽ οὔ τινά φημι λελεῖφθαι.
πεντήκοντά μοι ἦσαν, ὅτ᾽ ἤλυθον υἷες Ἀχαιῶν·   495
ἐννεακαίδεκα μέν μοι ἰῆς ἐκ νηδύος ἦσαν,
τοὺς δ᾽ ἄλλους μοι ἔτικτον ἐνὶ μεγάροισι γυναῖκες·
τῶν μὲν πολλῶν θοῦρος Ἄρης ὑπὸ γούνατ᾽ ἔλυσεν·
ὃς δέ μοι οἶος ἔην, εἴρυτο δὲ ἄστυ καὶ αὐτούς,
τὸν σὺ πρῴην κτείνας ἀμυνόμενον περὶ πάτρης,   500
Ἕκτορα· τοῦ νῦν εἵνεχ᾽ ἱκάνω νῆας Ἀχαιῶν
λυσόμενος παρὰ σεῖο, φέρω δ᾽ ἀπερείσι᾽ ἄποινα.
ἀλλ᾽ αἰδεῖο θεούς, Ἀχιλεῦ, αὐτόν τ᾽ ἐλέησον,
μνησάμενος σοῦ πατρός· ἐγὼ δ᾽ ἐλεεινότερός περ,

499 αὐτός a

ἔτλην δ᾿ οἷ᾿ οὔ πώ τις ἐπιχθόνιος βροτὸς ἄλλος,   505
ἀνδρὸς παιδοφόνοιο ποτὶ στόμα χεῖρ᾿ ὀρέγεσθαι."
    Ὣς φάτο, τῷ δ᾿ ἄρα πατρὸς ὑφ᾿ ἵμερον ὦρσε γόοιο·
ἁψάμενος δ᾿ ἄρα χειρὸς ἀπώσατο ἧκα γέροντα.
τὼ δὲ μνησαμένω, ὁ μὲν Ἕκτορος ἀνδροφόνοιο
κλαῖ᾿ ἁδινὰ προπάροιθε ποδῶν Ἀχιλῆος ἐλυσθείς,   510
αὐτὰρ Ἀχιλλεὺς κλαῖεν ἑὸν πατέρ᾿, ἄλλοτε δ᾿ αὖτε
Πάτροκλον· τῶν δὲ στοναχὴ κατὰ δώματ᾿ ὀρώρει.
αὐτὰρ ἐπεί ῥα γόοιο τετάρπετο δῖος Ἀχιλλεύς,
καί οἱ ἀπὸ πραπίδων ἦλθ᾿ ἵμερος ἠδ᾿ ἀπὸ γυίων,
αὐτίκ᾿ ἀπὸ θρόνου ὦρτο, γέροντα δὲ χειρὸς ἀνίστη,   515
οἰκτίρων πολιόν τε κάρη πολιόν τε γένειον,
καί μιν φωνήσας ἔπεα πτερόεντα προσηύδα·
"ἆ δείλ᾿, ἦ δὴ πολλὰ κάκ᾿ ἄνσχεο σὸν κατὰ θυμόν.
πῶς ἔτλης ἐπὶ νῆας Ἀχαιῶν ἐλθέμεν οἶος,
ἀνδρὸς ἐς ὀφθαλμοὺς ὅς τοι πολέας τε καὶ ἐσθλοὺς   520
υἱέας ἐξενάριξα; σιδήρειόν νύ τοι ἦτορ.
ἀλλ᾿ ἄγε δὴ κατ᾿ ἄρ᾿ ἕζευ ἐπὶ θρόνου, ἄλγεα δ᾿ ἔμπης
ἐν θυμῷ κατακεῖσθαι ἐάσομεν ἀχνύμενοί περ·
οὐ γάρ τις πρῆξις πέλεται κρυεροῖο γόοιο·
ὣς γὰρ ἐπεκλώσαντο θεοὶ δειλοῖσι βροτοῖσι,   525
ζώειν ἀχνυμένους· αὐτοὶ δέ τ᾿ ἀκηδέες εἰσί.
δοιοὶ γάρ τε πίθοι κατακείαται ἐν Διὸς οὔδει
δώρων οἷα δίδωσι, κακῶν, ἕτερος δὲ ἑάων·
ᾧ μέν κ᾿ ἀμμείξας δώῃ Ζεὺς τερπικέραυνος,
ἄλλοτε μέν τε κακῷ ὅ γε κύρεται, ἄλλοτε δ᾿ ἐσθλῷ·   530
ᾧ δέ κε τῶν λυγρῶν δώῃ, λωβητὸν ἔθηκε,
καί ἑ κακὴ βούβρωστις ἐπὶ χθόνα δῖαν ἐλαύνει,
φοιτᾷ δ᾿ οὔτε θεοῖσι τετιμένος οὔτε βροτοῖσιν.
ὣς μὲν καὶ Πηλῆϊ θεοὶ δόσαν ἀγλαὰ δῶρα
ἐκ γενετῆς· πάντας γὰρ ἐπ᾿ ἀνθρώπους ἐκέκαστο   535
ὄλβῳ τε πλούτῳ τε, ἄνασσε δὲ Μυρμιδόνεσσι,
καί οἱ θνητῷ ἐόντι θεὰν ποίησαν ἄκοιτιν.

526 ἀχνυμένοις a   528 κηρῶν ἔμπλειοι, ὁ μὲν ἐσθλῶν, αὐτὰρ ὁ
δειλῶν Plato

ἀλλ᾽ ἐπὶ καὶ τῷ θῆκε θεὸς κακόν, ὅττι οἱ οὔ τι
παίδων ἐν μεγάροισι γονὴ γένετο κρειόντων,
ἀλλ᾽ ἕνα παῖδα τέκεν παναώριον· οὐδέ νυ τόν γε   540
γηράσκοντα κομίζω, ἐπεὶ μάλα τηλόθι πάτρης
ἧμαι ἐνὶ Τροίῃ, σέ τε κήδων ἠδὲ σὰ τέκνα.
καὶ σέ, γέρον, τὸ πρὶν μὲν ἀκούομεν ὄλβιον εἶναι·
ὅσσον Λέσβος ἄνω, Μάκαρος ἕδος, ἐντὸς ἐέργει
καὶ Φρυγίη καθύπερθε καὶ Ἑλλήσποντος ἀπείρων,   545
τῶν σε, γέρον, πλούτῳ τε καὶ υἱάσι φασὶ κεκάσθαι.
αὐτὰρ ἐπεί τοι πῆμα τόδ᾽ ἤγαγον Οὐρανίωνες,
αἰεί τοι περὶ ἄστυ μάχαι τ᾽ ἀνδροκτασίαι τε.
ἄνσχεο, μηδ᾽ ἀλίαστον ὀδύρεο σὸν κατὰ θυμόν·
οὐ γάρ τι πρήξεις ἀκαχήμενος υἷος ἑῆος,   550
οὐδέ μιν ἀνστήσεις, πρὶν καὶ κακὸν ἄλλο πάθῃσθα.''
  Τὸν δ᾽ ἠμείβετ᾽ ἔπειτα γέρων Πρίαμος θεοειδής·
''μή πώ μ᾽ ἐς θρόνον ἷζε, διοτρεφές, ὄφρα κεν Ἕκτωρ
κεῖται ἐνὶ κλισίῃσιν ἀκηδής, ἀλλὰ τάχιστα
λῦσον, ἵν᾽ ὀφθαλμοῖσιν ἴδω· σὺ δὲ δέξαι ἄποινα   555
πολλά, τά τοι φέρομεν· σὺ δὲ τῶνδ᾽ ἀπόναιο καὶ ἔλθοις
σὴν ἐς πατρίδα γαῖαν, ἐπεί με πρῶτον ἔασας.''
[αὐτόν τε ζώειν καὶ ὁρᾶν φάος ἠελίοιο]
  Τὸν δ᾽ ἄρ᾽ ὑπόδρα ἰδὼν προσέφη πόδας ὠκὺς Ἀχιλλεύς·
''μηκέτι νῦν μ᾽ ἐρέθιζε, γέρον· νοέω δὲ καὶ αὐτὸς   560
Ἕκτορά τοι λῦσαι, Διόθεν δέ μοι ἄγγελος ἦλθε
μήτηρ, ἥ μ᾽ ἔτεκεν, θυγάτηρ ἁλίοιο γέροντος·
καὶ δέ σε γιγνώσκω, Πρίαμε, φρεσίν, οὐδέ με λήθεις,
ὅττι θεῶν τίς σ᾽ ἦγε θοὰς ἐπὶ νῆας Ἀχαιῶν.
οὐ γάρ κε τλαίη βροτὸς ἐλθέμεν, οὐδὲ μάλ᾽ ἡβῶν,   565
ἐς στρατόν· οὐδὲ γὰρ ἂν φυλάκους λάθοι, οὐδέ κ᾽ ὀχῆας
ῥεῖα μετοχλίσσειε θυράων ἡμετεράων.
τῶ νῦν μή μοι μᾶλλον ἐν ἄλγεσι θυμὸν ὀρίνῃς,
μή σε, γέρον, οὐδ᾽ αὐτὸν ἐνὶ κλισίῃσιν ἐάσω
καὶ ἱκέτην περ ἐόντα, Διὸς δ᾽ ἀλίτωμαι ἐφετμάς.''   570
  Ὣς ἔφατ᾽, ἔδεισεν δ᾽ ὁ γέρων καὶ ἐπείθετο μύθῳ.

558 om. a   566 ὀχῆα a

Πηλεΐδης δ' οἴκοιο λέων ὣς ἆλτο θύραζε,
οὐκ οἶος, ἅμα τῷ γε δύω θεράποντες ἕποντο,
ἥρως Αὐτομέδων ἠδ' Ἄλκιμος, οὕς ῥα μάλιστα
τῖ' Ἀχιλεὺς ἑτάρων μετὰ Πάτροκλόν γε θανόντα,   575
οἳ τόθ' ὑπὸ ζυγόφιν λύον ἵππους ἡμιόνους τε,
ἐς δ' ἄγαγον κήρυκα καλήτορα τοῖο γέροντος,
κὰδ δ' ἐπὶ δίφρου εἷσαν· ἐϋξέστου δ' ἀπ' ἀπήνης
ᾗρεον Ἑκτορέης κεφαλῆς ἀπερείσι' ἄποινα.
κὰδ δ' ἔλιπον δύο φάρε' ἐΰννητόν τε χιτῶνα,   580
ὄφρα νέκυν πυκάσας δοίη οἶκόνδε φέρεσθαι.
δμῳὰς δ' ἐκκαλέσας λοῦσαι κέλετ' ἀμφί τ' ἀλεῖψαι,
νόσφιν ἀειράσας, ὡς μὴ Πρίαμος ἴδοι υἱόν,
μὴ ὁ μὲν ἀχνυμένῃ κραδίῃ χόλον οὐκ ἐρύσαιτο
παῖδα ἰδών, Ἀχιλῆϊ δ' ὀρινθείη φίλον ἦτορ,   585
καί ἑ κατακτείνειε, Διὸς δ' ἀλίτηται ἐφετμάς.
τὸν δ' ἐπεὶ οὖν δμῳαὶ λοῦσαν καὶ χρῖσαν ἐλαίῳ,
ἀμφὶ δέ μιν φᾶρος καλὸν βάλον ἠδὲ χιτῶνα,
αὐτὸς τόν γ' Ἀχιλεὺς λεχέων ἐπέθηκεν ἀείρας,
σὺν δ' ἕταροι ἤειραν ἐϋξέστην ἐπ' ἀπήνην.   590
ᾤμωξέν τ' ἄρ' ἔπειτα, φίλον δ' ὀνόμηνεν ἑταῖρον·
"μή μοι, Πάτροκλε, σκυδμαινέμεν, αἴ κε πύθηαι
εἰν Ἀϊδός περ ἐὼν ὅτι Ἕκτορα δῖον ἔλυσα
πατρὶ φίλῳ, ἐπεὶ οὔ μοι ἀεικέα δῶκεν ἄποινα.
σοὶ δ' αὖ ἐγὼ καὶ τῶνδ' ἀποδάσσομαι ὅσσ' ἐπέοικεν."   595
    Ἦ ῥα, καὶ ἐς κλισίην πάλιν ἤϊε δῖος Ἀχιλλεύς,
ἕζετο δ' ἐν κλισμῷ πολυδαιδάλῳ, ἔνθεν ἀνέστη,
τοίχου τοῦ ἑτέρου, ποτὶ δὲ Πρίαμον φάτο μῦθον·
"υἱὸς μὲν δή τοι λέλυται, γέρον, ὡς ἐκέλευες,
κεῖται δ' ἐν λεχέεσσ'· ἅμα δ' ἠοῖ φαινομένηφιν   600
ὄψεαι αὐτὸς ἄγων· νῦν δὲ μνησώμεθα δόρπου.
καὶ γάρ τ' ἠΰκομος Νιόβη ἐμνήσατο σίτου,
τῇ περ δώδεκα παῖδες ἐνὶ μεγάροισιν ὄλοντο,
ἓξ μὲν θυγατέρες, ἓξ δ' υἱέες ἡβώοντες.
τοὺς μὲν Ἀπόλλων πέφνεν ἀπ' ἀργυρέοιο βιοῖο   605
578 ἐϋσσώτρου a

χωόμενος Νιόβῃ, τὰς δ᾽ Ἄρτεμις ἰοχέαιρα,
οὕνεκ᾽ ἄρα Λητοῖ ἰσάσκετο καλλιπαρήῳ·
φῆ δοιὼ τεκέειν, ἡ δ᾽ αὐτὴ γείνατο πολλούς·
τὼ δ᾽ ἄρα καὶ δοιώ περ ἐόντ᾽ ἀπὸ πάντας ὄλεσσαν.
οἱ μὲν ἄρ᾽ ἐννῆμαρ κέατ᾽ ἐν φόνῳ, οὐδέ τις ἦεν   610
κατθάψαι, λαοὺς δὲ λίθους ποίησε Κρονίων·
τοὺς δ᾽ ἄρα τῇ δεκάτῃ θάψαν θεοὶ Οὐρανίωνες.
ἡ δ᾽ ἄρα σίτου μνήσατ᾽, ἐπεὶ κάμε δάκρυ χέουσα.
νῦν δέ που ἐν πέτρῃσιν, ἐν οὔρεσιν οἰοπόλοισιν,
ἐν Σιπύλῳ, ὅθι φασὶ θεάων ἔμμεναι εὐνὰς   615
νυμφάων, αἵ τ᾽ ἀμφ᾽ Ἀχελώϊον ἐρρώσαντο,
ἔνθα λίθος περ ἐοῦσα θεῶν ἐκ κήδεα πέσσει.
ἀλλ᾽ ἄγε δὴ καὶ νῶϊ μεδώμεθα, δῖε γεραιέ,
σίτου· ἔπειτά κεν αὖτε φίλον παῖδα κλαίοισθα,
Ἴλιον εἰσαγαγών· πολυδάκρυτος δέ τοι ἔσται.᾽᾽   620
  Ἦ, καὶ ἀναΐξας ὄϊν ἄργυφον ὠκὺς Ἀχιλλεὺς
σφάξ᾽· ἕταροι δὲ δερόν τε καὶ ἄμφεπον εὖ κατὰ κόσμον,
μίστυλλόν τ᾽ ἄρ᾽ ἐπισταμένως πεῖράν τ᾽ ὀβελοῖσιν,
ὤπτησάν τε περιφραδέως, ἐρύσαντό τε πάντα.
Αὐτομέδων δ᾽ ἄρα σῖτον ἑλὼν ἐπένειμε τραπέζῃ   625
καλοῖς ἐν κανέοισιν· ἀτὰρ κρέα νεῖμεν Ἀχιλλεύς.
οἱ δ᾽ ἐπ᾽ ὀνείαθ᾽ ἑτοῖμα προκείμενα χεῖρας ἴαλλον.
αὐτὰρ ἐπεὶ πόσιος καὶ ἐδητύος ἐξ ἔρον ἕντο,
ἤτοι Δαρδανίδης Πρίαμος θαύμαζ᾽ Ἀχιλῆα,
ὅσσος ἔην οἷός τε· θεοῖσι γὰρ ἄντα ἐῴκει·   630
αὐτὰρ ὁ Δαρδανίδην Πρίαμον θαύμαζεν Ἀχιλλεύς,
εἰσορόων ὄψίν τ᾽ ἀγαθὴν καὶ μῦθον ἀκούων.
αὐτὰρ ἐπεὶ τάρπησαν ἐς ἀλλήλους ὁρόωντες,
τὸν πρότερος προσέειπε γέρων Πρίαμος θεοειδής·
῾῾λέξον νῦν με τάχιστα, διοτρεφές, ὄφρα καὶ ἤδη   635
ὕπνῳ ὕπο γλυκερῷ ταρπώμεθα κοιμηθέντες·
οὐ γάρ πω μύσαν ὄσσε ὑπὸ βλεφάροισιν ἐμοῖσιν
ἐξ οὗ σῆς ὑπὸ χερσὶν ἐμὸς πάϊς ὤλεσε θυμόν,
ἀλλ᾽ αἰεὶ στενάχω καὶ κήδεα μυρία πέσσω,

614-17 iniuria damnati   616 Ἀχελήϊον **a**: Ἀχελήσιον **b**

αὐλῆς ἐν χόρτοισι κυλινδόμενος κατὰ κόπρον.   640
νῦν δὴ καὶ σίτου πασάμην καὶ αἴθοπα οἶνον
λαυκανίης καθέηκα· πάρος γε μὲν οὔ τι πεπάσμην."
῞Η ῥ᾽, ᾽Αχιλεὺς δ᾽ ἑτάροισιν ἰδὲ δμῳῆσι κέλευσε
δέμνι᾽ ὑπ᾽ αἰθούσῃ θέμεναι καὶ ῥήγεα καλὰ
πορφύρε᾽ ἐμβαλέειν, στορέσαι τ᾽ ἐφύπερθε τάπητας,   645
χλαίνας τ᾽ ἐνθέμεναι οὔλας καθύπερθεν ἕσασθαι.
αἱ δ᾽ ἴσαν ἐκ μεγάροιο δάος μετὰ χερσὶν ἔχουσαι,
αἶψα δ᾽ ἄρα στόρεσαν δοιὼ λέχε᾽ ἐγκονέουσαι.
τὸν δ᾽ ἐπικερτομέων προσέφη πόδας ὠκὺς ᾽Αχιλλεύς·
"ἐκτὸς μὲν δὴ λέξο, γέρον φίλε, μή τις ᾽Αχαιῶν   650
ἐνθάδ᾽ ἐπέλθῃσιν βουληφόρος, οἵ τέ μοι αἰεὶ
βουλὰς βουλεύουσι παρήμενοι, ἦ θέμις ἐστί·
τῶν εἴ τίς σε ἴδοιτο θοὴν διὰ νύκτα μέλαιναν,
αὐτίκ᾽ ἂν ἐξείποι ᾽Αγαμέμνονι ποιμένι λαῶν,
καί κεν ἀνάβλησις λύσιος νεκροῖο γένηται.   655
ἀλλ᾽ ἄγε μοι τόδε εἰπὲ καὶ ἀτρεκέως κατάλεξον,
ποσσῆμαρ μέμονας κτερεϊζέμεν ῞Εκτορα δῖον,
ὄφρα τέως αὐτός τε μένω καὶ λαὸν ἐρύκω."
Τὸν δ᾽ ἠμείβετ᾽ ἔπειτα γέρων Πρίαμος θεοειδής·
"εἰ μὲν δή μ᾽ ἐθέλεις τελέσαι τάφον ῞Εκτορι δίῳ,   660
ὧδέ κέ μοι ῥέξας, ᾽Αχιλεῦ, κεχαρισμένα θείης.
οἶσθα γὰρ ὡς κατὰ ἄστυ ἐέλμεθα, τηλόθι δ᾽ ὕλη
ἀξέμεν ἐξ ὄρεος, μάλα δὲ Τρῶες δεδίασιν.
ἐννῆμαρ μέν κ᾽ αὐτὸν ἐνὶ μεγάροις γοάοιμεν,
τῇ δεκάτῃ δέ κε θάπτοιμεν δαινῦτό τε λαός,   665
ἑνδεκάτῃ δέ κε τύμβον ἐπ᾽ αὐτῷ ποιήσαιμεν,
τῇ δὲ δυωδεκάτῃ πολεμίξομεν, εἴ περ ἀνάγκη."
Τὸν δ᾽ αὖτε προσέειπε ποδάρκης δῖος ᾽Αχιλλεύς·
"ἔσται τοι καὶ ταῦτα, γέρον Πρίαμ᾽, ὡς σὺ κελεύεις·
σχήσω γὰρ πόλεμον τόσσον χρόνον ὅσσον ἄνωγας."   670
῞Ως ἄρα φωνήσας ἐπὶ καρπῷ χεῖρα γέροντος
ἔλαβε δεξιτερήν, μή πως δείσει᾽ ἐνὶ θυμῷ.
οἱ μὲν ἄρ᾽ ἐν προδόμῳ δόμου αὐτόθι κοιμήσαντο,
661 ῥέζων a

κῆρυξ καὶ Πρίαμος, πυκινὰ φρεσὶ μήδε᾽ ἔχοντες.
αὐτὰρ Ἀχιλλεὺς εὗδε μυχῷ κλισίης ἐϋπήκτου·   675
τῷ δὲ Βρισηῒς παρελέξατο καλλιπάρῃος.
Ἄλλοι μέν ῥα θεοί τε καὶ ἀνέρες ἱπποκορυσταὶ
εὗδον παννύχιοι, μαλακῷ δεδμημένοι ὕπνῳ·
ἀλλ᾽ οὐχ Ἑρμείαν ἐριούνιον ὕπνος ἔμαρπτεν,
ὁρμαίνοντ᾽ ἀνὰ θυμὸν ὅπως Πρίαμον βασιλῆα   680
νηῶν ἐκπέμψειε λαθὼν ἱεροὺς πυλαωρούς.
στῆ δ᾽ ἄρ᾽ ὑπὲρ κεφαλῆς καί μιν πρὸς μῦθον ἔειπεν·
"ὦ γέρον, οὔ νύ τι σοί γε μέλει κακόν, οἷον ἔθ᾽ εὕδεις
ἀνδράσιν ἐν δηΐοισιν, ἐπεί σ᾽ εἴασεν Ἀχιλλεύς.
καὶ νῦν μὲν φίλον υἱὸν ἐλύσαο, πολλὰ δ᾽ ἔδωκας·   685
σεῖο δέ κε ζωοῦ καὶ τρὶς τόσα δοῖεν ἄποινα
παῖδες τοὶ μετόπισθε λελειμμένοι, αἴ κ᾽ Ἀγαμέμνων
γνώῃ σ᾽ Ἀτρεΐδης, γνώωσι δὲ πάντες Ἀχαιοί."
Ὣς ἔφατ᾽, ἔδεισεν δ᾽ ὁ γέρων, κήρυκα δ᾽ ἀνίστη.
τοῖσιν δ᾽ Ἑρμείας ζεῦξ᾽ ἵππους ἡμιόνους τε,   690
ῥίμφα δ᾽ ἄρ᾽ αὐτὸς ἔλαυνε κατὰ στρατόν, οὐδέ τις ἔγνω.
Ἀλλ᾽ ὅτε δὴ πόρον ἷξον ἐϋρρεῖος ποταμοῖο,
[Ξάνθου δινήεντος, ὃν ἀθάνατος τέκετο Ζεύς,]
Ἑρμείας μὲν ἔπειτ᾽ ἀπέβη πρὸς μακρὸν Ὄλυμπον,
Ἠὼς δὲ κροκόπεπλος ἐκίδνατο πᾶσαν ἐπ᾽ αἶαν,   695
οἱ δ᾽ ἐς ἄστυ ἔλων οἰμωγῇ τε στοναχῇ τε
ἵππους, ἡμίονοι δὲ νέκυν φέρον. οὐδέ τις ἄλλος
ἔγνω πρόσθ᾽ ἀνδρῶν καλλιζώνων τε γυναικῶν,
ἀλλ᾽ ἄρα Κασσάνδρη, ἱκέλη χρυσέῃ Ἀφροδίτῃ,
Πέργαμον εἰσαναβᾶσα φίλον πατέρ᾽ εἰσενόησεν   700
ἑσταότ᾽ ἐν δίφρῳ, κήρυκά τε ἀστυβοώτην·
τὸν δ᾽ ἄρ᾽ ἐφ᾽ ἡμιόνων ἴδε κείμενον ἐν λεχέεσσι·
κώκυσέν τ᾽ ἄρ᾽ ἔπειτα γέγωνέ τε πᾶν κατὰ ἄστυ·
"ὄψεσθε, Τρῶες καὶ Τρῳάδες, Ἕκτορ᾽ ἰόντες,
εἴ ποτε καὶ ζώοντι μάχης ἐκ νοστήσαντι   705
χαίρετ᾽, ἐπεὶ μέγα χάρμα πόλει τ᾽ ἦν παντί τε δήμῳ."
Ὣς ἔφατ᾽, οὐδέ τις αὐτόθ᾽ ἐνὶ πτόλεϊ λίπετ᾽ ἀνὴρ

681 πυλαουρους p   693 om. a

οὐδὲ γυνή· πάντας γὰρ ἀάσχετον ἵκετο πένθος·
ἀγχοῦ δὲ ξύμβληντο πυλάων νεκρὸν ἄγοντι.
πρῶται τόν γ᾽ ἄλοχός τε φίλη καὶ πότνια μήτηρ   710
τιλλέσθην, ἐπ᾽ ἄμαξαν ἐΰτροχον ἀΐξασαι,
ἁπτόμεναι κεφαλῆς· κλαίων δ᾽ ἀμφίσταθ᾽ ὅμιλος.
καί νύ κε δὴ πρόπαν ἦμαρ ἐς ἠέλιον καταδύντα
Ἕκτορα δάκρυ χέοντες ὀδύροντο πρὸ πυλάων,
εἰ μὴ ἄρ᾽ ἐκ δίφροιο γέρων λαοῖσι μετηύδα·   715
"εἴξατέ μοι οὐρεῦσι διελθέμεν· αὐτὰρ ἔπειτα
ἄσεσθε κλαυθμοῖο, ἐπὴν ἀγάγωμι δόμονδε."
    Ὣς ἔφαθ᾽, οἱ δὲ διέστησαν καὶ εἶξαν ἀπήνῃ.
οἱ δ᾽ ἐπεὶ εἰσάγαγον κλυτὰ δώματα, τὸν μὲν ἔπειτα
τρητοῖς ἐν λεχέεσσι θέσαν, παρὰ δ᾽ εἷσαν ἀοιδοὺς   720
θρήνων ἐξάρχους, οἵ τε στονόεσσαν ἀοιδήν –
οἱ μὲν ἄρ᾽ ἐθρήνεον, ἐπὶ δὲ στενάχοντο γυναῖκες.
τῇσιν δ᾽ Ἀνδρομάχη λευκώλενος ἦρχε γόοιο,
Ἕκτορος ἀνδροφόνοιο κάρη μετὰ χερσὶν ἔχουσα·
"ἆνερ, ἀπ᾽ αἰῶνος νέος ὤλεο, κὰδ δέ με χήρην   725
λείπεις ἐν μεγάροισι· πάϊς δ᾽ ἔτι νήπιος αὔτως,
ὃν τέκομεν σύ τ᾽ ἐγώ τε δυσάμμοροι, οὐδέ μιν οἴω
ἥβην ἵξεσθαι· πρὶν γὰρ πόλις ἥδε κατ᾽ ἄκρης
πέρσεται· ἦ γὰρ ὄλωλας ἐπίσκοπος, ὅς τέ μιν αὐτὴν
ῥύσκευ, ἔχες δ᾽ ἀλόχους κεδνὰς καὶ νήπια τέκνα,   730
αἳ δή τοι τάχα νηυσὶν ὀχήσονται γλαφυρῇσι,
καὶ μὲν ἐγὼ μετὰ τῇσι· σὺ δ᾽ αὖ, τέκος, ἢ ἐμοὶ αὐτῇ
ἕψεαι, ἔνθα κεν ἔργα ἀεικέα ἐργάζοιο,
ἀθλεύων πρὸ ἄνακτος ἀμειλίχου, ἤ τις Ἀχαιῶν
ῥίψει χειρὸς ἑλὼν ἀπὸ πύργου λυγρὸν ὄλεθρον,   735
χωόμενος, ᾧ δή που ἀδελφεὸν ἔκτανεν Ἕκτωρ
ἢ πατέρ᾽, ἠὲ καὶ υἱόν, ἐπεὶ μάλα πολλοὶ Ἀχαιῶν
Ἕκτορος ἐν παλάμῃσιν ὀδὰξ ἕλον ἄσπετον οὖδας.
οὐ γὰρ μείλιχος ἔσκε πατὴρ τεὸς ἐν δαῒ λυγρῇ·
τῶ καί μιν λαοὶ μὲν ὀδύρονται κατὰ ἄστυ,   740
ἀρητὸν δὲ τοκεῦσι γόον καὶ πένθος ἔθηκας,

721 θρήνους a

Ἕκτορ· ἐμοὶ δὲ μάλιστα λελείψεται ἄλγεα λυγρά.
οὐ γάρ μοι θνῄσκων λεχέων ἐκ χεῖρας ὄρεξας,
οὐδέ τί μοι εἶπες πυκινὸν ἔπος, οὗ τέ κεν αἰεὶ
μεμνῄμην νύκτας τε καὶ ἤματα δάκρυ χέουσα.''   745
  ῝Ως ἔφατο κλαίουσ᾽, ἐπὶ δὲ στενάχοντο γυναῖκες.
τῇσιν δ᾽ αὖθ᾽ Ἑκάβη ἀδινοῦ ἐξῆρχε γόοιο·
'' Ἕκτορ, ἐμῷ θυμῷ πάντων πολὺ φίλτατε παίδων,
ἦ μέν μοι ζωός περ ἐὼν φίλος ἦσθα θεοῖσιν·
οἱ δ᾽ ἄρα σεῦ κήδοντο καὶ ἐν θανάτοιό περ αἴσῃ.   750
ἄλλους μὲν γὰρ παῖδας ἐμοὺς πόδας ὠκὺς Ἀχιλλεὺς
πέρνασχ᾽, ὅν τιν᾽ ἕλεσκε, πέρην ἁλὸς ἀτρυγέτοιο,
ἐς Σάμον ἔς τ᾽ Ἴμβρον καὶ Λῆμνον ἀμιχθαλόεσσαν·
σεῦ δ᾽ ἐπεὶ ἐξέλετο ψυχὴν ταναήκεϊ χαλκῷ,
πολλὰ ῥυστάζεσκεν ἑοῦ περὶ σῆμ᾽ ἑτάροιο,   755
Πατρόκλου, τὸν ἔπεφνες· ἀνέστησεν δέ μιν οὐδ᾽ ὥς.
νῦν δέ μοι ἑρσήεις καὶ πρόσφατος ἐν μεγάροισι
κεῖσαι, τῷ ἴκελος ὅν τ᾽ ἀργυρότοξος Ἀπόλλων
οἷς ἀγανοῖσι βέλεσσιν ἐποιχόμενος κατέπεφνεν.''
  ῝Ως ἔφατο κλαίουσα, γόον δ᾽ ἀλίαστον ὄρινε.   760
τῇσι δ᾽ ἔπειθ᾽ Ἑλένη τριτάτη ἐξῆρχε γόοιο·
'' Ἕκτορ, ἐμῷ θυμῷ δαέρων πολὺ φίλτατε πάντων,
ἦ μέν μοι πόσις ἐστὶν Ἀλέξανδρος θεοειδής,
ὅς μ᾽ ἄγαγε Τροίηνδ᾽· ὡς πρὶν ὤφελλον ὀλέσθαι.
ἤδη γὰρ νῦν μοι τόδ᾽ ἐεικοστὸν ἔτος ἐστὶν   765
ἐξ οὗ κεῖθεν ἔβην καὶ ἐμῆς ἀπελήλυθα πάτρης·
ἀλλ᾽ οὔ πω σεῦ ἄκουσα κακὸν ἔπος οὐδ᾽ ἀσύφηλον·
ἀλλ᾽ εἴ τίς με καὶ ἄλλος ἐνὶ μεγάροισιν ἐνίπτοι
δαέρων ἢ γαλόων ἢ εἰνατέρων εὐπέπλων,
ἢ ἑκυρή – ἑκυρὸς δὲ πατὴρ ὣς ἤπιος αἰεί –,   770
ἀλλὰ σὺ τὸν ἐπέεσσι παραιφάμενος κατέρυκες,
σῇ τ᾽ ἀγανοφροσύνῃ καὶ σοῖς ἀγανοῖς ἐπέεσσι.
τῶ σέ θ᾽ ἅμα κλαίω καὶ ἔμ᾽ ἄμμορον ἀχνυμένη κῆρ·
οὐ γάρ τίς μοι ἔτ᾽ ἄλλος ἐνὶ Τροίῃ εὐρείῃ
ἤπιος οὐδὲ φίλος, πάντες δέ με πεφρίκασιν.''   775
764 ὤφελλ᾽ ἀπολέσθαι a

Ὣς ἔφατο κλαίουσ', ἐπὶ δ' ἔστενε δῆμος ἀπείρων.
λαοῖσιν δ' ὁ γέρων Πρίαμος μετὰ μῦθον ἔειπεν·
"ἄξετε νῦν, Τρῶες, ξύλα ἄστυδε, μηδέ τι θυμῷ
δείσητ'· Ἀργείων πυκινὸν λόχον· ἦ γὰρ Ἀχιλλεὺς
πέμπων μ' ὧδ' ἐπέτελλε μελαινάων ἀπὸ νηῶν,   780
μὴ πρὶν πημανέειν, πρὶν δωδεκάτη μόλῃ ἠώς."
Ὣς ἔφαθ', οἱ δ' ὑπ' ἀμάξῃσιν βόας ἡμιόνους τε
ζεύγνυσαν, αἶψα δ' ἔπειτα πρὸ ἄστεος ἠγερέθοντο.
ἐννῆμαρ μὲν τοί γε ἀγίνεον ἄσπετον ὕλην·
ἀλλ' ὅτε δὴ δεκάτη ἐφάνη φαεσίμβροτος ἠώς,   785
καὶ τότ' ἄρ' ἐξέφερον θρασὺν Ἕκτορα δάκρυ χέοντες,
ἐν δὲ πυρῇ ὑπάτῃ νεκρὸν θέσαν, ἐν δ' ἔβαλον πῦρ.
Ἦμος δ' ἠριγένεια φάνη ῥοδοδάκτυλος Ἠώς,
τῆμος ἄρ' ἀμφὶ πυρὴν κλυτοῦ Ἕκτορος ἤγρετο λαός.
αὐτὰρ ἐπεί ῥ' ἤγερθεν ὁμηγερέες τ' ἐγένοντο,   790
πρῶτον μὲν κατὰ πυρκαϊὴν σβέσαν αἴθοπι οἴνῳ
πᾶσαν, ὁπόσσον ἐπέσχε πυρὸς μένος· αὐτὰρ ἔπειτα
ὀστέα λευκὰ λέγοντο κασίγνητοί θ' ἕταροί τε
μυρόμενοι, θαλερὸν δὲ κατείβετο δάκρυ παρειῶν.
καὶ τά γε χρυσείην ἐς λάρνακα θῆκαν ἑλόντες,   795
πορφυρέοις πέπλοισι καλύψαντες μαλακοῖσιν·
αἶψα δ' ἄρ' ἐς κοίλην κάπετον θέσαν, αὐτὰρ ὕπερθε
πυκνοῖσιν λάεσσι κατεστόρεσαν μεγάλοισι·
ῥίμφα δὲ σῆμ' ἔχεαν, περὶ δὲ σκοποὶ εἴατο πάντῃ,
μὴ πρὶν ἐφορμηθεῖεν ἐϋκνήμιδες Ἀχαιοί.   800
χεύαντες δὲ τὸ σῆμα πάλιν κίον· αὐτὰρ ἔπειτα
εὖ συναγειρόμενοι δαίνυντ' ἐρικυδέα δαῖτα
δώμασιν ἐν Πριάμοιο, διοτρεφέος βασιλῆος.
Ὣς οἵ γ' ἀμφίεπον τάφον Ἕκτορος ἱπποδάμοιο.

789 ἔγρετο codd. fere omnes   790 om. a; fortasse delendus

COMMENTARY

1–5 The opening is like 677–81; 2.1–4; 10.1–4. But this sleeplessness springs from emotional turmoil, not merely watchful concern. These lines also look back to 23.257–8 αὐτὰρ ᾿Αχιλλεὺς | αὐτοῦ λαὸν ἔρυκε καὶ ἵҳανεν εὐρὺν ἀγῶνα, which is the beginning of the games. There a gathering is formed, here it is broken up; there the people are kept back, here they scatter; there Achilles is with the people, here separate from them. Further, the contrast of wakeful Achilles with the rest of the Greeks recalls 23.57–61. Here as there, his passions re-emerge in his solitude.

1 Λῦτο 'was broken up', aorist middle/passive of λύω, with epic lengthening and without augment (= ἔλῦτο). See further 707 n.

ἀγών 'the gathering': cf., e.g., 23.617; Hes. *Theog.* 91 and West ad loc.

2–3 ἰέναι...ταρπήμεναι: the infinitive, as often in Homer, expresses the consequence of the main verb; cf., e.g., 15, 36, 611, 663, 716: translate (literally) 'they scattered, so as to go; *they* took care of supper and sweet sleep, so as to take pleasure (in them)'.

6–9 were condemned as an interpolation by the Alexandrian critics, Aristophanes of Byzantium (*c.* 257–180 B.C.) and Aristarchus (*c.* 217–145 B.C.). Their case, though not all their reasoning, is strong. These words are clearly meant to enlarge on φίλου ἑτάρου μεμνημένος (4); but they add nothing of any force: contrast the vivid and pointed memories of Patroclus in 19.315–18. Here the vividness is created by the description of Achilles' tossing and turning. Granted that the lines are suspect, two other considerations, which are not in themselves arguments against their authenticity, may reinforce the suspicions. (1) The sense runs on admirably and smoothly from line 5 to line 10. (2) 8 = *Od.* 8.183; 13.91, 264 (the sea-journeys concerned here would be expeditions against other cities during the siege of Troy; cf. *Il.* 9.328–9; 18.342; *Od.* 3.105–8). Line 558, a clear interpolation, is likewise drawn (in part) from the *Odyssey* (13.360).

6 ἀδροτῆτα = ἀνδροτῆτα 'manhood': cf. 16.857. It seems likely that this was the original form of the word in the text, even though our older

85

MSS have ἀνδροτῆτα. For the loss of the nasal cf. 14.78 where ἁβρότη = ἀμβρότη or 10.65 where ἀβροτάξομεν = ἀμβροτάξομεν. See further J. Latacz, *Glotta* 43 (1965) 62–76. For a different explanation, see G. C. Horrocks, *P.C.P.S.* 206 (1980) 10.

6–8 Two zeugmas. (1) ποθέων governs ὁπόσα…ἄλγεα as well as Πατρόκλου…ἀδροτῆτά τε καὶ μένος ἠΰ, though it is only the notion of 'remembering' implicit in 'missing' which is relevant in the former case. (2) πείρων ('crossing') governs both 'wars' and 'waves', though it is strictly appropriate only to 'waves'. For zeugma in Homer see 8.506; 4.282 and van Leeuwen ad loc.

12 δινεύεσκ' ἀλύων: a sign of longing; cf. Sappho 96.15 Lobel–Page; Menander, *Misumenos* 7; also *Il.* 2.778–9. At this point the description of one night merges into the description of a series of nights (-εσκε, -ασκετο, -εσκετο are frequentative imperfects, denoting repeated action). The transition is made with ease and delicacy.

παρὰ θῖν' ἁλός: the sea-shore is the characteristic place for Achilles' isolation in the *Iliad*; cf. 1.350; 23.59.

14 The optative denotes repeated past action: 'whenever/each time he yoked…'; cf., e.g., 768; 3.216; 8.270.

15 δ(έ) marks the resumption of the main sentence, after the subordinate clause (ἐπεί…ἵππους), as often in Homer: cf. Denniston 179. On the infinitive ἕλκεσθαι, see 2–3 n.

16 Cf. 23.13–14 οἱ δὲ τρὶς περὶ νεκρὸν ἐΰτριχας ἤλασαν ἵππους | μυρόμενοι: this is part of the lamentation for Patroclus; for the ritual cf. *Beowulf* 3169–72; Jordanes, *Getica* ch. 49 (the funeral of Attila the Hun). So when Achilles drags the corpse three times round the tomb here, that is a sort of tribute to Patroclus and sign of his yearning for him, as well as a degradation of Hector. This gives his action a meaning deeper than that of the first dragging (22.395–404), which was merely an immediate gesture of triumph and hatred.

17 τόνδε means no more than 'him': cf. 264 n.; 403; 20.302.

18 προπρηνέα: part of the disgrace. A corpse prepared for burial is laid on its back: Achilles inverts the funeral rite, as he did before in 23.25.

Aristotle explained Achilles' action by reference to a Thessalian

custom of dragging murderers round tombs: see Callim. fr. 588 and
Pfeiffer ad loc. If there was such a custom, and if Homer knew of it,
that does not explain or justify Achilles' behaviour in the *Iliad*, which
is clearly seen as wrongful (cf. 50–4).

18–21 Cf. 23.184–91. This passage differs in two respects from the
earlier one:

(1) There both Aphrodite and Apollo protect the corpse, here only
Apollo. That is because Apollo alone counts in what immediately
follows here. In other words, the event is described in the way most
relevant to the context: cf., e.g., 18.84 'the gods' gave Thetis to Peleus
as his wife, in 18.432 'Zeus' did, in 24.60 Hera did.

(2) There Aphrodite keeps off the dogs and anoints the corpse with
divine oil, ἵνα μή μιν ἀποδρύφοι ἑλκυστάζων, while Apollo covers the
whole area with a cloud to stop the sun shrivelling up its flesh: here
Apollo covers the whole corpse (πάντα) with the aegis, ἵνα μή μιν κτλ.
The aegis, then, in the hands of Apollo alone produces the effects which
both gods had produced in Book 23, each by different means. This is
again because it is he, and not she, who matters here.

So the episode as recounted in Book 24 recalls, but abridges and
modifies, the version of it in Book 23. There is a rather similar relation
between the divine assemblies which begin *Od.* 1 and *Od.* 5: cf.
M. J. Apthorp, *C.Q.* n.s. 27 (1977) 1–9.

19 ἄπεχε χροῒ 'kept away from his flesh': the dative is used as in
ἀμύνειν τί τινι; cf. *Od.* 20.263.

φῶτ' 'the man', 'him'; cf., e.g., 4.139.

20 The aegis, whose original meaning seems to be 'goat-skin', is worn
round the shoulders in 5.738 and 18.204; perhaps we should imagine
it wrapped like a shroud round the body here. It is golden, because
divine things are characteristically golden: cf. 341; 5.727; 8.19, 69.
Apollo uses it again at 15.318, 361, though there Zeus has given it him
(229). In general on the aegis, see N. Prins, *De oorspronkelijke beteekenis
van de aegis* (Diss. Utrecht 1931); H. Borchhardt, *AH* E 53–6.

23–6 'The gods' turns out not to include Hera, Poseidon and Athena;
for this form of exposition, see 498 n. On Hermes' role, see 334–5 n.

24 Ἀργειφόντην 'slayer of Argus'. The traditional explanation of the
epithet is satisfying: cf. N. J. Richardson on *H.H.Dem.* 335. Hermes

killed Argus whom the jealous Hera had set to watch over Io, one of
the mortal women loved by Zeus.

25 ἐήνδανεν 'it was pleasing' (Attic ἐδόκει), imperfect of ἀνδάνω.

25-30 These lines were condemned by Aristarchus. But the origin of
Hera's and Athena's hatred for Troy comes effectively at the end of the
poem: ἀλλ' ἔχον ὡς σφιν πρῶτον... – their enmity went on implacably
from its very beginning. Like the Attic tragedians after him (see, e.g.,
Soph. *El.* 504–15; Eur. *Med.* 1–15; *Or.* 807–18, 982–1012; *I.A.* 573–89,
1283–1318 – the judgement of Paris again), Homer heightens and
extends his tragedy by taking us back to where it started. This reminds
us that even if for the moment 'the gods' are to unite in allowing the
ransom of Hector's body, the gods hostile to Troy still have reason to
be as angry as ever; and the city they hate must fall (cf. 728–9 n.). No
motive for Poseidon's resentment is given: that is because one already
has been in 21.441–60, namely the deceit of Laomedon. (The curt and
elliptical style is natural when, as here, a story is only mentioned, not
told: cf., e.g., 9.566–7; *Od.* 8.76–82; also 608–9 n.). See further,
K. Reinhardt, *Das Parisurteil* (Frankfurt a. M. 1938) = *Tradition und
Geist* (Göttingen 1960) 16–36; M. Davies, *J.H.S.* 101 (1981).

26 Ποσειδάων': the final iota of the dative singular is elided, as
sometimes happens in Homer, though not in other Greek verse: cf., e.g.,
4.259; 11.544; 23.693.

27-8 There is a powerful antithesis between the accumulated Ἴλιος
ἱρή | καὶ Πρίαμος καὶ λαός and the single 'Αλεξάνδρου. The gods' anger
with one citizen and his folly affects the whole city (cf. 611 n.), a point
to which Aeschylus gave powerfully tragic expression in the *Agamemnon*
(390–6, 532–7, 823–4), as did Euripides in the *Hecuba* (641–9), recalling
the judgement of Paris. In the *Iliad*, cf. above all 6.55–60, where
Agamemnon's vindictive words against Troy are said to be just (62),
but are also felt to be terrible.

ἔχον 'they hung on, persisted': cf. 12.433.

ἄτης 'folly', 'madness': the word ἀρχῆς appears in all manuscripts
at 3.100, and in some here and at 6.356, after 'Αλεξάνδρου ἕνεκ'. In
3.100 ἀρχῆς should be kept; Hdt. 8.142.2 probably guarantees the sense
'initiative' for it, and that passage may, moreover, be an echo of
Homer. But it may have crept in as a variant, here and at 6.356, from

3.100. Aristarchus objected (see the scholia here and on 3.100) to the reading ἄτης, that it sounds like an excuse for Paris: it could imply that he was 'carried away' rather than fully responsible for what he did. Perhaps that is why ἀρχῆς is put in the mouth of the man he offended, Menelaus, in 3.100; but it is not a reason for doubting ἄτης here or in 6.356. Homer is very far from exculpating Paris (see 29–30 n. on μαχλοσύνην); and ἄτη may take away a person's wits, but not his responsibility: cf. 9.115–20; 19.137–8.

29–30 νείκεσσε elsewhere commonly means 'upbraided' (e.g. 249), but here 'found fault with', just as μέμφομαι can be used of both expressed and unexpressed blame.

ᾔνησ' likewise means 'approved of, found best' (cf. 8.9), not 'praised'. Note also that 'say' in Greek commonly corresponds to 'think' in English: e.g. 5.473; 8.497; 12.165; 20.262.

θεάς 'the (other two) goddesses': for a similar elliptical form of expression see 531 n.

μέσσαυλον 'inner courtyard', where cattle were kept. This happens on Mount Ida; for the noble youth as a herdsman, cf. 11.104–6; 15.547–8 – again sons of Priam.

μαχλοσύνην 'randiness'. The word is properly used of women; but cf. Lucian, *Alex.* 11. If the implication is that Paris is a 'ladies' man', that fits the Paris of the *Iliad* well (cf. esp. 3.39–55). And we see how seductive his lust can be in 3.437–47. Now the myth as reported by Proclus from the *Cypria* says that Paris made Aphrodite the winner in the beauty-contest of the three goddesses which he judged, because she promised him marriage with Helen: προκρίνει τὴν Ἀφροδίτην ἐπαρθεὶς τοῖς Ἑλένης γάμοις. These lines allude to the same story, but in such a way as to stress Paris' error: Aphrodite gave him not so much the most desirable of women, as 'randiness', i.e. made him a seducer and uxorious. Such a harsh view of Paris is characteristic of the *Iliad*, where he forms a counterpart to Hector, the brave warrior and good husband (cf. 704–6 n.). And just as Paris' folly brings Hector death and Troy destruction, so here it causes Hector's body to lie unburied.

31 ἐκ τοῖο here, as in 1.493, is elastically used: it refers to the day Hector was killed. The funeral of Patroclus and the games had occupied a day each after it, and the gods' quarrelling lasted nine days (107–8). Such loose-sounding references are quite common in Homer and after

him, sometimes with considerable poetic or rhetorical effect: cf. 8.9 τάδε
ἔργα where Zeus does not care to reveal his aims; 23.190 πρίν, which
hints at the events of Book 24; *Od.* 3.303 ταῦτα...λυγρά, mentioned
in this vague way by Nestor, are reserved for Menelaus' tale in Book
4 (519–33); 8.79 ὥς, which merely hints at what Apollo's prophecy said.
See further 264 n.; for later parallels, e.g. Soph. *O.C.* 1435 (τάδε); Ar.
Thes. 13 (τότε); Dem. 6.33 (τοῦτο); 9.36 (τότε).

33–76 Apollo begins by complaining of the gods' ingratitude to
Hector, and sets him, the worshipper of the gods who should now enjoy
their pity, against Achilles, whose pitilessness should make him hateful
to the gods. Hera counters by setting Achilles, the son of a goddess,
against Hector, a mere common mortal; she concludes by complaining
of the gods', above all Apollo's, inconstancy towards Achilles and his
parents. Zeus effects a settlement: he allows Hector his privileges, while
granting that Achilles' will be greater; and he sets aside the notion of
stealing the body. This opens the way for the meeting between Achilles
and Priam.

In a sense, then, this is a clash between two partisans, in which they
each champion their own man, followed by a compromise. But the
argument is framed so as to bring out deeper issues: what is decided
will represent what the gods stand for. The question is where their
friendship should go: to an ordinary mortal who had deserved it by his
piety, or to the son of a goddess who is by nature closer to the
Olympians. This question contains a larger one: are they to uphold
human civilization, or let it be flouted? By allowing Hector's burial they
show that they do make humanity their concern, and that they do
reward their friends (cf. 425–31, 749–50 nn.). It remains true that
Hector has died and been dragged, and that Troy will fall a prey to
the gods who hate it.

33–4 Cf. *Od.* 5.118 (Calypso complaining to Hermes because the gods
have commanded her to let Odysseus go) σχέτλιοί ἐστε, θεοί, ζηλήμονες
ἔξοχον ἄλλων and *Od.* 1.60–1 (Athena remonstrating with Zeus on
Odysseus' behalf) οὐ νύ τ' Ὀδυσσεὺς | Ἀργείων παρὰ νηυσὶ χαρίζετο
ἱερὰ ῥέζων ; For the piety of Hector or the Trojans cf. 4.48–9; 22.169–72.

θεοί: the vocative here and in 39 has a certain rhetorical force. Apollo
is aiming to make Athena, Hera and Poseidon conform with ' the gods '
as a whole; and in his view the gods, as guarantors of morality, should

be shocked at Achilles' treatment of Hector. Hera in 57 counters with a different notion of the gods: for her their nature and duty is to show their superiority to men.

36 ἦ . . . ᾧ: the repetition, like σῇ . . . σοῖς in 772, brings out how much Hector is missed; so does the division into five (cf. 495–7 n.) of those who miss him.

38 The termination -αιεν (rather than -ειαν) for the third person plural of the aorist optative occurs only here in Homer, though τίσαιεν may have been an ancient reading in 1.42 (see scholia ad loc.). κήειαν is unattested, as are κήειας and κήειε; κήαι occurs in 21.336. Perhaps κήαιεν was preferred for phonetic reasons; κτερίσαιεν was then naturally attracted to the form of κήαιεν just before. This attraction could, however, be due to a scribe, not to the poet, since κτερίσειαν is a variant.

ἐπί is adverbial, 'moreover'.

κτέρεα κτερίσαιεν: for the cognate accusative, expressing the internal object, i.e. the substance of the action contained in the verb, cf. 172 n. In the singular κτέρας means 'possession' (cf. 235); in the plural the word comes to have the specific sense 'funeral honours', presumably *via* the meaning 'funeral gifts'. For such gifts, cf. 23.166–75.

40–1 νόημα | γναμπτόν: a good man knows how to yield (cf. 15.203 στρεπταὶ μέν τε φρένες ἐσθλῶν). The epithet recalls Phoenix' appeal to Achilles in Book 9: 'even the gods can be deflected' (497 στρεπτοί); 'give that honour to the Prayer-goddesses which bends (514 ἐπι-γνάμπτει) even strong men's hearts'. Achilles seems as obdurate as he was in Book 9.

42–3 In 8.230–4 and 17.658–64 a temporal clause after a relative is complemented by no main sentence; here, conversely, the ἐπεί-clause is completed by no verb: it ends with εἴξας. This kind of freedom lends naturalness and flexibility to Homer's style; for similar phenomena see 212–13, 509–11, 721–2 nn.

A human characteristic is here transferred to the animal: the lion 'gives in' to his strength and pride because he represents the man who is the enemy of other men. For the same reason βροτῶν is no mere line-filler.

δαῖτα 'dinner': the word is properly used of a human meal. Here and in 1.5 (cf. R. Pfeiffer, *A history of classical scholarship* 1 (Oxford 1968) 111) it is used of animals' prey with sinister effect.

44 ἔλεον...αἰδώς: the two words are linked again at 207–8; 22.123–4 referring to Achilles' implacability. When they recur finally in 503, Achilles responds to the appeal.

ἀπώλεσεν 'he has lost', rather than 'he has destroyed'; cf. 15.129 νόος δ' ἀπόλωλε καὶ αἰδώς.

45 Cf. Hes. *W.D.* 318 (αἰδώς ἥ τ' κτλ.). In that place the stress is on σίνεται, i.e. on the bad sort of shame; here on ὀνίνησι, i.e. on the good sort of shame. The phrase is then a form of 'polar' expression: i.e. one which says, for greater emphasis, 'neither *x* nor *y*', or 'both *x* and *y*' – *y* being the opposite of *x* – where the relevant notion is only either *x* or *y*; cf. Wilamowitz on Eur. *H.F.* 1106; F. Leo, *Kleine Schriften* 1 (Rome 1960) 158–62; G. E. R. Lloyd, *Polarity and analogy* (Cambridge 1966) 90–4. In Homer, cf. 10.249 μήτ' ἄρ με μάλ' αἴνεε μήτε τι νείκει (where there was no question of blame); 15.98–9; *Od.* 15.72–3.

Some scholars have suspected that this line has been interpolated from Hesiod; and it is true that Hesiod's previous line (317) αἰδώς δ' οὐκ ἀγαθὴ κεχρημένον ἄνδρα κομίζειν leads naturally up to the idea of a 'shame which does both great harm and great good to men', but the phrase is no less appropriate, in its different way, in *Iliad* 24. It is striking that *W.D.* 317 too is close to a line of Homer, *Od.* 17.347 αἰδώς δ' οὐκ ἀγαθὴ κεχρημένῳ ἀνδρὶ παρεῖναι. It is not absurd to think that Hesiod was echoing his contemporary: this seems to have happened in Hes. *Theog.* 84–92 (cf. *Od.* 8.170–3); the relation between the two passages is well discussed by P. Cauer, *Grundfragen der Homerkritik*³ (Leipzig 1923) 653–5. In general, see G. P. Edwards, *The language of Hesiod* (Oxford 1971) 166–89.

If the line *is* an interpolation, it would fall into a common type, which expands on a phrase that could seem too brief (οὐδέ οἱ αἰδώς here): cf. 558; 7.353; 14.217; Aesch. *Ag.* 1226 and Fraenkel ad loc. But it is not necessary, and may well be wrong, to suppose that it is spurious.

46 μέλλει μέν πού τις...ὀλέσσαι 'I suppose a man must have lost...before now'; cf. 18.362; *Od.* 4.378. Here the turn of phrase is heavily sarcastic.

48 μεθέηκε 'he relented', literally 'he let go': aorist indicative of μεθίημι.

49 τλητόν 'patient, enduring'. For the unusual active sense of the verbal adjective, cf. *Od.* 4.494 ἄκλαυτον 'without weeping'; 10.3 πλωτῆ 'floating'; Soph. *O.T.* 969 and Jebb ad loc.; Wackernagel I 288. For the thought cf. 549 ἄνσχεο, which, in its context, shows that Achilles has learned Apollo's lesson.

Μοῖραι (plural) occurs only here in Homer. The Moirai, like the Erinyes in 19.418, are a source of right order in the world. (Moira and Erinys are connected in 19.87.) They have a place here also because Apollo would obstruct his aim of arousing the gods' pity if he said that 'the gods' gave men endurance. This line is echoed in Archil. fr. 13.5–7, where θεοί is the subject.

52 οὐ...ἄμεινον 'that will discredit and damage him', literally 'that is not more honourable or more advantageous for him'. This form of expression, which looks like a weighty understatement, seems particularly proper to solemn or serious warnings: cf. οὐ...κέρδιον ἡμῖν in 7.352; οὐ γὰρ ἄμεινον in Hes. *W.D.* 750 (cf. 759 οὔ τοι λώϊον) and Hdt. 1.187.2; 3.71.2, 82.5. In positive form, Hdt. 3.72.5 ὃς ἄν...ἑκὼν παρίῃ, αὐτῷ οἱ ἄμεινον...ἔσται.

53 '(Let him take care) that noble though he is, our just anger does not strike him.' μή with a first-person subjunctive here introduces a warning: cf. 1.26.

ἀγαθῷ 'noble/excellent/powerful', not a term of *moral* commendation. It emerges from this passage, as from this book and the whole poem, that to be merely ἀγαθός is not enough (cf. Eur. *Supp.* 594–7); note also ἀγαθός περ ἐών as used in 1.131, 275; 19.155. There too neither Achilles nor Agamemnon was right to over-assert his 'excellence' (ἀρετή); cf. A. A. Long, *J.H.S.* 90 (1970) 121–39, esp. 128.

οἱ is placed unusually late in the sentence; one would expect it to come after μή: cf. J. Wackernagel, *Kleine Schriften* I (Göttingen 1953) 1–104, esp. 4–8. But μή, which is emphatic, since it marks and introduces a warning, forms a separate initial colon, or 'up-beat', to the sentence (see Ed. Fraenkel, *S.B.A.W.* 1965, Heft 2, 41), as in Plat. *Prot.* 313c καὶ ὅπως γε μή, | ὦ ἑταῖρε, | ὁ σοφιστής...ἐξαπατήσῃ ἡμᾶς; *Crat.* 430d; Aeschin. 3.156; and ἀγαθῷ περ ἐόντι is a subordinate clause. Cf. also Hdt. 1.90.2 εἰ ἐξαπατᾶν τοὺς εὖ ποιεῦντας νόμος ἐστί οἱ, where heavy emphasis falls on 'deceiving his benefactors'.

ἡμεῖς is emphatic: 'we (the just and powerful gods)' as opposed to 'him', the erring and impotent mortal. For the antithetical juxtaposition of the two pronouns at the end of the phrase cf., e.g., *Od.* 11.390 ἔγνω δ' αἶψ' ἐμὲ κεῖνος; Ar. *Clouds* 1233.

54 κωφήν... γαῖαν 'the dumb, inert earth', i.e. the corpse, since man is made of water and earth (see 7.99 with Leaf's note; cf. Hes. *W.D.* 61). For this use of γαῖαν, cf. Soph. *El.* 244 γᾶ τε καὶ οὐδὲν ὢν | κείσεται τάλας. For the sense of κωφήν, cf. 14.16 κύματι κωφῷ used 'of the ground swell...as opposed to the splash and rush of the wave-tops before a wind' (Leaf); κωφόν means 'inert, ineffectual' in 11.390. The gods protect the shiftless, suppliants or strangers or beggars (cf. *Od.* 14.58; 16.422) – and so also the inanimate and speechless dead, who can neither act, nor even raise a cry for help (βοή), on their own behalf. In Homer Hector threatens Achilles that divine wrath will fall on him if he refuses his corpse burial (22.358; cf. *Od.* 11.73); elsewhere there is said to be a 'law of the gods' which requires that all corpses be buried (Soph. *Aj.* 1343; *Ant.* 450–5; Eur. *Supp.* 563). Similarly, the gods who show pity (19, 23, 332) expect men to show pity (44).

Lines 53–4 are echoed by Aeschylus in fr. 266 Nauck (from the *Ransoming of Hector*). There the speaker, Hermes, says that no harm can be done to the dead, since they feel neither pleasure nor pain; however, divine νέμεσις executes their wrath for them. If this is an attempt to reproduce exactly Homer's thought, it suggests that Aeschylus took κωφήν to mean 'insensible', and ἡμεῖς ('we, the vigilant and powerful gods') to be in antithesis to κωφήν... γαῖαν. This is not entirely happy, since if κωφήν means that the dead *feel* nothing, that tends to play down both Achilles' misdeed and the importance of the gods' intervention; and that Aeschylus attributes wrath (κότον) to the dead, even just after saying that they are subject to neither pleasure nor pain, shows that he was in some measure conscious of this difficulty himself.

56–7 Heavily sarcastic: even what Apollo said could be true, if the same status is to be given to Achilles and Hector – which is absurd. The sarcasm is heightened if, as may well be, Hera's words are a variation on an everyday formula: cf. *Od.* 15.435, where εἴη κεν καὶ τοῦτ' εἰ... expresses qualified agreement to a proposal; *Od.* 11.348, where τοῦτο μὲν οὕτω δὴ ἔσται ἔπος αἴ κεν ἔγωγε | ...ἀνάσσω expresses emphatic agreement. For similar formulae see 139, 373, 669 nn.

57 Hera switches abruptly from addressing Apollo to addressing all the Olympians. For such sudden apostrophe cf. 741: 2.235; 9.636; 17.29; Dem. 18.208 (Αἰσχίνη); Cat. 87.4 (*tuo*). Here, as there, it quickens the emotional pulse of the utterance. See further 'Longinus', *On the sublime* 27.3–4, who quotes *Od.* 4.681–9 and [Dem.] 25.27.

58 γυναῖκα... μαζόν: for the double accusative, of the whole and the part, see, e.g., 170; cf. 61 n.

θήσατο ('sucked') seems deliberately to echo θήσετε (57), so as to stress the contrast Hera is making: for similar echoes cf. 390 n.; 21. 523–5 ἀνῆκε... ἔθηκε... ἐφῆκε. Hdt. 1.41.1–42.2 (Croesus' speech) ἀχάριτι... χρηστά... χρηστοῖσι... χρήζω... χρεόν, (Adrastus' reply) κεχρημένον... χαρίζεσθαι... χρηστοῖσι is a highly elaborate parallel from later prose.

59–60 The story that Hera brought up Thetis is mentioned by Ap. Rhod. 4.790–8 and Apollodorus 3.13.5. It may have figured in the *Cypria* (fr. 2), where it is said that Thetis refused to marry Zeus as a favour to Hera. Those passages are all clearly based on this one; and it seems likely that Homer invented this story to give Hera a motive for her goodwill to Thetis here: cf. B. K. Braswell, *C.Q.* n.s. 21 (1971) 23. When in 14.303 Hera says she was herself brought up by Oceanus and Tethys, that is probably a similar *ad hoc* invention.

61 περὶ κῆρι φίλος... ἀθανάτοισι 'very dear to the gods' heart': περί is adverbial; cf. 236, 423, 435. For the double dative of the whole and part see, e.g., 197; cf. 58 n.

62–3 We have already been told that Apollo will cause Achilles' death (21.277–8; 22.359). So behind Hera's rhetoric there is tragedy, as Aeschylus brought out in a lost play, famously quoted by Plato, *Rep.* 383a–b.

θεοί follows forcefully on θεᾶς γόνος and φίλος ἀθανάτοισι, and strongly contrasts with θνητός and ἀνδρί. This is where favour of 'the gods' should go.

δαίνυ(ο) 'you feasted' second person singular of the imperfect of δαίνυμαι; on the form of the termination, see Chantraine 1 §227.

κακῶν ἕταρ': presumably because he favours the Trojans, including Paris. This is the retort to 39, where Apollo was indignant that the gods

could favour 'the evil Achilles'; it also looks like a standard form of
blame (cf. Hes. *W.D.* 716).

αἰὲν ἄπιστε too is a retort. Apollo said that Achilles was savage; Hera
says that Apollo is treacherous. So also, if Achilles was like the lion who
took his 'dinner' from men's herds (43), Apollo, who 'dined' with
Peleus and Thetis, then betrays his hosts.

αἰέν as used here is the typical 'you always...' of quarrels, which
Homer, as a keen student of life, reproduces; cf. 1.107, 177, 541; 8.361;
12.211.

66 The special honour Achilles will have is in the first instance the
honour he will win by releasing Hector's body (110). There may also
be an allusion to his funeral, where he is lamented by the Nereids and
the Muses, his bones are put in a golden jar made by Hephaestus, etc.:
see *Od.* 24.36–92, which concludes μάλα γὰρ φίλος ἦσθα θεοῖσιν.

ἀλλὰ καὶ Ἕκτωρ 'but Hector, for his part...', i.e. Hector too has
a claim on the gods' favour. For the use of καί cf. 16.623 εἰ καὶ ἐγώ σε
βάλοιμι 'if *I* strike *you* (rather than you me)'; Denniston 304.

68 **ὡς γὰρ ἔμοιγ'** 'so he was to me, at least'; for this use of γάρ, see
Denniston 66–7.

69–70 = 4.48–9, Zeus speaking of Priam, as he gives up Troy to his
wife's anger. Here he is granting the Trojans' piety some reward: cf.
425–31 n.

71 **ἐάσομεν** 'let us forget about...'; cf., e.g., 19.8; *Od.* 4.212. On the
form of the termination, see 357 n.

κλέψαι is treated as a noun (τὸ κλέψαι in Attic prose): cf., e.g., 242;
1.258; *Od.* 2.117.

72–3 'His mother is always beside him.' 17.408 mentions frequent
visits of Thetis to Achilles, but 'always' is, as often in life and in
Homer (cf. 62–3 n.), an exaggeration. So too in 4.11, where αἰεὶ παρ-
μέμβλωκε recurs. Homer is in general artful in his use of rhetorical
overstatement: e.g. in 8.475–6 Zeus, to cow Hera, prophesies 'they will
fight over Patroclus' body on the sterns of their ships', whereas in 18.172
the fighting goes on 'in front of the ships'; in 16.558 the dead Sarpedon
is called, to heighten the sense of his loss, 'the man who first leapt over
the Achaeans' wall', whereas in 12.438 it was Hector. Here Zeus's
bringing in Thetis (as if she were unavoidable) shows his good will

towards her and her son (cf. 110–11). That good will was in Book 1
the cause of 'ten thousand sufferings'; here its effects are happy.

παρμέμβλωκεν: perfect of παραβλώσκω.

ἦμαρ in the phrase νύκτας τε καὶ ἦμαρ (always at the end of the line)
is treated as a plural for metrical convenience, and perhaps under the
influence of ποσσῆμαρ, ἐννῆμαρ etc.

74 εἰ + optative introduces a request: cf. 10.111; 15.571; 16.559. Zeus
does not give a direct order to Iris, because that would seem high-handed
in a context where his aim is to be diplomatic: εἴ τις appears to leave
it to the gods whether anyone is to summon Thetis.

78–82 The sea 'groans' as Iris touches down on it; she is like an object
that brings 'death' to 'man-eating' fish. But her mission is peaceful
(though she finds mourning); and the 'man-eater' (207) and groaning
mourner (123) Achilles relents. For an analogous contrast between
simile and narrative see 17.674–81: Menelaus looking around in
friendly concern to see if his companion is alive is compared to an eagle
looking for a hare who finally swoops on it and kills it.

78 Σάμου: i.e. Samothrace (not Samos); cf. 753; 13.12.

79 μείλανι = μέλανι: an epic lengthening found only here in all
Greek. But Μειλανίων (Latin Mīlanion) is a by-form of the name
Μελανίων.

ἐπεστονάχησε: a definite, if not emphatic, metaphor; cf. 2.95, 784;
16.391, where the earth or rivers 'groan'. In general on Homeric
metaphors, see Parry, *MHV* 365–75, though he underrates their force.

80–3 There is no good reason for preferring Plato's (*Ion* 538d) version
of these lines, or any part of it: cf. van der Valk II 323–4.

81 κατ'...κέρας ἐμβεβαυῖα 'set over a (piece of) horn'. The lead
serves to sink the bait; the horn, also mentioned in *Od.* 12.253, stops
fish biting through the line. Cf. H.-G. Buchholz et al., *AH* J 169. For
other fishing similes see 16.406–8; *Od.* 12.251–4. Homeric men eat
meat – the heroic diet; the simile, as similes in Homer often do, gives
us a glimpse of everyday life.

84–6 Thetis laments Achilles among her companions already in
18.35–64: so too Hector is lamented before his time (6.500–2). The
great deaths of the *Iliad* – Sarpedon's, Patroclus', Hector's – are all

heavily foreshadowed; likewise Achilles', which looms over the whole
end of the poem. For an exhaustive collection of references to Achilles'
death see Kullmann 308–13, 320–5; for a fine analysis, Schadewaldt,
HWW 261. In this book, see 131–2, 540, and more obliquely 93–4, 104–5.

84 εἴαθ' 'they were sitting'; third person plural of the imperfect of
ἧμαι (Attic ἧντο); cf. 99, 799. On the form of the stem, see West on
Hes. *Theog.* 622.

85 οἱ: 'ethic' dative, expressing the involvement of the person
concerned; cf. 253, 599, 716, 749.

86 τηλόθι πάτρης: cf. 541. On this motif in the *Iliad* see Griffin
106–12. Achilles' fate sums up the lot of the Iliadic hero; cf. 538–42.

88 Ζεὺς ἄφθιτα μήδεα εἰδώς: the phrase occurs only here in Homer;
it seems to carry more sense of authority than, e.g., (καλέει σε) Κρόνου
πάϊς ἀγκυλομήτεω would have done. Hesiod uses it three times in
twenty lines to stress Zeus's superiority over Prometheus, the would-be
deceiver of the god (*Theog.* 545, 550, 561).

90–1 Thetis is embarrassed to disturb the blissful ease of the gods. The
two δέ's are explanatory ('for'), as often in Homer: cf. 236, 561, 611
and Denniston 169.

92 μέν stresses the assertion, here with an adversative implication: 'I
will go, despite my misgivings'; cf. 289. The line is similar to *Od.* 2.318
(Telemachus defying the suitors) εἶμι μέν, οὐδ' ἁλίη ὁδὸς ἔσσεται ἣν
ἀγορεύω.

94 The black is for mourning: cf. Hes. *Theog.* 406 and West ad loc.
Thetis does not try to conceal her grief, despite her embarrassment; and
the Olympians respond with tact, even if such grief is foreign to them.

96 ἀμφὶ δ'...θαλάσσης 'the swell of the sea receded on either side
of them'. For this portent cf. 13.29 (the sea makes way for Poseidon);
18.66–7 (for Thetis and the Nereids).

98–9 are deliberately worded like 83–4, to contrast the happy gods
and the mourning Thetis. The phrase μάκαρες θεοὶ αἰὲν ἐόντες, which
occurs four times in *Od.* but only here in *Il.*, is chosen to stress the same
contrast.

100 'She sat down beside Zeus, and Athena gave her her place': a *hysteron proteron*; cf. 206–7 n. Athena sits at Zeus's right hand: cf. Pind. fr. 146.

101–2 For the form of the welcome cf. 15.84–9; that Hera should welcome Thetis is in accord with 59–60.

102 ὤρεξε πιοῦσα 'she handed it (back) when she had drunk'.

104 ἤλυθες: the regular formula of greeting in Homer; cf. 3.428; *Od.* 16.23, 461; 17.41. Also outside Homer: cf. Alcaeus fr. 350.1 Lobel–Page; Theognis 511; Ar. *Birds* 680; Theoc. 12.1–2.

105 οἶδα καὶ αὐτός both forestalls complaints (cf. *Od.* 10.457; similar, *Il.* 19.421; *Od.* 5.215) and expresses understanding (cf. *Od.* 17.193; Soph. *O.C.* 1615). Thetis' misgivings are echoed and met with both firmness and sympathy.

107 ἐννῆμαρ: see 31 n.

108 Ἕκτορος...νέκυι: cf. 17.240 νέκυος...Πατρόκλοιο where the genitive Πατρόκλοιο probably depends on νέκυος. νέκυς + genitive ('the body of *x*') is not found elsewhere in Homer; but cf., e.g., Hdt. 1.140.1 ἀνδρὸς Πέρσεω ὁ νέκυς.

109 (= 24) ὀτρύνεσκον: the ὀτρύνουσιν of two ancient editions is probably a fussy correction: cf. van der Valk II 167. And here too the imperfect is in fact more appropriate than the present: this is what gods *were* doing before the debate and before Zeus's intervention.

110 κῦδος: this consists partly in the gifts Achilles receives, but much more in the generosity with which he treats the suppliant, for magnanimous behaviour does good to a person's reputation: cf., e.g., 9.257–8 (Achilles will be more honoured if he gives up his quarrel); *Od.* 14.402–5, 21.331–3 (good repute is lost if strangers are maltreated). Only limited importance is in fact accorded to the gifts, either by Homer or by Achilles: cf. 119, 594 nn.

προτιάπτω (Attic προσάπτω) 'I am going to attach'. The present tense refers to an immediate future: cf. 8.541; 9.261; 16.850; *Od.* 20.156.

111 '(with the aim of) keeping your respect and friendship for the future'. μετόπισθε goes with the nouns rather than with the verb: cf. 6.450 Τρώων...ἄλγος ὀπίσσω ('the Trojans' future sufferings'); 22.19

τίσιν...ὀπίσσω ('punishment to come'); also 617 n. For the participle expressing an aim cf., e.g., 1.159; 19.312.

116 αἴ κέν πως 'an expression of studied courtesy in the mouth of Zeus' (Leaf, comparing 1.207, where Athena says αἴ κε πίθηαι to Achilles). It is designed to soften the peremptory tone of 112–15.

117–18 'I will send Iris (to tell him) to ransom...': the infinitive goes with the command implicit in the sending of Zeus's messenger.

119 τά κε θυμὸν ἰήνῃ (a final clause) 'which may gladden his heart'; cf. 19.174 of Agamemnon's recompense to Achilles. Zeus expects that Achilles will be pleased with the gifts and will fear the divine command (116); what he does not predict is the fellow-feeling which will join Achilles and Priam. This is true to Homer's vision of the difference between gods and men (cf. 460–7 n.); it also leaves something fresh to emerge in the actual narrative of the event.

123–5 As in 2–3, Achilles grieves while others prepare to eat. (The point of mentioning these preparations is clearly that Achilles does not intend to eat when they are over; cf. 128–30.) In 19.205–14 he refuses to take food before the battle, a refusal repeated in 19.304–8. In 23.42–53 he reluctantly accepts food but refuses a bath.

125 ἱέρευτο 'had been sacrificed': pluperfect.

128–32 Thetis soothes Achilles' grief before delivering Zeus's orders, just as Zeus had shown sympathy to her before issuing them.

128 τέο μέχρις...: contrast Thetis' words to Achilles in 1.362 and 18.73: τέκνον, τί κλαίεις; τί δέ σε φρένας ἵκετο πένθος; There she is merely condoling; here she is admonishing.

129 σὴν ἔδεαι κραδίην: cf. 6.202; Od. 9.75; 10.143. Here, as in Od. 10.379, 'eating your heart' is contrasted with literal eating; for a similar contrast see 523 n. The phrase may echo colloquial speech: cf. Ar. Wasps 286 μηδ' οὕτω σεαυτὸν | ἔσθιε μηδ' ἀγανάκτει, and our own 'eating your heart out'.

130–1 'food and sex' is picked up by 'sex' alone: see 456 n.

περ goes with the whole phrase γυναικί...μίσγεσθαι ('sleeping-with-a-woman'), not γυναικί in particular; and it implicitly contrasts 'sex' with 'death': cf. Denniston 482. See further on περ, besides Denniston, H. Fränkel, *Glotta* 14 (1925) 6–13; also 749–50 n.

131–2 = 16.852–3 (οὔ θην οὐδ' αὐτός κτλ.). One of a number of links between the deaths of Patroclus, Hector and Achilles: see esp. 16.829–61 with 22.330–66. The words which in Book 16 were a grim prophecy here serve to reconcile Achilles with life and with men.

131 βέῃ 'you will live'.

134 ἑέ = ἕ; cf. 20.171. A metrically convenient form, but not necessarily an invented one: see Chantraine I §124.

139 'Let whoever brings the ransom come here (τῇδ' εἴη) and take away the corpse.' For the use of εἰμί cf. *Od.* 14.407–8 τάχιστά μοι ἔνδον ἑταῖροι | εἶεν; and for the use of the optative, 149; *Od.* 4·735; 14.408; Chantraine II §320.

This line is usually punctuated with a stop after τῇδ' εἴη. Those words would then mean 'so be it', a form of acceptance more resigned than 669 ἔσται τοι καὶ ταῦτα: cf. Fraenkel, *BA* 78 n. 1, and esp. Plat. *Gorg.* 513e ἔστω, εἰ βούλει, σοὶ οὕτως (a very reluctant acceptance). But this would be the only place in Homer where τῇδε means 'thus' (though note 373 etc. πῃ = 'somehow' and *Od.* 8.510 τῇ = 'in which manner'). Elsewhere it means 'here'; and in this line ὧδε – cf. 7.34 ὧδ' ἔστω – would have served perfectly well instead.

ὃς ἄποινα φέροι: Priam is not named here. His entry must be a profound surprise (cf. 480–4).

140 πρόφρονι θυμῷ: for the sense of πρόφρων cf., e.g., 8.23. Achilles feels he is making a concession to Zeus's earnest insistence; but as in Book 1 (216–18), he obeys the divine command without demur.

141–2 A variant on ὣς οἱ μὲν τοιαῦτα πρὸς ἀλλήλους ἀγόρευον (8 times in *Il.*, 17 in *Od.*). The phrasing suggests that the conversation was substantial (πολλά) and intimate (μήτηρ τε καὶ υἱός). This is in keeping with Zeus's picture of a Thetis 'forever at Achilles' side' (72–3).

πολλά does not so much imply a long exchange as one full of import: cf. Soph. *Aj.* 1049 τόσονδε...λόγον was a bold and offensive speech, but only two lines long; Ar. *Lys.* 356 τοσαυτί were brave words, but again only two lines long.

145 Ἴλιον εἴσω: to be construed with the notion of 'going' implicit in ἄγγειλον: cf. *Od.* 4.775 μή πού τις ἐπαγγείλησι καὶ εἴσω.

148 For the shift from indirect speech to direct in this line cf., e.g., 4.303; 20.197; Kühner–Gerth II § 595.5. It was this that probably gave rise to the variant reading οἷος here and in 177.

149 γεραίτερος: Priam's companion must be old; this makes the 'young man' Hermes' intervention the more valued (cf. 368). This line qualifies the emphatic 'let him go alone' of 148: cf. 498 n.

152 θάνατος...τάρβος are a kind of hendiadys (i.e. 'fear and death' = 'fear of death'): cf. 5.171 ποῦ τοι τόξον ἰδὲ πτερόεντες ὀϊστοὶ | καὶ κλέος; ('your fame in archery'); *Od.* 11.202–3 ἀλλά με σός τε πόθος σά τε μήδεα, φαίδιμ' Ὀδυσσεῦ, | σή τ' ἀγανοφροσύνη μελιηδέα θυμὸν ἀπηύρα ('the yearning for your wisdom and kindness').

154–5 ἄξει...ἄγων...ἀγάγῃσιν: the key-word is repeated; cf. πομπός...πομπόν in 437–9; also 11.380–1; 13.114–21; 15.561–3; 16.104–5. For the long syllable of ὅς (though ἄξει has no digamma) cf. 22.236.

ἠός κεν...πελάσσῃ 'until he brings him to Achilles'. Hermes cannot join in the actual meeting of Priam and Achilles; cf. 460–7 n.

ἀγάγῃσιν = ἀγάγῃ: on the form of the termination see Chantraine I § 219.

157 The triple negation is highly emphatic; cf. 9.63 ἀφρήτωρ ἀθέμιστος ἀνέστιος. Zeus as it were rehabilitates Achilles after Apollo's attack (39–54) which was left unanswered in the debate: before the great quarrel, Achilles was far from cruel, as emerges from his treatment of Calchas (1.84–91), the dead Eetion (6.414–16) or of suppliants on the battlefield (see 751–3 n.); and in the end he learns to 'endure' too (49 n.).

οὔτε...ἄφρων οὔτ' ἄσκοπος, words which refer to practical wisdom, have also a moral dimension. This is characteristic of Greek: cf., e.g., 40, 114, 377, and in later usage, σώφρων = both 'sensible' and 'restrained, temperate' or ἀμαθής = both 'uninstructed' and 'brutal'.

158 πεφιδήσεται 'he will spare': reduplicated future of φείδομαι; cf. Chantraine I § 212.

159-70 The scene is a version of an Iliadic type: Iris' arrival –
description of the scene she finds – approach and address to the person
sought: cf. 77–87; 2.786–95; 3.121–9; 11.195–9.

159 = 8.409. Likewise, 144 βάσκ'...ταχεῖα = 8.399; 188 = 8.425.

160 ἐς Πριάμοιο 'to (the house) of Priam': cf. 309, 482, 593.

κίχεν δ' ἐνοπήν τε γόον τε 'she found cries and wailing': as with
Thetis (83–6), so with Priam. The situation in Troy is as it was in Book
22 (163–5 picks up 22.414): likewise Achilles at the beginning of Book
24 had returned to the condition he was in before the games.

162–4 ἐντυπάς 'closely': the word is probably connected with τύπος.
If it means that the contours, the 'impression', of the body shows
through the cloak, that is certainly true of the mourner's huddled
posture: see, e.g., Johansen, figs. 41, 58, 63 (also p. 168); *Od.* 8.85; Eur.
H.F. 1214–32.

Priam's covering himself with dung (as in 22.414) is an extreme form
of the self-defilement that goes with mourning: cf. 18.23–7, Achilles
mourning for Patroclus. In Hdt. 6.58, which describes the funeral rites
for Spartan kings, and (ed.) F. Sokolowski, *Lois sacrées des cités grecques*
(Paris 1969) 97 A 25, a Cean funerary law, (κατα)μιαίνεσθαι is used of
what mourners normally do.

168 κέατο: from κεῖμαι, third person plural of the imperfect cf. 610;
84 n.

170 τυτθὸν φθεγξαμένη 'speaking softly', literally 'small' (a 'loud
voice' in Greek being μεγάλη φωνή), so as not to be heard by the
children and daughters-in-law. This motif is not used in 1.194–201
where Athena is speaking to Achilles in the presence of others, because
it would detract from the grandeur of her apparition. In *Od.* 16.59
Athena beckons Odysseus out of the house before talking to him. For
the aorist participle, where the action it denotes is not prior to the main
verb but coincident with it, cf. 121, 477, 661 (see Barrett on Eur.
Hipp. 289–92); προσηύδα is in effect an aorist, since imperfect and aorist
can be used indifferently in narrative (cf. 689 n.).

τὸν δέ...γυῖα: fear is natural in a man who sees a god or a portent;
cf. 20.130; *Od.* 16.179; 24.533; Hdt. 8.38. For the double accusative,
see 58 n.

172 τόδ' ἱκάνω 'I have come (on) this (errand)': τόδ' is 'internal' object of the verb; cf. 38 n., 235, 421, 451, 652, 735.

175–87 are exactly modelled on Zeus's instructions in 146–58, in the normal Homeric manner; cf. 113–15 and 134–6.

181–7 Priam does not tell Hecuba of these assurances; they both feel the need to make a libation to Zeus before he leaves; and when he meets Hermes, he fails to guess who the helpful stranger is. This is partly because, though there is no doubt that the command to go comes from Zeus, what the gods say can always mislead; hence men easily discount or forget divine promises. Thus in 5.714–18 we learn that Hera and Athena promised Menelaus that he would sack Troy and return safely home; but no human being in the *Iliad* ever recalls this. And in Book 2 the dream was sent by Zeus precisely in order to deceive. Similarly in the *Aeneid*, when Aeneas has just had Creusa's prophecy (2.780–4), the Trojans are still *incerti quo fata ferant* (3.7): cf., e.g., 1.209–10, after oracles have made still clearer and firmer what Creusa said. There are also artistic reasons why lines 181–7 should be ignored in what follows. We and the characters are to experience Priam's journey as a great and dangerous enterprise; if he were serenely confident in Zeus's aid, and transmitted his confidence to those around him, that would detract from the awesomeness of the event. At the same time it would be improper not only for Iris to suppress Zeus's assurances, but also for Zeus not to give them. If the god sent Priam on his journey with a bare command, he would fail to show the pity and understanding which characterize him in this book and in this speech (174). See further below, 288–9, 327–8, 373–7, 519 nn.

191 ἐς θάλαμον κατεβήσετο 'he went down to the treasure-chamber': cf. 6.288–92; *Od.* 2.337–47, 15.99–105. 'The private homes excavated at Mycenae...have basements' (Wace, *CH* 490).

192 κεχάνδει 'contained': pluperfect of χανδάνω. The form κεχόνδει is found in a papyrus; it could be genuine (cf. λέλογχα, πέπονθα), but κεχανδότα is the reading of all manuscripts at 23.268; *Od.* 4.96.

194 δαιμονίη does not ascribe any particular quality, or express any particular attitude, to the person addressed; rather it puts the speaker in a certain relation to the hearer, adding warmth to appeals, challenges, protests, invitations etc. So here to Priam's request for advice to Hecuba. Cf. E. Brunius-Nilsson, ΔAIMONIE (Uppsala 1955).

197   τί τοι...εἶναι; 'what do *you* think?: cf. Ar. *Peace* 925 τί δαὶ δοκεῖ; *Birds* 1676 τί δαὶ σύ φῆς; The epic style lightly veils a colloquial turn of phrase.

198   αὐτόν stresses the spontaneity of what is done (cf. 218, 360, 560). Neither Priam's nor Achilles' actions (cf. 157–8) in this book are mere obedience to a divine command.

200   ἀμείβετο μύθῳ: cf. 424 ἠμείβετο μύθῳ. This phrase occurs at the end of the line 8 times in *Od.*, only in this book in *Il.* But for the same pattern of line see 571 = 1.33; and τὸν δ' ἠμείβετ' ἔπειτα is common in *Il.*

201–2   Priam's former wisdom is not something the rest of the poem particularly brings out; and 282 (= 674) is hardly enough to characterize him as wise. The point here is to stress his present folly, as Hecuba sees it: cf. 23.440, 570, 603–4 (Antilochus was 'wise before' because foolish now); 22.233–4 (Deiphobus was Hector's 'dearest brother before' because Athena in the shape of Deiphobus is to betray him now); 17.587–8 (Menelaus was 'a feeble fighter before' because Hector should be ashamed of avoiding him now).

ἔκλε(ο) 'you were famed' = ἐκλέεο: cf. 1.275 ἀποαίρεο; Chantraine I § 227.

οἷσιν ἀνάσσεις = (ἐκείνους) οἷσιν ἀνάσσεις.

203–5   Cf. 519–21 n; for sons of Priam killed by Achilles 751–3 n.

οἷος: it is as if Hecuba had heard part of Zeus's command (148, 177). The character is made to know something the poet has told us: thus in 1.380–1 Achilles knows that Chryses has prayed to Apollo, because the poet said so in 1.35: see further Bowra in *CH* 70.

205   σιδήρειον: cf. 20.372; 22.357; *Od.* 4.293; 5.191; 12.280; 23.172. Probably a colloquial as much as a high poetic metaphor: cf. Lysias 10.20 'εἰ μὴ σιδηροῦς ἐστι, he will have noticed....'; Aeschin. 3.166 'ὦ σιδηροῖ, how could you endure...?', passages which do not look as if they were influenced by Homer; and weapons in the heroic world of the *Iliad* are not made of iron.

206 'if he lays hands on you and sets eyes on you': *hysteron proteron*, i.e. the two notions come in order of importance or intensity rather than in temporal sequence. Similarly ὠμηστής καὶ ἄπιστος in 207: 'an eater of raw flesh and untrustworthy'. Cf. 100, 346, 685, and, e.g., 21.537 'they opened the gates and pushed aside the bolts'; 22.466–72 'she fainted and fell; and she cast the bands from her head...'; *Od.* 5.264; 19.535. For the same tendency to thrust forward the main point, cf. 498 n.

207–8 οὔ σ' ἐλεήσει...αἰδέσεται: cf. 44 n. For the asyndeton, as here, with a reinforcing phrase, cf. 9.70 ἔοικέ τοι, οὔ τοι ἀεικές.

208 ἄνευθεν 'apart' – reinforced by ἑῶν ἀπάνευθε τοκήων in 211 – because a dead man's relatives would normally have his body with them as they lamented.

209 ἥμενοι suggests 'helplessly, idly': see 542 n.

209–10 For life as spun by destiny cf. 20.127–8; *Od.* 7.197–8; Hes. *Theog.* 218–19 and West ad loc.

212–13 The wish, 'I could eat you raw!', recalls 22.346–7 (Achilles to Hector). It seems to be based on popular speech: cf. the misanthrope in Men. *Dysc.* 468 Γε. μὴ δάκῃς. Κν. ἐγώ σε νὴ Δία, | καὶ κατέδομαί γε ζῶντα; also Xen. *Hell.* 3.3.6; *Anab.* 4.8.14; and in English, Shakespeare, *Much ado about nothing* IV i 'O God that I were a man! I would eat his heart in the market-place.' It comes forcefully and abruptly after the resignation of 208–12; and it strikingly echoes ὠμηστής (207): the thought of Achilles' savagery provokes Hecuba's.

There is anacoluthon (cf. 42–3 n.) after κρατερῷ: Hecuba's threat violently breaks off the resigned and melancholy train of thought. For similar anacoluthon cf. 18.107; 22.122, again in passages of strong emotion.

213–14 'Then my son would be avenged', literally 'Then there would be work of vengeance for my son.' The form must be ἄντιτα, not ἂν τιτά: cf. *Od.* 17.51 = 60, where αἴ κε...ἂν is out of the question. The plain optative here denotes a possibility: cf., e.g., 15.197; 19.321.

214–16 Hector's flight in Book 22 is forgotten. As the scholia comment, Hecuba's words make the outrage done to his corpse seem the more horrifying and reveal her motherly love. What remains in her mind is the impression of him standing outside the walls and waiting for Achilles: 'but he waited for Achilles...so Hector with unquenchable spirit stood firm' (22.92–6).

φόβου 'flight' (not 'fear'), as always in Homer.

218–24 Though Priam asked for Hecuba's advice, it emerges here that his mind was already made up. That he should consult his wife all the same is natural in a husband; it also makes possible Hecuba's bitter and moving speech. In 22.77–89 when Hector goes out to meet Achilles, Hecuba again vainly tries to prevent the departure; but this time her failure is all to the good.

218–19 αὐτή 'gratuitously'; cf. 198 n.

ὄρνις...κακός 'a bird of ill omen': Hecuba's warning in 206–8 is treated as if it would bring about the result it envisages; so, for the superstitious, any mention of death could cause death.

ἐνὶ μεγάροισι, because the flight of birds would normally be watched out of doors, and because a man does not expect to harbour bringers of bad luck in his own home.

219 οὐδέ με πείσεις is a blunt refusal; cf., e.g., 18.126. In everyday language, cf. Ar. *Clouds* 119 οὐκ ἂν πιθοίμην; *Eccl.* 1011; *Plut.* 600 οὐ γὰρ πείσεις, οὐδ' ἢν πείσῃς (a hyperbolic form).

220 ἄλλος ἐπιχθονίων 'a mortal rather (than a god)', not 'any other mortal': cf. LSJ s.v. ἄλλος II 8.

220–2 Lines 218–19, and the word αὐτή there, gain in force from this passage: they are not spoken by a superstitious man.

222 For the refusal to trust oracles cf., e.g., *Od.* 1.415–16; Hes. fr. 303 'no *mantis* can know the mind of Zeus'; Soph. *O.T.* 497–506. Priam is being sensible, not irreverent. Greek attitudes to *manteis* are well explored by A. D. Nock, *Collected papers* (Oxford 1972) 542; K. J. Dover, *J.H.S.* 93 (1973) 64.

223 ἐσέδρακον is aorist of ἐσδέρκομαι.

224 εἶμι...ἔσσεται = 92. Priam's daring comes out the more strongly when the same words have been used in a weaker way before. Thetis merely obeys: Priam resolves.

226–7 Priam's words are related to a common turn of phrase: 'if only I could first achieve such-and-such, I would gladly die': cf. *Od.* 7.224–5; *H.H.Aphrod.* 153–4; Solon fr. 33.5–7; Aesch. *Ag.* 1610–11; *Cho.* 438. Here, where the wish for death is a real one (cf. 244–6), the common locution is given new life.

βούλομαι 'I want to' (not 'I am willing'): cf. LSJ s.v., I 1.

227 'When I had released (ἐξ...εἴην, from ἐξίημι, with tmesis) my desire to bewail him'. For ἐπήν with the aorist optative cf. 19.208.

228 ἀνέῳγεν is imperfect of ἀνοίγω.

229–31 δώδεκα...τόσσους...τόσσα...τόσους: for this kind of repetition to give an effect of quantity, cf. 11.678–81; *Od.* 14.100–1; 24.276–7. Note also 495–7 n.

230–1 = *Od.* 24.276–7, except that καλά there replaces λευκά. καλά is also a variant here; but it is redundant after περικαλλέας in 229 and before περικαλλές in 234. Contrariwise, it is in place in *Od.* 24.277 when no word for 'beautiful' precedes or follows it.

232 is very close to 19.247 (χρυσοῦ δὲ στήσας Ὀδυσεὺς δέκα πάντα τάλαντα, with φέρον in the next line). It is suspect here. (1) στήσας 'having weighed it out' is less pointed here where no definite quantity of gold has been promised (see 9.122). (2) ἔφερεν cannot mean 'carried out (of the house)', because the sons do that in 275; but then it is not at all clear what it does mean. (3) ἐκ...ἐκ (233–4) follow more naturally from ἔξελε (229), if ἔφερεν has not intervened. It is true that we might expect gold to form part of the ransom: cf. 6.48; 11.124, 134; 22.351; *Od.* 22.58; 24.274. But, by the same token, it would be natural for someone to interpolate this line. It is best deleted.

235 ἐξεσίην ἐλθόντι 'to him when he went (there) on an embassy'. ἐξεσίην is internal object of the verb: cf. 172 n.

236 ὁ γέρων rather than Πρίαμος (which is metrically equivalent here), because 'the old man' creates more pathos in this very pathetic sentence: cf. scholion on 1.33.

περὶ δ' ἤθελε θυμῷ 'he greatly wished in his heart'. περί is adverbial; cf. 61 n. On the use of δέ, see 90–1 n.

237–8 In 22.412–13 the Trojans restrained Priam from going to

Achilles. Here, with the new purpose that Zeus's message has given him, he has regained authority. That makes him impatient with those who were sharing his inactivity and his mourning before (161–2; 22.429), first the citizens, then his sons. But his anger also springs, as both his speeches make clear (cf. 493–4 n.), from the violence of his grief, which he cannot share with others. That is what he will now learn to do with Achilles.

239 ἔρρετε 'get out!'. The word is blunt and not at all elevated, as emerges from its use in Attic (e.g. Ar. *Lys.* 1240); cf. 8.164; 9.377; 20.349; 22.498; 23.440 – always where strong feelings are expressed.

239–40 'Haven't you enough to weep about at home, without coming to cause me misery?', literally 'Is there not wailing for you at home? (I say this) because you have come...'; for the use of ὅτι cf., e.g., 16.35; also below, 376, 388, 683 nn.

κηδήσοντες is a fine sarcasm, if we recall that κήδεα = 'mourning' in Homer: here the mourners *cause* grief.

241 οὔνεσθ' 'do you think it a light matter...?'. This is second person plural – with epic lengthening – of ὄνομαι; a papyrus reads οὔνο[σθ' which would be the same thing. The scholia tell us that Aristarchus read ὀνόσασθ' which may well be an attempt to regularize the unusual form: cf. van der Valk 1 565–6. Possibly ὤνεσθ' (imperfect) is the correct reading: ου and ω would both have been written as Ο in the earliest texts (cf. 789 n.).

242 παῖδ' ὀλέσαι τὸν ἄριστον 'losing the best of my sons'. The phrase is in apposition to ἄλγεα in 241: cf. 71 n.

γνώσεσθε 'you'll learn', i.e. by bitter experience: cf. 1.185; 7.226; 8.406.

243 ῥηΐτεροι...μᾶλλον: for the strengthened comparative, see LSJ s.v. μάλα II 2; cf. 334 n.

244–6 βαίην is more forceful as a wish ('may I go...') than as a potential future ('I would go...'). 'May I go under the earth before...' – like 'may the earth cover me before/when...' in 4.182; 6.464–5; 8.150 – may well be a colloquial, though intense, rather than a high poetic form of expression: cf. Xen. *Cyrop.* 5.5.9; *Anab.* 7.1.30 ἐγὼ μὲν τοίνυν εὔχομαι πρὶν ταῦτα ἐπιδεῖν ὑφ' ὑμῶν γενόμενα μυρίας ἐμέ γε κατὰ τῆς γῆς ὀργυιὰς γενέσθαι.

247 διέπ' 'he controlled them', i.e. shepherded them away: cf. 2.207 δίεπε στρατόν of Odysseus checking the Greeks' stampede with the help of the σκῆπτρον (cf. 2.186, 199).

249–51 Agathon, Antiphonus and Pammon are mentioned only here in Homer. It is not clear which of δῖον and ἀγαυόν is the noun, and which the epithet; Pherecydes (*FGH* 3 F 137) took Dios to be the name. Neither name recurs in Homer.

For the list of names cf. the much longer string of nymphs at 18.39–49. Perhaps the main function of such lists is to give a sense of reality to the narrative: the poet can put a name to Priam's sons or Thetis' companions, so they seem to be not merely 'extras'. So too before the Catalogue of Ships Homer invokes the Muses because they 'are there and know everything' (2.485): this indicates that the long list of names which follows is certainly meant to have the feel of history, and is probably believed to be history.

253 The first four feet of the line have the same syntactical and metrical pattern as those of 239. That stresses how both speeches express the same mood.

κατηφόνες 'disgraces', i.e. causes of shame; cf. 16.498 κατηφείη καὶ ὄνειδος. The termination -ών designates 'a living being as...possessing the quality of the primitive adjective' – i.e. κατηφής in this case – 'often referring to qualities that meet with disapproval' (C. D. Buck and W. Petersen, *A reverse index of Greek nouns and adjectives* (Chicago 1945) 247).

254 ἀντί goes with Ἕκτορος: the preposition is 'postponed': cf., e.g., 349, 397, 705.

255–6 Cf. 493–4 n.

256 οὔ τινα: the overstatement is then corrected in 260–2; see 498 n.

257 Mestor and Troilus are mentioned only here in Homer; it is quite unclear what stories, if any, he associated with them. Troilus' death at Achilles' hands figured in the *Cypria* and it is often treated in early art: see K. Schefold, *Myth and legend in early Greek art* (London 1966) 44, 61, 87 (with illustrations).

258–9 Hector, for Hera so decidedly a mere man (58), was for Priam like a god: the emphatic θεός...θνητοῦ...θεοῖο echoes the main theme of the goddess' speech. And yet Hector was mortal and is dead: cf. 534–8 n.

261 ψεῦσται 'liars'; i.e. tellers of stories (cf. *Od.* 19.203)? Or Don Juans (cf. 3.39; 13.769 ἠπεροπευτά)? Or big talkers and poor doers (cf. 19.107)? In 3.106 Priam's sons are called ὑπερφίαλοι καὶ ἄπιστοι ('arrogant and untrustworthy'), where a truce is to be made.

ἄριστοι bitterly echoes ἀρίστους in 255. The superlative seems to be particularly apt to carry a sarcastic force: cf. 3.39 = 13.769 εἶδος ἄριστε; 23.483 νεῖκος ἄριστε; Hdt. 3.80.4 διαβολὰς ἄριστος ἐνδέκεσθαι; Thuc. 3.38.5 ἀπατᾶσθαι ἄριστοι.

262 ἐπιδήμιοι ἁρπακτῆρες 'robbers in your own country', i.e. because they eat up the sheep and goats. A sarcastic oxymoron; for the idea, cf. Ar. *Peace* 1189–90 'lions at home, (foxes in battle)'. Robbing *foreigners'* livestock is of course far from disgraceful; cf. 11.670–84, where Nestor proudly recalls his exploits as a cattle-rustler.

263–4 Priam's sons have done nothing about his orders of 189–90. This neatly makes room for the old man's speech and motivates his impatience in these lines.

οὐκ ἄν... ; introduces a command: cf. 3.52; 5.456; Soph. *Aj.* 1051. Like English 'Why don't you...?' it can convey a gentle suggestion or, as in these passages, a contemptuous challenge.

263 Cf. *Od.* 6.57 (Nausicaa's request to Alcinous for a waggon). Likewise, 150 = *Od.* 6.37 (ἡμιόνους καὶ ἄμαξαν); 275 is like *Od.* 6.74–5.

264 ταῦτα 'these things', though the objects are not visible. Cf. 17, 31 nn.; Ar. *Wasps* 798. The deictic pronoun denotes what is uppermost in the speaker's mind: cf. O. Taplin, *The stagecraft of Aeschylus* (Oxford 1977) 150–1.

ἵνα πρήσσωμεν ὁδοῖο 'so that we can be on our way'. πρήσσω is used, as commonly in Homer, of 'covering' ground; the genitive is used of the space within which the movement happens: cf., e.g., 13.64 πεδίοιο διώκειν 'pursue over the plain'.

266–74 'Priam's cart...has a detachable body (πείρινς)...and a single shaft (ῥυμός) to which a yoke for two mules is bound on with a long cord or strap (ζυγόδεσμον ἐννεάπηχυ). The yoke has a central knob (ὀμφαλός), and at the outer ends of it are hooks or rings (οἴηκες) to guide the outside reins...we may understand the κρίκος as a ring or eye at one end of the ζυγόδεσμον, placed over a peg (ἕστωρ) on the front of the chariot frame; that once in position, the ζυγόδεσμον is carried forward to form a stay...and the rest of its otherwise excessive length of nine cubits used to bind the yoke to the shaft' (Stubbings in *CH* 540–1, with illustrations).

The elaborate description of how the cart was assembled is designed as a relief after the pain and rage of Priam's speeches; the libation and the portent which follows it then create, for the time being, a calmer and happier mood. The account of how the meal was prepared in 621–7 has a rather similar effect.

273–4 I.e. they fastened the ζυγόδεσμον to the central knob of the yoke by winding it round it three times; they then wound it repeatedly (ἐξείης = 'one (bit) after another') round the shaft, and finally tucked in the end (γλωχῖνα) of the cord or strap. Cf. J. Wiesner, *AH* F 7–10.

281 ζευγνύσθην 'they had them yoked', cf. διδάσκομαι 'I have someone taught': a typical use of the middle.

282 πυκινὰ φρεσὶ μήδε' ἔχοντες = 674. Apparently a decorative epithet, like πεπνυμένος, which has no specific reference to the context.

283–320 Libations are normal before departures: cf. *Od*. 13.54–6; 15.147–50; and, e.g., Thuc. 6.32.1. The wording of 284–6 is very close to *Od*. 15.148–50; and, as in *Od*. 15, a portent follows. This passage is significantly linked to the other libation before a departure in the *Iliad*, 16.220–52. In both places there is a prayer to Zeus, introduced by identical words (306–7a = 16.231–2a); but in Book 16 Zeus denies a safe return; here he grants it and announces his intentions by a portent. Once again, in Book 24 we see the gods' kinder face.

284 δεξιτερῆφι: the case ending -φι(ν) is one of Homer's archaisms. It is used in a variety of senses: here and at 600 it is equivalent to a dative, in 268 and 576 to a genitive. See further Chantraine I §§ 104–8.

285 χρυσέῳ ἐν δέπαϊ: in *Od*. 15.149 the order of noun and adjective in this phrase is reversed in some MSS, which removes the harsh epic lengthening (δέπαϊ) with hiatus.

ὄφρα λείψαντε κιοίτην 'so that they might make a libation before going'. The emphasis is on the participle; cf. 309 n.

288–9 Hecuba treats the journey as simply Priam's initiative, ignoring Zeus's command. She wants confirmation that this really is the god's will, as well as reassurance about what may happen to her husband. For the use of μέν, see 92 n.

291 Zeus 'watches' Troy from Ida here not as the spectator of the fighting (as, e.g., in 11.337; 13.157), but as the protector of the city; cf. ἐσκατορᾷς in Anacreon, *PMG* 348.6; ἐπορῶσι in Hdt. 1.124.1; δέδορκε in Eur. *Supp.* 190.

292–3 ταχύν: the variant ἑόν is inappropriate before ὅς τέ οἱ αὐτῷ κτλ.; in 296 the word is in place because no such phrase follows. Probably ἑόν got into the text here from confusion with 296. For the same reason it is a variant – a very weakly attested one – in 310 (where it could mean 'your'; cf. 550 n.; West on Hes. *W.D.* 381).

ὅς τε...καί εὐ 'who...and whose...'. But whereas English repeats the relative pronoun in such phrases, Greek starts what has the air of a fresh sentence ('who...and his...'): cf. 1.78–9; 17.35–7; Soph. *El.* 444–6 and Jebb ad loc.; Kühner–Gerth II §561.1.

296 οὐ used after εἰ, where μή would be normal, gives more precise emphasis: 'if Zeus does *not* give you his messenger...'; cf., e.g., 15.162; Kühner–Gerth II §511.4b.

εὐρύοπα: here, as sometimes, a nominative; that seems to be an artificial extension of its use as an accusative (cf. 98).

300 Epic style lightly veils the polite language of everyday (cf. 660–1, 669 nn.): for this formula of agreement see 23.95–6; Plat. *Symp.* 193e ἀλλὰ πείσομαί σοι; Ar. *Clouds* 90 πείσομαι; *Birds* 1371 καὶ πείσομαί σοι. Similar expressions are collected by Fraenkel, *BA* 81–2.

301 χεῖρας ἀνασχέμεν 'to hold up one's arms' in effect means 'pray', since raising the arms is the normal ancient gesture of prayer: cf. e.g., 1.450; 3.275; 18.75.

302–7 For the washing of the cup and the hands before a prayer cf. 6.266; 16.228–30; *Od.* 2.261; 12.336.

304 The line χέρνιβα δ' ἀμφίπολος προχόῳ ἐπέχευε φέρουσα occurs six times in *Od.* The form χέρνιβον seems to be invented for metrical convenience here, where there is no δ'.

306 μέσῳ ἕρκεϊ: the court outside the μέγαρον; an altar of Zeus Herkeios might stand there (*Od.* 22.334–5; cf. *Il.* 11.772–5).

307 οὐρανὸν εἰσανιδών 'looking up to the sky', as normal in praying; cf., e.g., 7.178. For this posture in art, see Neumann 78, with illustration.

308 Ἴδηθεν μεδέων: Priam prays to Zeus as the god of his homeland; cf. 291 n.

309 'Let me find friendship and pity when I come to Achilles' house': the emphasis is on the adjectives; cf. 285 n. For the phrasing cf. *Od.* 6.327; and 314a = *Od.* 6.328a. Hecuba told Priam to pray for a safe return (287–8); in fact Priam prays for what is uppermost in his thoughts – the success of his supplication; cf. 460–7 n.

315 = 8.247. Zeus is τέλειος, 'the accomplisher' (see Aesch. *Supp.* 525–6; *Ag.* 973 and Fraenkel ad loc.); and Zeus's bird is like him: so too, at 293, its power is greatest as his is. It may also be implied that the eagle brings the 'most perfect' augury, the one that is most surely fulfilled: cf. LSJ s.v. τελήεις.

316 περκνόν 'dark', 'livid (in colour)'. The type of eagle is presumably the same as the one called μέλανος in 21.252 and κελαινός in Aesch. *Ag.* 115. See further Fraenkel's note ad loc.; W. G. Arnott, *C.Q.* n.s. 29 (1979) 7–8.

319 εἴσατο 'appeared', aorist of εἴδομαι.

320b–21 = *Od.* 15.164b–5.

322 γεραιὸς ἑοῦ: there is a particular point in ἑοῦ here, where Priam and Idaios have separate vehicles. ἑοῦ (δ') ἐπεβήσετο δίφρου recurs in 8.44; 13.26.

323 = *Od.* 3.493; 15.146, 191. ἐριδούπου 'resounding' may well refer in all these passages to the clatter of chariot-wheels echoing in the portico; if so, when it is used with αἴθουσα in *Od.* 3.399; 7.345; 20.176, 189, where there is no driving or noisy activity, that is a secondary development.

324–7 The two-wheeled, horse-drawn δίφρος is a lighter thing than the four-wheeled, mule-drawn ἀπήνη. The ἀπήνη serves to carry the gifts, which are bulky (228–37), and to bring back the corpse (150–1, 697). That Priam has a vehicle to himself allows Hermes to become his driver (440).

327–8 The portent of 315–21 is apparently forgotten; see 181–7 n.

θάνατόνδε 'to his death': the word is used elsewhere in the *Iliad* only before the deaths of Patroclus and Hector (16.893; 22.287). As Priam goes out on his enterprise, he seems like one of the great warriors of the poem.

332 ἰδὼν δ' ἐλέησε γέροντα: the sight of Priam gives a fresh impulse to Zeus's pity (cf. 174); this is also the answer to Priam's prayer (301 αἴ κ' ἐλεήσῃ). Hence Homer does not say 'Zeus remembered his promise' or the like, which would also be flatter.

334–5 Contrast *Od.* 5.27–8 ἦ ῥα, καὶ Ἑρμείαν, υἱὸν φίλον, ἀντίον ηὔδα· | "Ἑρμεία, σὺ γὰρ αὖτε τά τ' ἄλλα περ ἄγγελός ἐσσι..." Here Hermes is not brought in as the messenger of the gods, which he never is in the *Iliad*, but as a god who is close to men. Thus he is the patron of travellers (cf. [Theoc.] 25.4–6 and Gow ad loc.); see also, e.g., Ar. *Peace* 394 ὦ...φιλανθρωπότατε δαιμόνων; *Clouds* 1478–81 (the first god Strepsiades turns to for help is 'dear Hermes'). In line 24 (cf. 109) the gods want him to steal the corpse. This shows up by contrast the way in which he in fact intervenes: with Priam he shows his friendliness to men, not merely his power to act by stealth; and this quality is amply exhibited in the scene between them. He thus properly represents the humaner mood of the Olympians in Book 24.

In the Battle of the Gods Hermes was ranged with the pro-Greek gods (20.35, 72; 21.497; cf. 15.214). His behaviour here is prepared for by lines 25–30: it was only Hera, Poseidon and Athena who were against letting Hector be buried.

334 μάλιστά γε φίλτατον: for the strengthened superlative, see LSJ s.v. μάλα III 3; cf. 243 n.

335 καί τ' ἔκλυες ᾧ κ' ἐθέλησθα 'and you listen to whomever you like'. For the 'timeless' aorist, used of a typical action, cf., e.g., 616; 1.218; 17.99. For the thought, cf. 344; Hes. *Theog.* 27 and West ad loc.: gods characteristically do things 'as they like', for they are free; men commonly act under constraint.

337   For the redundant τε after μήτε, cf. 5.89. See further Chantraine
II §502.

338   **Πηλεϊωνάδ':** the -δε (cf. 287, 328) is only here used with a
person. But the formation is guaranteed by Ap. Rhod. 3.647 αὐτο-
κασιγνήτηνδε.

339-48   339-45 = *Od.* 5.43-9; 340-2 = *Od.* 1.96-8; 343b-4 = *Od.*
24.3b-4; 347b-8 = *Od.* 10.278b-9. Two elements in this description are
clearly more purposeful here than in the *Odyssey* passages. (1) The wand
is in fact used in *Il.* 24 to put people to sleep (445), but not in *Od.* 5
or 24. (2) In *Il.* 24 Hermes is a young man because of the relationship
this creates between him and Priam, the old man; in *Od.* 10 his youth
has no such point.

346   **Τροίην τε καὶ Ἑλλήσποντον:** cf. 206-7 n.

347   **αἰσυμνητῆρι:** in *Od.* 8.258 αἰσυμνηταί seem to be 'overseers' of
the games. That is too specialized a meaning for this context; so it
should be translated 'ruler, prince', like αἰσυμνητής in later Greek. So
too in *Od.* 13.223 Athena is 'soft-skinned like the children of kings'. The
proper form of the word here could, however, be αἰσυητῆρι, which
occurs in most manuscripts: cf. the name Αἰσυήτης in 2.793.

348   Hermes' youthfulness is a disguise, not a manifestation, of his
nature. In early Greek art he is regularly depicted as a full-bearded
man.

349   For the tomb of Ilus see 10.415; 11.166, 372. For his genealogy,
20.230-40.

   παρέξ 'alongside' goes with σῆμα: cf. 254 n.

354-5   The asyndeton in these lines conveys urgency: cf. 16.126-9;
Aesch. *Cho.* 887-90; Xen. *Hell* 7.1.30.

354   **φράζεο...φραδέος:** this kind of repetition is typical of maxims:
cf. 7.282 = 293; 11.793; 13.115; 15.203; Hes. *W.D.* 352, 369. φραδέος
is probably an artificial epic formation on the model of ἀριφραδής,
ἀφραδής etc.; the word occurs only here in Greek.

355   **διαρραίσεσθαι:** 'shall be destroyed': cf. 728-9 n.

357   **λιτανεύσομεν** 'let us supplicate': -ομεν/-ετε for -ωμεν/-ητε in the subjunctive of aorists of weak verbs is common in Homer: cf. 71, 523, 667.

359 ἐνὶ γναμπτοῖσι μέλεσσι = 11.669; *Od.* 11.394; 13.398, 430; 21.283. The stock epithet γναμπτοῖσι 'flexible' is enlivened here by the antithesis with ὀρθαί.

360 ἐριούνιος is always a title of Hermes. It probably means 'swift-running'; οὔνει/οὔνιος/οὖνον are recorded in Hesychius' glossary as Arcadian or Cypriot words = 'run!/runner/race', and ἐρι- is the common strengthening prefix. This epithet may well be one of those archaisms whose meaning was not clear to the poet himself.

361 The gesture is one of reassurance: cf. 671–2 n.

362 πάτερ is common enough as a respectful form of address to an older man (e.g. *Od.* 7.28). But it is rather more than that when picked up by 371 φίλῳ δέ σε πατρὶ ἐΐσκω (cf. 398 γέρων δὲ δὴ ὡς σύ περ ὧδε) and 373 φίλον τέκος, 425 ὦ τέκος. (1) The dialogue which follows revolves around Hector, who is always except in 390 referred to as 'my son/your son' (385, 388, 408, 422, 426). So Hermes becomes something like Hector to Priam, both as his defender and as the good 'son'. (2) When Priam meets Achilles, he compares himself, and is compared, to Peleus: Achilles' feeling for him has something of a son's for his father. Here too we have a meeting of two men who are, for a short while, like father and son. Thus this episode sets off the later one because it lacks all that is tragic there: here there is nothing like Priam's violent grief and self-pity, or Achilles' compassion and suppressed rage. As so often in Homer, what characterizes the gods and their works is ease and grace: that is both their glory and their limitation.

363 = 10.83, 386 (except that ἀμβροσίην replaces ὀρφναίην).

366 θοὴν διὰ νύκτα μέλαιναν = 653; 10.394, 698. The choice of θοήν may be influenced by phrases like θοὴν ἀνὰ νῆα μέλαιναν (*Od.* 2.430; cf. 10.244, 332 etc.). But 'swift' is also an epithet more appropriate to night(-fall) in Greece than further north; note also 14.261 Νυκτὶ θοῇ.

367 τίς ἂν δή τοι νόος εἴη; 'what sort of state would you be in then?'; cf. Virg. *Aen.* 4.408 (an echo of this line) *quis tibi tum, Dido, cernenti talia sensus...?*; Plat. *Symp.* 219d τίνα οἴεσθέ με διάνοιαν ἔχειν...; *Rep.* 492c with Stallbaum, and Adam, ad loc.; Ovid, *A.A.* 3.713 *quid tibi mentis erat...?*

369 = *Od.* 16.72; 21.133; cf. *Il.* 19.183. The infinitive construes with γέρων: '(too) old to defend himself'; cf., e.g., 662-3 n; 13.483 καρτερός...ἐναίρειν; 15.570 ἄλκιμος...μάχεσθαι.

371 φίλῳ...πατρί 'my own father' echoes πάτερ in 362; on ring-composition, see 549-51 n. The structural device here brings out an important aspect of the whole episode (see 362 n.).

373-7 Priam does not guess that this is Hermes from Zeus's message in 181-7; likewise in *Od.* 3.21ff. Telemachus apparently fails to guess that 'Mentor' is a god, although he seems to have done the day before (2.297). Both episodes require this ignorance; and where gods are at work it is not surprising; cf. 587-9 n.

373 The polite and epic fulness of expression thinly masks the everyday οὕτως (γε πως) or ἔστι ταῦτα = 'yes': cf., e.g., Plat. *Theaet.* 160a, 165c; *Soph.* 244d; Xen. *Oec.* 1.9.

φίλον τέκος need not imply intimacy: cf. 7.279; 10.192; *Od.* 15.509. But it is a significant response to φίλῳ πατρί in 371 (see further 362 n.), which it echoes with a slight variation of sense, τέκος being metaphorical, πατρί literal (cf. 553-5 n.).

374 ἀλλ' gives lively assent: 'why, then...'; cf. Denniston 18-19.
ἔτι...καὶ ἐμεῖο 'still...even me'; i.e. after all the misfortunes the gods have given him.

376-7 οἷος...τοκήων 'such as you (are), wonderful in stature and beauty, and you are wise...'; the relative clause develops into a main sentence, in the normal Greek manner; cf. 292-3 n.

377 μακάρων: dramatic irony, since the word is a typical epithet of gods. Calling the parents 'happy' is a way of complimenting a young person: cf. *Od.* 6.154-5; Eur. *Ion* 308.

379 Equivalent to the ὀρθῶς γε or ὀρθῶς λέγεις of Attic conversation (e.g. Plat. *Theaet.* 197b, 201a); cf. 373 n.
κατὰ μοῖραν 'expresses the gods' approval of Priam's pious senti-ments' (Leaf); it also indicates, with Olympian irony, that μακάρων δ' ἔξ ἐσσι τοκήων is true in a sense Priam did not imagine.

381-4 Hermes' questions remains unanswered: cf. 4.31-3; 6.254; 14.42-3; *Od.* 3.214-15; 7.237-9 (no answer to 'who are you?'). The reason is clear: a reply could only be flat; and Hermes' last words naturally prompt a counter-question from Priam.

385 σὸς πάϊς is emphatic at the beginning of the line and before a stop; cf. 362 n.

οὐ...'Αχαιῶν 'he was not missing/did not hang back from battle with the Greeks'; for the phrase cf. 13.310; 17.142; 23.670. For the use of the genitive in 'Αχαιῶν, cf. 11.542; Kühner–Gerth II §414.4.

388 ὅς has explanatory force here: cf. 434; also 240 n. The variant ὥς ('How well...!') is also possible.

καλά 'well' seems to imply that Hermes has shown an understanding of what Hector's death means to Priam. But it might rather mean 'properly', i.e. with no misguided attempt to spare Priam's feelings (cf. εὖ in *Od.* 4.327); similarly in 407 the old man wants 'the whole truth'.

ἀπότμου = δυσπότμου, as in *Od.* 1.219; 20.140. Compare also πανάποτμος (255 = 493), ἄμμορον (6.408).

390 'You are testing me: it's *Hector* you're asking about.' Hermes knows that what Priam wants to find out is not, for its own sake, who the stranger is, but whether he is someone who can give good information about Hector's body. At the same time he works in an answer to 387 in 396–40. The assonance πειρᾷ...γεραιέ...εἴρεαι is striking: it is echoed in 433.

Ἕκτορα δῖον: for the accusative of the person or thing asked about cf. 6.239; *Od.* 13.238; Ar. *Birds* 167; Plat. *Euthyd.* 271b6.

καί introduces an explanation of what was said immediately before it; cf. 766; 18.9; Thuc. 1.1.1 '...starting my history as soon as the war began καὶ ἐλπίσας μέγαν τε ἔσεσθαι καὶ ἀξιολογώτατον τῶν προγεγενημένων'; 1.90.1, 109.4.

391–404 Hermes makes it clear that he knows not only Hector's name, but what he looks like. He also implies that as a subject of Achilles, he will know what has now happened to Hector's body; Priam pursues this implication in 406–9. At the same time the god enlarges on his admiring remarks about Hector in 383–4, recalling the Trojan's successes of Books 15–16. He gains Priam's trust not only because he persuades the old man that he can help, but also, more subtly, because he accommodates his words to Priam's feelings about his son.

391–3 Perhaps a designed contrast to 22.373–4 when the Greeks, as they stab Hector's dead body, recall with bitter mockery how he once set fire to their ships.

397 Hermes never gives his 'name'; paternity is sufficient identification; cf. 6.145–211; 21.153–60; *Od.* 6.196.

398 Hermes' 'father' is rich, like Priam; Hermes has noted Priam's wealth (381–2). Another touch by which the god deftly relates himself to the man.

γέρων...ὧδε : cf. 362 n. For the redundant ὧδε after ὡς cf. 2.258. See also 149 n.

400 λάχον ἐνθάδ' ἕπεσθαι 'I drew it as my lot to follow (Achilles) here.'

401–4 These lines remind us that the war must go on, and Troy fall, whatever happens between Achilles and Priam: cf. 667, 728–9, 800 nn. But Achilles does in fact delay the resumption of battle (670).

403 καθήμενοι 'sitting idle': cf. 542 n.

407 εἶς carries some emphasis at the beginning of the line before a pause: it implies 'you *really are*'; cf. 6.224–5 τῷ νῦν σοὶ μὲν ἐγὼ ξεῖνος φίλος Ἄργεϊ μέσσῳ | εἰμί, σὺ δ' ἐν Λυκίῃ ('so I *really am* your guest-friend, and you mine'); 16.515 εἶς ('you may *be* in Lycia or in Troy, but you can *hear* from anywhere'); *Od.* 4.95 εἰσίν ('are *alive*'); 17.159 ἔστιν ('is *present*'; the word is also stressed by hyperbaton there).

408–9 ἠέ μιν...'Ἀχιλλεύς: in 23.182–3 Achilles promises Patroclus that he will give Hector's body to the dogs. But Priam imagines Achilles behaving with even more ferocity than he actually has; this brings out the more his magnanimity in what follows.

413–14 'He has been lying there for eleven days', literally 'this (is) the twelfth day for him lying'; cf. 765.

δυωδεκάτη...ἥδε 'this is the twelfth (day)': cf., e.g., 665–7; *Od.* 2.374. The variant ἠώς looks like a reminiscence of 1.493 and 21.80; but this is night-time.

416 ἑοῦ ἑτάροιο φίλοιο like ἑοῦ...ἑτάροιο in 755, indicates a certain sympathy for Achilles; contrast the more neutral Μενοιτιάδαο θανόντος in 21.28; 24.16; *Od.* 24.77.

418 **θηοῖο** is second person singular of the present optative of θηέομαι (the Ionic form of θεάομαι).

419 **περὶ δ' αἷμα νένιπται:** for the syntax see 292–3 n.

421 'The other Greeks' all stab Hector's corpse in 22.369–71; cf. 391–3 n.

422–3 The culmination – in rhetoricians' language, the ἐπιφώνημα – of the speech: till now the gods are not mentioned, and the preservation of Hector's body remains unexplained. In accordance with lines 23–78 (cf. 113) it is seen as the will of all the gods rather than of Aphrodite and Apollo alone. The thought is reinforced by 749–50.

422 **ἐῆος** 'your'; cf. 550; 1.393; 15.138; 19.342. The meaning is beyond doubt, but the form of the termination is puzzling: see Chantraine 1 § 128 (p. 274).

425–31 Priam draws a moral conclusion from Hermes' words. The gods let men suffer and die (cf. 525 – 6); but men can expect something in return if they venerate them (cf. 66–70). Book 24 here, as in general, affirms in the midst of the tragic suffering that the gods are in some measure good and just.

425 **διδοῦναι:** a unique form of διδόναι, though 16.745 ζευγνῦμεν is analogous. It is probably an epic lengthening: cf. Chantraine 1 §§ 45 (c), 235.

426 **εἴ ποτ' ἔην γε** 'if he ever was'; cf. 3.180; 11.762; *Od.* 15.268; 19.315; 24.289. A pathetic turn of phrase apparently peculiar to Homer. What is lost is so much missed that it can seem never to have been there at all.

428 **τῶ** 'therefore': see Chantraine 1 § 115.

   οἱ: dative, because ἀπομνήσαντο (sc. χάριν; cf. Hes. *Theog.* 503 and West ad loc.) is equivalent to 'paid back the favour'.

   καὶ ἐν θανάτοιό περ αἴσῃ 'if only after his death'. The gods did show their concern, but late: cf. 20, 750.

429 ἄλεισον: this cannot be the same cup as the one mentioned in 234–5; that one is too precious for this purpose.

430 σύν γε θεοῖσιν 'if, that is, the gods will it': again dramatic irony (cf. 377 n.). The whole situation is ironic too. Priam, who has just concluded that men should offer gifts to the gods, offers a gift to someone he does not know is a god. But in fact in this case the gift would be improper, to Hermes the god as it is to Hermes the man (cf. 433–6); for the gods are now themselves *repaying* a favour.

433 echoes 390. As there, it is not really Priam, but Hermes who is 'probing', i.e. subtly evoking reactions from his interlocutor. In both places, Hermes' reply is a tactful way of asserting his divine superiority without revealing his divinity. Here, as there, there is assonance, but of a slightly different kind (πειρᾷ... γεραιέ... πείσεις).

435 δείδοικα καὶ αἰδέομαι: no conflict is felt between fear of punishment and shame or respect; cf. Eumaeus' words about his master Telemachus in *Od.* 17.188–9: ἀλλὰ τὸν αἰδέομαι καὶ δείδια, μή μοι ὀπίσσω | νεικείῃ· χαλεπαὶ δὲ ἀνάκτων εἰσὶν ὁμοκλαί. This mixture of considerations of reverence or honour with considerations of prudence is not 'primitive', but candid and life-like. In Homer, cf. also 1.331; 3.172; 15.657–8; 18.394; *Od.* 7.305; 8.22; 14.234; and after Homer, *Cypria* fr. 23 ἵνα γὰρ δέος ἔνθα καὶ αἰδώς; Thuc. 2.37.3 and Gomme ad loc.

437–9 A sharp antithesis to what goes before: 'I will not rob him, but I will escort you'; it is stressed by the repetition πομπός... πομπόν. That word is a hint of a reminder to Priam of Zeus's message (182).

437 ἄν... κε: for the double particle, see Chantraine II § 503. ἄν... ἄν is common in Attic.

   Ἄργος: i.e. 'all the way home'. Ἄργος is used in a broad sense as 'Greece' when it is a question of being far away or of going back: e.g. 2.287, 348; 12.70; 14.70; 19.329.

439 The protasis ('if I *did* escort you in that way...') is left unexpressed: cf. 3.53; 5.885–7; 20.94–6.

440–1 Hermes said he would be Priam's πομπός: he now translates his words into action by taking the reins of the old man's chariot.

Peisistratus, Telemachus' πομπός in the *Odyssey* (3.325; 4.162), is also his driver (3.482–3).

ἐπαΐξας 'leaping up on to'; cf. 711; 17.481.

446 ἄφαρ: the gods' actions and movement are characteristically swift: cf. 346, 691; 13.18, 62–5; *Od.* 1.410. Also 567 n. This would be no quick business for a mortal, as Achilles points out in 566–7.

448–56 Achilles' dwelling is described here, rather than in Book 1 or 9 or 16, because Priam's entering it is so great an enterprise (cf. 574–5 n.); and the description is not merely decorative. (1) The Myrmidons 'made it for their lord' (the repeated ποίησαν ἄνακτι carries a certain emphasis). This indicates that Achilles is a king who commands the loyalty of his subjects (cf. 435–6). (2) The κλισίη is in effect a house with a πρόδομος (673) or αἴθουσα (644) and a μέγαρον (647); it is called οἶκος (572) and δώματα (512). This lends dignity to Achilles through his environment; it is also functional in the following narrative: see 583–4 n., 673–6 n. (3) The account of the bolt brings out Achilles' great strength. Thus the whole passage prepares us for the man who is to arouse Priam's wonder (629–30). For descriptions likewise significantly framed and placed see, e.g., 6.240–50 (Priam's great palace and flourishing family: what follows is heavy with foreboding of the fall of Troy); *Od.* 5.55–75 (Calypso's cave: Hermes has just arrived there, and Odysseus is about to leave its peace and its pleasures for the horrors and dangers of the sea); *Od.* 7.84–133 (Alcinous' miraculous palace and garden: Odysseus is about to enter the house as an all-too-human sufferer and suppliant).

450–6 ἀτάρ κτλ.: the relative clause is expanded loosely in the normal Greek manner: cf. 292–3 n. Such lengthy expansion is typical of Homer. ὅτε (448) is eventually picked up by δή ῥα τόθ' (457).

450–1 ἔρεψαν…ὄροφον, 'they covered it (with) a roof'; the accusative marks the internal object (cf. 172 n.). So there is no need to suppose a special sense 'reeds' for the word here.

454–6 A typically Homeric way of setting heroic strength in relief: cf. 5.303–4 'two common men of our time could not carry it; Diomede brandished it alone with ease'; 11.636–7; 12.447–9; 16.141–2 = 19.388–9; 20.286–7.

455 μεγάλην κληῗδα 'the great bolt': this is the same as the ἐπιβλής of 453. For the syntactical connection of this line with the succeeding one, cf. 450–6 n.

456 ἐπιρρήσσεσκε on its own corresponds to the pair ἐπιρρήσσεσκον ...ἀναοίγεσκον: cf. 475 n.; 130–1 γυναικὶ ἐν φιλότητι μίσγεσθαι corresponding to οὔτε σίτου οὔτ' εὐνῆς; 15.660–3 ὑπὲρ τοκέων corresponding to παίδων ἠδ' ἀλόχων καὶ κτήσιος ἠδὲ τοκήων; 19.160–7 σιτοῗο corresponding to σίτου καὶ οἴνοιο...οἴνοιο...καὶ ἐδωδῆς. Further, Hdt. 1.32.6; Eur. H.F. 1374–81; Ar. Birds 78–9.

460–7 Hermes now reveals that he is a god: he does not merely disappear leaving Priam to guess it, which is what happens at, e.g., 13.62–75; 17.322–41; 22.294–9; Od. 1.319–23; 3.371–9. His speech serves to show Priam that the help Zeus promised was in fact given. At a deeper level, it shows up the difference between men and gods. A god cannot receive a human welcome (464–5); nor of course can he make an appeal like Priam's. Fellow-feeling, like suffering (cf. 525–6), is peculiar to men; the gods can pity, and require that men show pity, as they do in this book, but no more. Thus Zeus had not envisaged that Hermes should be present at the meeting of Achilles and Priam (154), and had not envisaged how much would happen at that meeting (cf. 119 n.).

465–7 refine on this difference. Hermes tells Priam to invoke Achilles' father and mother and child; in fact, Priam only mentions the father. Further, Hermes only tells him to clasp Achilles' knees; in fact, Priam also kisses his hands. What the god commands is a conventional supplication. What the man does over and above that is to appeal as a father to his son's killer. For similar discrepancies between instructions and execution see 1.503–10; 9.225–306. Thetis does not, for diplomatic reasons, bring in explicitly the argument Achilles had told her to use (1.394–412); but Achilles' mentioning it both emphasizes her tact and makes clear why she has a claim on Zeus's favour. Likewise, Odysseus omits, again for diplomatic reasons, the conclusion of Agamemnon's message which insists that he is king (9.158–61). The omission also helps us understand why Achilles thinks Agamemnon is lying (9.308–14, 345, 375–6). Note also 309 n.

460 εἰλήλουθα 'I have come', perfect of ἔρχομαι (Attic ἐλήλυθα).

Where gods are concerned, 'coming' often implies coming to help: cf., e.g., Sappho 1.5 (as often in prayers) ἀλλὰ τυίδ' ἐλθέ. For the form of divine self-revelation cf. *Od.* 11.252; *H.H.Dem.* 268-9.

462 εἴσομαι 'I shall hasten' (not to be confused with the future of οἶδα).

463-4 'It would be offensive (sc. to the gods) that mortal men should entertain an immortal god face to face in that way.' Hesiod says of an age *earlier* than that of the *Iliad* (fr. 1.6-7): 'In those days mortal men sat and dined together with the immortal gods.' (In later poetry, cf. *Cat.* 64.384-408.) The wedding of Peleus and Thetis (cf. 62) is an example; this is also the privilege of the fairy-land Phaeacians (*Od.* 7.201-6). In Homer gods do not customarily even appear to men in their true shape: cf. 20.131; *Od.* 3.222-3; 16.161.

467 τέκεος : Neoptolemus is mentioned, with great pathos, in 19. 326-33 (also *Od.* 11.505-40). But Peleus alone is to count here.

469 No time is spent on Priam's reaction to Hermes' speech. The whole thrust of the narrative goes towards his meeting with Achilles. For such economy, cf. 690-1 n.

472-6 To serve Achilles' meals had formerly been Patroclus' task, as Achilles himself recalls in lamenting his friend's death (19.315-18; cf. 9.205-17). The contrast with Book 9 is suggestive. There Patroclus sits with Achilles, who is singing (186-91): here Automedon and Alkimos, who have taken Patroclus' place (cf. 574-5), are only with Achilles to clear away the table, and he is quite inactive. However, he is no longer groaning, as when Thetis arrived (122-3), and he has eaten, as she encouraged him to do (128-30): that the table is still there quietly stresses the point with a visual detail. So the scene-setting again prepares us for what is to follow: Patroclus is lost, and Achilles withdrawn into himself; but the full violence of his grief has passed.

474 Ἄλκιμος = Ἀλκιμέδων. The short form of the name is used (cf. 574; 19.392) to avoid the jingle Αὐτομέδων...Ἀλκιμέδων: cf. 16.298 στεροπηγερέτα for νεφεληγερέτα after νεφέλην; 23.168 μεγάθυμος for πόδας ὠκὺς before ἐς πόδας.

475 ἐδωδῆς: partitive genitive (cf., e.g., 641), the object of ἔσθων καὶ

πίνων. There is no word for 'drink', to correspond to ἐδωδῆς: cf. 456 n.,
Od. 5.196–7 ἐτίθει παρὰ πᾶσιν ἐδωδὴν | ἔσθειν καὶ πίνειν, οἷα βροτοὶ
ἄνδρες ἔδουσιν. Similar, *Il.* 12.319–20; *Od.* 20.312–13. The line was
suspected in antiquity because elsewhere in Homer the tables are not
cleared away before the diners have risen. But since a convivial evening
is clearly not in store here, the tables have served their purpose. So the
scholia and Athenaeus (12b) are essentially right in explaining the
discrepancy by reference to Achilles' mourning.

477 ἔλαθ' εἰσελθών 'he came in without being seen'; for the
aorist participle, cf. 681; 170 n. A visitor in Homer is normally seen
straightaway by his host: see 1.330; 9.193; 11.645; 18.382; *Od.* 1.113;
3.34; 4.22; 5.77–8; 17.31, 328. See further 576 n.

Πρίαμος μέγας: cf. 629–32 n.

477–8 Grasping the knees is the basic and characteristic gesture of
supplication. For kissing the knees cf. 8.371; *Od.* 14.279. These lines and
504–6 are enough to explain why the *hands* are kissed here.

478–9 χεῖρας…ἀνδροφόνους: these words recur in 18.317, 23.18,
again with sharp pathos.

479 The line is a 'tricolon crescendo', i.e. each part of the phrase is
longer than the preceding one: δεινὰς | ἀνδροφόνους, | αἳ οἱ…υἷας. This
pattern sometimes goes, as here, with an effect of climax: cf., e.g.,
4.125–6 λίγξε βιός, | νευρὴ δὲ μέγ' ἴαχεν, | ἆλτο δ' ὀϊστὸς ὀξυβελής…;
5.740–2; 2.62–4. See further E. Fraenkel, *Horace* (Oxford 1957) 351 n. 1.

480–4 The simile heightens the moment by contrasting a more usual
situation with this one. The person in the simile has killed someone and
arrives seeking refuge with a rich man who will take him into his
household (cf. 16.572–4; *Od.* 15.272–8): the bystanders are amazed
simply at the unexpectedness of the arrival (cf. 9.193; 11.776; *Od.*
16.12). But Priam is a suppliant in his own homeland; he has entered
an environment he knows to be hostile; and the amazement here is that
he should be supplicating the killer of his son (cf. 519–21). Moreover,
he is himself the rich man (cf. 398 n.; 543–6 etc.), who is bringing part
of that wealth with him.

480 ἄτη 'folly', naturally refers to the impulse which made the man
commit murder. The relative clause then, unusually, expresses the

consequence of the sentence it is attached to: cf. 13.336; 21.353–5. But if the phrasing naturally suggests that ἄτη causes what the man does *after* the murder, that is purposeful. For in Priam's case it is precisely his coming to Achilles' tent which seems mad (201–5) or incredible (519–21). So the simile is worded to fit the narrative, even at the risk of losing some of its internal clarity.

πυκινή 'strong', literally 'compact, tight', because its grip is hard to escape from: cf. 16.599 πυκινὸν δ᾽ ἄχος ἔλλαβ᾽ Ἀχαιούς.

483 θεοειδέα 'god-like'. The epithet is more than a generic and decorative one. It corresponds to Achilles' wonder; and it makes Priam his equal (cf. 629–32): Priam in his turn addresses him as 'god-like' (486). In 680 a metrical equivalent, βασιλῆα, is used: there, where the old man is the object of a god's concern, θεοειδέα would be out of place. θεοειδής is used eight times of Priam in the *Iliad*, and only in this book: that is presumably because this is his ἀριστεία.

486–506 Priam's argument is: 'Remember your father, and pity me. We are both old men, deprived of their sons; but my suffering is worse than his, for I have no hope of seeing my son again.' This thought is unfolded in 486–502, and then repeated in summary form in 503–6, when the gods are invoked too. It was prepared for in 22.416–28, where Priam thought of going to ransom Hector's body. The difference between the preparation in Book 22 and the event here is significant. What distinguishes this speech is its even more intense concentration on Hector, the 'only' son, and Priam's claim that his suffering is worse than Peleus'. It is precisely these points that Achilles' speech is designed to answer. Priam is overwhelmed by what he has been through at Hector's death and for Hector's body – 'things such as no man on earth has ever yet endured' (505); he has yet to learn to bear his suffering through the knowledge that it is typically human.

486 The speech begins straightaway with its main point; supplications in Homer are normally introduced in a more elaborate way; see 15.662–3; 22.338; *Od.* 11.67–8; 15.261–2. The abruptness betokens intense feeling.

487 ἐγών: for the nominative cf., e.g., 376; 6.477.

ἐπὶ γήραος οὐδῷ 'on the threshold of old age' (defining genitive). The phrase recurs once in the *Iliad*, in Priam's appeal to Hector in Book 22 (60); for another echo of that speech see 516 n.

488-9   These lines press the analogy between Priam and Peleus: two
helpless old men harassed by those around their home. The word
τείρουσι is used of what the Greeks do to Troy in 6.255. So although
Homer could have had in mind stories about what happened to Peleus
after Achilles' death (Eur. *Tro.* 1126–8; Apollod. *Epit.* 6.13), he need
not have done. *Od.* 11.494–503, where the dead Achilles wonders if
Peleus is being 'dishonoured', is based on this passage.

488   περιναιέται ἀμφὶς ἐόντες: for this type of pleonasm cf. 9.123–4
ἵππους | πηγοὺς ἀθλοφόρους, οἳ ἀέθλια ποσσὶν ἄροντο; *Od.* 1.299–300;
2.65–6; Hdt. 1.79.2; 8.4.1. See also 673 n.

489   οὐδέ τίς ἐστιν...ἀμῦναι 'and there is no one to keep off...': for
the use of the infinitive, cf. 610–11.

493-4   = 255–6 (ὤμοι ἐγώ κτλ.). There Priam used the phrase in
bitterness against his surviving sons: here simply in sorrow (υἷας
ἀρίστους applies to all his sons). That indicates that the angry mood
of 253–64 is a transient one and stresses the deeper feeling which
underlay it.

495-7   By numbering and classifying his sons Priam gives more weight
to his loss: cf. Arist. *Rhet.* 1365a10 'a single subject when divided into
parts seems more impressive' (quoting 9.592–4); also, e.g., 36–7 n.,
228–37; 11.677–81; 21.350–1.
   If Priam has many concubines, that seems to reflect the practice of
eastern kings like Solomon (I Kings 11: 1–4). But if he has so many
sons, that has a definite poetic purpose. Fathers are bereaved in war:
this is something frequently mentioned in the *Iliad*, and it finds its
culminating expression in Book 24, where Priam is the bereaved father
par excellence and where the loss of his 'only' son stands out the more
against the loss of so many other sons. Cf. Deichgräber 99–103; Griffin
123–5; also Griffin's article in *C.Q.* n.s. 26 (1976) 165, 168 n. 29.
Similarly, Achilles represents all the unfamilied warriors of the poem
in this book (cf. 86 n.).

497   γυναῖκες: two of these are mentioned in the *Iliad*, Laothoe (21.85;
22.48) and Kastianeira (8.305). They are of inferior status to Hecuba;
the poem speaks of several 'bastard' sons of Priam (4.499 etc. νόθον).

498   Many sons of Priam besides Hector are killed in the *Iliad*: see

4.498–500; 5.159–60; 8.302–8; 11.101–9, 490; 16.737–43; 20.407–18; 21.116–19. In 24.257 the deaths of Troilus and Mestor are mentioned.

τῶν μὲν πολλῶν corrects the emotional exaggeration (οὔ τινα) of 494. For the pattern of exposition in which flat statement is followed by qualification see, e.g., 149, 256; 4.397; 7.185–9; 11.328–35; *Od.* 15.4–8. It is one form of the parataxis typical of Homer; but it is not confined to oral poetry: see, e.g., Thuc. 1.97.2 'everyone before me omitted this period... and the one man who did handle it, Hellanicus, did so cursorily and inaccurately'; Hdt. 4.188; 5.99.1–2; 8.113.3; Ar. *Frogs* 692–6. That Priam goes on nonetheless to treat Hector as his 'only' son has argumentative and emotive value. It stresses the analogy between himself and Peleus; it also represents the strength of his grief at losing Hector.

In 22.423 Priam spoke of 'so many' (τόσσους) of his sons killed by Achilles. So the formulation of this line, with 'Ares' as the subject, is tactful: elsewhere the subject of γούνατ' ἔλυσεν is a specific hero (5.176; 15.291; 16.425). But it also prepares for the climax 'the most precious of my sons was the one you killed'.

499 ἄστυ καὶ αὐτούς 'the city and the citizens': cf. 14.47 νῆας...καὶ αὐτούς; *Od.* 9.40 πόλιν ἔπραθον, ὤλεσα δ' αὐτούς. The variant αὐτός could mean 'alone' (cf., e.g., 8.99), but καὶ αὐτός after οἶος seems fussy, and has little manuscript support.

501 Ἕκτορα: the name is effectively delayed till this late point in the speech; and it is stressed by its position, first in the line before a pause: cf. Ἕκτορ in Andromache's lament (742).

504 ἐλεεινότερός περ 'still more pitiable': cf. Denniston 482.

506 The line must correspond to 478–9, in order to recall the gesture which sums up the meaning of Priam's enterprise; it therefore means 'to reach his hands to my mouth'. The force of the middle voice in ὀρέγεσθαι is felt, though not in the usual way. Elsewhere the word, without χεῖρα or the like, means 'reach out (my own hands) to get for myself', here, with χεῖρ', 'reach out (to bring to myself) someone else's hands'; it is also logical that χεῖρ' ὀρέγεσθαι should not mean the same as χεῖρ' ὀρέγειν ('reach out one's own hands').

ἀνδρὸς παιδοφόνοιο goes with χεῖρ'; for the interlaced word-order cf. 284; 2.314; 8.10–11; 11.89, 327; 12.177–8; 23.339–40. In an

Argivo-Corinthian relief of 575–550 B.C. Priam touches Achilles' chin (cf., e.g., 1.501): see Johansen 49. But since the artist has used his freedom to vary on the text (Priam and Achilles are both standing; Priam does not clasp Achilles' knees etc.), that proves nothing about the meaning of this line. It does look as though Virgil took the line to mean 'reach out my hands to his mouth' (see *Aen.* 1.487 *tendentemque manus Priamum conspexit inertis*); but from Virgil's time – and it may well be modelled on a fifth-century B.C. original – we have the fine silver cup which shows Priam kneeling and kissing Achilles' hands: see A. D. Trendall and T. B. L. Webster, *Illustrations of Greek Drama* (London 1971) 57.

507 = *Od.* 4.113.

πατρὸς...ἵμερον...γόοιο 'a desire to bewail his father'.

508 Achilles' first gesture is not to accept the supplication – that he does at 515 by taking Priam's hand and lifting him up (cf. *Od.* 7.167–8; Thuc. 1.137.1) – but to push the old man away. ἀπωθεῖν is used of rejecting a supplicant in 6.62; *Od.* 15.280; only ἦκα ('gently') makes it clear that Achilles is ridding himself of Priam just for the present, to let go the feelings the old man's speech has aroused.

509–11 Both men have to indulge their own grief if they are to feel for the other's; for such weeping satisfies a natural desire: hence τετάρπετο (cf. 23.10, 98).

τὼ δέ...ὁ μὲν...αὐτὰρ 'Αχιλλεύς: for the pattern of sentence cf. 7.306–7; 12.400–4; *Od.* 8.361–2. At line 511 the sentence loses contact with the initial participle (μνησαμένω) and develops independently: cf., e.g., 5.592–4; Kühner–Gerth II §§ 490.4, 602.1. For similar phenomena see 292–3, 419, 450–6 nn.

510 ἐλυσθείς 'curled up' (cf. *Od.* 9.433) or perhaps 'crouching'. Priam's posture at this point is as humiliating as can be: cf. 22.220–1 ...οὐδ' εἴ κεν μάλα πολλὰ πάθοι ἑκάεργος 'Απόλλων | προπροκυλινδόμενος πατρὸς Διὸς αἰγιόχοιο. The abasement belongs to the act of supplication: cf. J. Gould, *J.H.S.* 93 (1973) 74–103.

514 Desire – like the θυμός itself, the vehicle of the emotions – is spread through the body (γυίων), but it belongs particularly to the πραπίδες as the seat of intelligence.

515 χειρὸς ἀνίστη 'raised him by the hand'; for the genitive cf., e.g., 735. On the gesture, see 508 n.

516 πολιόν τε κάρη πολιόν τε γένειον: for this kind of emphatic repetition cf., e.g., 771–2 n.; 23.790. The same phrase recurs in 22.74, in Priam's appeal to Hector; for another echo of that speech see 487 n.

518–51 Achilles' first words are an expression of the wonder described at 480–4 and also a warmly felt response to Priam's speech: πῶς ἔτλης (519) echoes ἔτλην (505); 520–1 ('I have killed many of your sons') echoes 498 ('many of my sons have died in battle') and 500–1 ('you killed Hector'). After this sympathetic beginning, Achilles goes on to answer Priam's argument. (1) He corrects Priam's exclusive concern with Hector. He has killed 'many fine sons' (520) of the old man; and Priam, unlike Peleus, still has sons left. So the suffering he has in common with Peleus consists not so much in the loss of Hector, as in something broader, the whole Trojan war (548; 488–9 n.): cf. *Od.* 20.18 'endure, my heart: you have endured worse before' (also *Od.* 12.208). It goes with this that though Achilles wept for Patroclus as well as Peleus (511–12), and though his whole speech implicitly shows how he has come to terms with his grief over his friend, he makes no reference to the sorrow of his which corresponds to Priam's over Hector. (2) Priam's suffering is not greater than Peleus' or than any man's (504–6); rather, both share the common lot of men (525–48): cf. *Od.* 1.353–5. This shows that suffering is a part of human life and the gods' will, and so must be borne with equanimity. It also extends the hearer's pity from himself towards another. Thus Achilles' feeling for Peleus serves not only to arouse his sympathy for Priam, but also to mitigate Priam's sorrow. (3) There is worse suffering than Peleus' or Priam's, that of the man who never knows the good fortune they have known (531–3). Beyond the world in which heroes face death in seeking glory, the *Iliad* envisages something worse, brute hunger and degradation; and its characters, like King Lear (IV iii '...O, I have ta'en | Too little care of this!'), must see it too, if they are to understand their condition.

Achilles' speech has much in common with later *consolationes*. These sometimes begin with warm expressions of condolence: e.g. Hor. *Od.* 1.24.1–4; Kassel 51. The arguments of lines 522–51 also find analogies there. For (1), see Kassel 99: e.g. Sen. *Ad Helv.* 2.2 *animum in omnium aerumnarum suarum conspectu collocare*; for (2), see Kassel 54–5, 70–2; e.g. Cic. *Tusc.* 3.79 *non tibi hoc soli*, 3.34 *humana humane ferenda*; (3) corresponds to [Plut.] *Cons. ad Ap.* 9 or Timocles, *CAF* II 453: just as the sufferings of legendary heroes are invoked to console ordinary men, so here the sufferings of ordinary men are invoked to console a legendary hero. See further 524, 549–51 nn. These similarities are not surprising: ever since there were grief and speech, there must have been an art of consolation; and Homer was a source of moral instruction to the ancient world (despite the battering he took from Plato).

518   ἅ δείλ': this form of address is a sign of strong feeling (cf. e.g., 17.201, 443). Later, in comforting or admonishing Priam, Achilles uses the drier γέρον (543, 546, 560, 569, 599, 650, 669) or γεραιέ (618).

ἄνσχεο 'you have endured': uncontracted and unaugmented aorist of ἀνέχομαι (= Attic ἀνέσχου).

519–21 (= 203–5 πῶς ἐθέλεις κτλ.). Though Achilles is later aware of it (563–7), here he ignores Hermes' presence on the journey. That represents the first flush of astonishment at Priam's coming, it also emphasizes that the gods' support does not make the old man's enterprise any less extraordinary: cf. 181–7 n.

522 A guest is normally seated as soon as he arrives: cf., e.g., 100; 9.200; 18.399; *Od.* 3.37; 4.51 (after a bath); 14.49. See further 576 n.

523   ἐν θυμῷ: i.e. in silence, cf. 3.8–9; *Od.* 22.411.

κατακεῖσθαι: the metaphor follows finely on κάτ' ἄρ' ἕζευ: the visible act of sitting means letting grief 'lie'.

524 The weeping had its place and gave a sort of pleasure (514); now it must be seen to be idle. Again a topic of consolation: cf. Soph. *El.* 137; Cic. *Tusc.* 3.64 *nihil profici maerendo* (cf. 77); Kassel 63.

525–6   ἐπεκλώσαντο 'they have spun out/allotted': the verb only here in the *Iliad*, but cf. 209–10 n.

ἀχνυμένους: the accusative seems more idiomatic than the dative (see app. crit.); cf. 6.207–8 καί μοι μάλα πόλλ' ἐπέτελλεν | ...ὑπείροχον ἔμμεναι ἄλλων; *Od.* 4.209–10; 14.193–5; also 146 above.

ἀκηδέες 'without sorrow', in antithesis to ἀχνυμένους: the gods, who in this book show their pity for men and demand that men pity each other, also will human suffering and never share it.

527–33 Pindar took these lines to imply that there were three jars, two of bad things, one of good, if *Pythian* 3.80–2 refers to this passage: μανθάνων οἶσθα προτέρων· | ἓν παρ' ἐσλὸν πήματα σύνδυο δαίονται βροτοῖς | ἀθάνατοι. Plato (*Rep.* 379d) and Plutarch (*Mor.* 24a) rightly understood that there were only two jars. The point is not that men have more bad fortune than good, but that they have either a mixture of good and bad, or else merely bad; and ἕτερος naturally suggests a contrast between each of two jars. So κακῶν is equivalent to ἕτερος μὲν κακῶν: cf. 7.420; 22.157 φεύγων, ὁ δ' ὄπισθε διώκων; and in prose, Plat. *Rep.* 369c1. The πίθοι are like the storage-jars sunk in the floors of Mycenean palaces. A rather similar symbolic πίθος figures in Hes. *W.D.* 94.

Plato (*Rep.* 379d) objected to this passage that it makes evil come from the gods. Whatever be thought of it as theology, it contains a moral idea of some substance. Men must both accept their own suffering and pity others', as Achilles is doing, because they are all alike weaker than the gods, who send it upon them: cf. *Od.* 18.130–50; Hdt. 1.86.6; Soph. *Aj.* 121–6; and the whole conclusion of Euripides, *Heracles*.

For similar thoughts as a consolation cf. *Od.* 4.236–7; 6.188–90. Also *Il.* 5.383–4 for a witty reversal: a god is comforted by being told how often gods have suffered at the hands of men.

The variant form in which Plato quotes this line cannot be right: see van der Valk II 356–8.

528 ἐάων 'of good things', apparently neuter genitive plural of ἐΰς: this form looks like an artificial epic creation; cf. Chantraine I §84.

531 τῶν λυγρῶν i.e. *only* bad things, by contrast with ἀμμείξας; cf. 608 δοιώ ('only two') by contrast with πολλούς.

532 βούβρωστις 'starvation', like βούλιμος. The prefix βου- means 'big', 'powerful'; cf. βούπαις, etc. and our 'strong as an ox' (perhaps too 'I could eat an ox'). Elsewhere βούβρωστις or βούλιμος is found as a *daimon*: see Plutarch, *Moralia* 693e–694b (cf. Semonides fr. 7.101–2 Λιμόν...δυσμενέα θεόν). It is striking that Plutarch mentions a religious rite called βουλίμου ἐξέλασις ('the driving out of famine'); here it is βούβρωστις which 'drives'.

Starvation is singled out among misfortunes above all for the degradation it brings (531 λωβητόν, 533); also because the starving man is a vagrant (533 φοιτᾷ). In all these respects there is a contrast with Priam and Peleus, who are, of course, not hungry either.

534–8 Note the complex pattern formed by words for 'god' and 'man' in these lines. The *gods* favoured Peleus above all *men* by giving him, a *mortal man*, a *goddess* for his wife. But the *god* brought him too suffering. Cf. 258–9 n.

ὡς μὲν καί... 'so also...': these words introduce the application of the general law stated in the whole of 525–33; 529–30 (not 531–3) are the lines which are particularly relevant to Peleus.

537 Peleus' marriage to Thetis is a token of supreme good fortune: cf. 60–1; Hes. fr. 211; Pind. *I.* 6.25 Πηλέος...εὐδαίμονος γαμβροῦ θεῶν.

538–40 There is a deliberate echo of 493–501 here: 'No sons...but one doomed to die young' answers 'no sons are left...most are dead...the only one is dead', Achilles' 'only' being literal, Priam's figurative.

539 κρειόντων i.e. sons who would take over the kingdom from him.

540 παναώριον corresponds to πανάποτμος (493): the implication in both cases, as in the whole passage, is that Peleus' sorrows are no less than Priam's. And if Priam imagined Peleus hoping to see Achilles return (490–2), that was an illusion: cf. 19.334–7 where Achilles thinks of Peleus as either dead or daily expecting news of his son's death.

542 ἧμαι 'I sit around', 'I am idle': cf. 403. There is a hint of colloquial speech in this use of the word: cf. Hdt. 3.151.2; [Dem.] 7.23; Ar. *Clouds* 1201 and Dover ad loc. It is used of Achilles' *absence* from the battle in 1.329, 416, 421 and above all, in his own mouth, in 18.104. It is a bitter paradox that Achilles is now far from idle at Troy, when he is killing Priam's sons (σέ τε κήδων ἠδὲ σὰ τέκνα), doing to him the opposite (κήδων) of what he should be doing for Peleus (κομίζω = κήδομαι). It is also a fine touch that Achilles sees both Priam's and Peleus' suffering as embodied in one and the same person: himself. This reinforces the argument that the two old men's misfortunes are equal; and it brings out how detached Achilles is from his role as the warrior.

544–5 ἄνω...καθύπερθε 'out to sea...inland'. Both words' basic meaning is 'up above', and so it seems confusing that each means the opposite of the other here. But ἀνάγειν can mean both 'carry inland'

and (more often ἀνάγεσθαι) 'put out to sea'. French là-bas ('down there') is used in a similarly loose way: I have even seen it applied to Heaven.

Μάκαρος: in myth the original colonist of Lesbos.

These lines give a southern (Lesbos), an eastern (Phrygia) and a northern and western (Hellespont) boundary to Priam's kingdom. 'Hellespont', as Homer used it, covers all the sea off Troy and Thrace, not just the Dardanelles: hence it is 'vast', as here, or 'broad' (7.86; 17.432).

546 κεκάσθαι 'you were supreme'. The infinitive refers to the past as is clear from πρίν in 543. The word picks up ἐκέκαστο in 535. Peleus was 'supreme in wealth'; Priam was 'supreme in wealth and sons'. But both wealth and sons are depleted now: cf. 18.288–92.

549–51 The end of the speech recalls its beginning. 549 ~ 518 (Priam *has* 'endured in his heart' coming to the Greek camp, now he *must* 'endure', not 'bewail in his heart', the death of his son); 550 ~ 524; 551 κακὸν ἄλλο ~ 518 πολλὰ κακά. For simpler examples of such ring-composition, see, e.g., 371, 570 nn.; 5.800 ~ 812–13; 16.745 ~ 750.

ἄνσχεο is aorist imperative of ἀνέχομαι (= Attic ἀνάσχου). A typical theme of consolation: cf. Hor. *Od.* 1.24.19–20; Kassel 55.

ἑῆος 'your': cf. 422 n.

551 'You will not bring him to life before more trouble has come upon you.' Again Achilles points Priam's thoughts to other sufferings than the death of Hector: this time to future ones, as to past and present ones in 548. He is hinting at the fall of Troy and Priam's death (cf. 728–9 n.) – he means, of course, that Priam will *never* raise his son from the dead: cf., e.g., Soph. *El.* 137–8; Hor. *Od.* 1.24.11–18.

553–5 The lines answer 522–3, not only by refusing Achilles' invitation to sit, but also in connecting κεῖται with ἷζε: there can be no sitting and no letting the grief lie, when Hector lies neglected. Also a retort to 551 οὐδέ μιν ἀνστήσεις: Priam cannot raise up Hector, but neither will he sit down.

Cf. *Od.* 10.383–7: Odysseus refuses to eat the food Circe has set before him until his companions are released. In 387 there the words λῦσον ἵν' ὀφθαλμοῖσιν ἴδω recur: they are more pointed in the *Iliad*, where

Priam's 'seeing' Hector is such a dangerous matter (583-6, cf. 600-1). For other coincidences with the Circe episode see 339-48 n.

557 ἔασας 'you have let me be', i.e. 'spared my life'. Cf. 569, 684; 16.731; *Od.* 4.744.

558 This line, omitted in some manuscripts and a papyrus, seems to be a misguided attempt to 'complete' the sense of ἔασας (cf. 45 n.): it is modelled on *Od.* 13.359-60 and *Il.* 18.61, 442. From the scholia it emerges that the major ancient critics did not have this line in their texts at all.

560-70 A sharp retort to Priam's words, brought out again by verbal echoes: 560 the negative command beginning the speech, as in 553; 569 οὐδ' αὐτὸν...ἐάσω ~ 557 ἐπεί με...ἔασας. Achilles knows his anger could flare up again: that is why he dwells on the divine will, which is to curb himself as much as it is to reassure Priam.

561 δέ 'for': cf. 90-1 n.

565-7 Cf. *Od.* 23.187-9. οὐδὲ μάλ' ἡβῶν is more pointed here, in words addressed to an old man.

ὀχῆας: the plural is the better attested reading than the singular ὀχῆα: cf. van der Valk II 158-9. Since it refers to the bolt of 453-5, the word should be taken as a 'poetic' plural, like δώματα, ὄχεα, λέχεα etc. The bolt or bolts in the gate in the Greek wall are likewise referred to as singular (12.121, 291; 13.124), and plural (12.455-62).

ῥεῖα: the gods characteristically do things 'easily': cf. 15.362; *Od.* 3.231; 10.574; Hes. *W.D.* 5-8 and West ad loc. See also 446 n.

568 τῷ: cf. 428 n.

ἐν ἄλγεσι goes with θυμόν rather than the verb: cf. 617 n.

θυμὸν ὀρίνῃς: θυμὸν ὀρίνειν was what Hermes told Priam to do in supplicating Achilles (467). From deep fellow-feeling to violent grief is only a step.

570 Achilles' respect for the gods comes out the more strongly for the contrast with Book 1. There Chryses invoked Apollo (21) and was rebuffed by Agamemnon (26-32). Here Achilles insists that the divine command will be obeyed.

Διός echoes Διόθεν in 561, by a form of ring-composition: cf. 549-51 n.

572 λέων ὥς may be meant to recall the lion-simile of 41–3. The savage Achilles is not far from the surface here, as the last speech has brought out. ὦρτο λέων ὥς is used of warriors in 11.129; 20.164.

574–5 The information about Automedon and Alkimos is reserved for here, where it emphasizes Achilles' respect for Priam and his gifts. For delayed information, cf. 448–56 n.; also 18.250–2: the details about Polydamas are kept back until his last speech of warning; Hes. *W.D.* 94: the jar is first mentioned when it becomes important; Fraenkel on Aesch. *Ag.* 59 (and Appendix A).

576 The unyoking would normally be the first thing on arrival (cf. 8.433–4; *Od.* 4.37–41), but the reception of Priam, like his supplication, follows an irregular course because of the powerful emotions it involves; cf. 477, 522, 596–620 nn.

ζυγόφιν: on the termination, see 284 n.

578 ἐϋξέστου: the variant ἐϋσσώτρου is unlikely to be right. It does not recur in Homer, and in a repetition of this kind (cf. 275b–6) it would be un-Homeric to vary the epithet.

580 The χιτών is worn next to the skin, and of the φάρεα, one is wrapped round him and one spread beneath him; cf. (ed.) F. Sokolowski, *Lois sacrées des cités grecques* (Paris 1969) 97 A 1–4, a fifth-century Cean inscription (cf. 162–4 n.): κατὰ τ]άδε θά[π]τεν τὸν θανόντα· ἐν ἐμα[τ]ίο[ις τρι]σὶ λευκοῖς, στρώματι καὶ ἐνδύματι [καὶ ἐ]πιβλέματι; similar is 18.352–3. In 588 only one φᾶρος is mentioned because the other is not put 'round' Hector, but under him on the bier (cf. στρώματι in the inscription).

583 A further reason why Achilles' dwelling is a full-scale house: the servants must wash Hector's body, but not in Priam's sight. Hence it is brought not into the μέγαρον, but another room.

ὡς μὴ Πρίαμος ἴδοι υἱόν corresponds to 555 ἵν' ὀφθαλμοῖσιν ἴδω. We would expect Achilles to hand over the body to Priam; but the two men cannot be together in the presence of the corpse; so Hector 'has been released' (599) before Priam sees him.

585 Ἀχιλῆϊ: the proper name is at first sight odd when Achilles is subject of the sentence, but it is used simply for clarity: cf. 9.269. Note also 20.27; 23.727.

586   ἀλίτηται: for the subjunctive after the optatives see 688 n.

587–9   Achilles in effect begins the funeral rites by having the body washed, and by himself laying it on the bier (cf. 720), which is often the mother's task (21.123–4; 22.352–3): this, together with his words to Patroclus, marks the end of his vengeance on Hector. It is doubly significant because he thus returns the corpse with his own hand: cf. in other solemn acts of giving back 1.440–1 τὴν μὲν ἔπειτα... | πατρὶ φίλῳ ἐν χερσὶ τίθει; Soph. *Phil.* 1287 δέχου δὲ χειρὸς ἐξ ἐμῆς βέλη τάδε. The more striking, then, that he does not return it directly to Priam: cf. 583, 649 nn.

Hector's corpse is washed, although it is clean and fresh (cf. 411–23). We should not ask why the slaves or Achilles are not said to notice this. Divine actions sometimes provoke no comment: e.g. 1.188–222 (Athena's conversation with Achilles); 5.506–8, 21.6–7 (mist or darkness spread over the battle). The washing emphasizes Achilles' humane concern: cf. Eur. *Supp.* 765–6 and Collard ad loc.; *Tro.* 1152.

591–5   Now Achilles can utter the name he suppressed before Priam. Patroclus' ghost in Book 23 did not demand any more vengeance; the thought that he might resent the ransoming of his killer's body is the residue of Achilles' own vindictive feeling. In 23.21, 182–3 giving Hector to the dogs was part of his promise to Patroclus.

592–4   The dead can know or hear what their living relatives or friends do: for this belief, expressed with varying degrees of confidence, see, e.g., Pind. *O.* 14.20–4, *P.* 5.101; Isoc. 19.42; Plato, *Laws* 927b; Arist. *E.N.* 1100a29–30, 1101a22–4. Further, K. J. Dover, *Greek popular morality* (Oxford 1974) 243–5.

εἰν Ἀϊδός περ ἐών: cf. 23.179 καὶ εἰν Ἀΐδαο δόμοισι (Achilles to the dead Patroclus again). The phrase conveys a hint of doubt: can the dead really hear? Cf. Aesch. *Cho.* 315–22.

594–5   This is not mere 'materialism'; rather, in the Homeric world, the improper thing would have been to refuse such an adequate (οὐ ...ἀεικέα, ἐπέοικεν) compensation, because it would be unsociable and inhuman to do so. That was what Achilles did in Book 9. Thus his satisfaction with the gifts is a motive for releasing Hector's body which complements his respect for the gods (560–70). It also serves to express his devotion to Patroclus (595).

596–620 The scene takes up where it left off (597 ἔνθεν ἀνέστη). Now Achilles invites Priam to eat. Ordinarily in Homer the guest is fed before any real conversation begins (cf. 9.199–221; 11.624; *Od.* 1.123–43; 3.65–6; 6.47–67; 7.167–77); that is the proper way to show hospitality. But here the meal has a further meaning: coming after the weeping and the consolation, it is the sign that both men have learned to live with their grief.

Achilles persuades Priam to eat with the example of Niobe. The story is adapted to fit his purpose better. 603–9 and 614–17 give, in compressed form, the usual version. Niobe who had twelve children compared herself favourably with the goddess Leto who had only two, Apollo and Artemis; as a punishment for her presumption, Artemis and Apollo shot down all Niobe's children with their arrows. She wept inconsolably; at last she was turned into a rock and her tears into a waterfall.

The story is expounded in a way characteristic of such exemplary tales: cf., e.g., 11.664–764. The main point of the example is made at the beginning and repeated at the end: 601–2 'Eat, for Niobe ate...' and 614 'she ate', 618–19 'let us eat'. The rest of the story is then strung from the initial comparison. It will be noted that 614–17 prevent the passage from forming a perfect 'ring' (cf. 549–51 n.) because they interrupt the echo of 601–2. But that is not an argument against their authenticity, because such a habit of composition is never a rigid law; and other considerations make it clear that they have a purpose (see 614–17 n.). What is added here is all for the sake of Priam. Niobe's children lie defiled and unburied for days because Hector did too (31; cf. 107). 'The gods' bury the children, because 'the gods' (113 = 134, 422, 749) have willed Hector's burial. Niobe ate after weeping, because Priam must eat too. See further M. M. Willcock, *C.Q.* n.s. 14 (1964) 141–54.

598 'against the opposite wall' (cf. 9.219; *Od.* 23.90): genitive of place.

599 λέλυται 'he is released'. The perfect denotes, as usual, an achieved state; it thus figures naturally in an expression of willing compliance: cf., e.g., Ar. *Ach.* 344.

601 μνησώμεθα: the 'we' here and in 618 denotes sympathetic

participation, especially since Achilles has himself recently eaten: cf.,
e.g., 15.553; Plat. *Gorg.* 527d–e (Socrates treats Callicles as a friend:
cf. 482a; 513c etc.); Catullus 96.3–4 (a poem of condolence). In
general, see Wackernagel 1 42–3.

603–9 All Niobe's many children were killed: so too Priam claimed
to have lost the 'single' son left to him of many (499). The children
of Leto, two only, correspond to Achilles, an only son. There is no
correspondence between Niobe's boast and Priam; but the motif has
to be included if the story is to make sense.

608–9 δοιώ...πολλούς...δοιώ...πάντας: the clipped and pointed
style sounds a note of grim pathos: cf. 11.136–7 ὡς τώ γε κλαίοντε
προσαυδήτην βασιλῆα | μειλιχίοις ἐπέεσσιν· ἀμείλικτον δ' ὅπ' ἄκουσαν;
17.196–7 ὁ δ' ἄρα ᾧ παιδὶ ὅπασσε | γηράς· ἀλλ' οὐχ υἱὸς ἐν ἔντεσι πατρὸς
ἐγήρα.

608 'she said that she (Leto) had borne (only) two; she herself had
borne many'. The sentence shifts from reported speech to direct
statement (though Niobe is surely taken to have said that she had borne
many children) in a way which is natural in Greek, if slightly
disconcerting to a modern reader: cf. 2.119–22; also 148 n. For the
omission of a subject for τεκέειν cf. 9.234–5 (Τρῶες)...οὐδ' ἔτι φασὶ |
σχήσεσθ' (sc. the Greeks); 12.106–7; 15.556–8. For δοιώ = 'only two'
cf. 531 n.

611 The people, as well as Niobe later, have to be turned into stone
partly to explain why the children remained unburied, partly to
introduce the motif of the gods' concern. The whole people must suffer
for an individual's guilt: cf. 1.43–52 (the whole Greek army is afflicted
with the plague after Agamemnon's misdeed); Hes. *W.D.* 240–3; also
27–8 n.

λαοὺς δὲ λίθους: a pun on λαός and λᾶας (= λίθος) seems to be
implicit here as in Hes. fr. 234; see further Merkelbach–West ad loc.
For the use of δέ see 91 n.

614–17 The traditional conclusion to the myth now follows, which is
also relevant, since as Homer tells it, Niobe's petrifaction is in no way
a release from her sorrows but a perpetuation of them. For Priam too
will continue to weep after he has eaten (619–20); likewise, κήδεα πέσσει
used of Niobe is echoed by 639 κήδεα...πέσσω in Priam's mouth.

Homer first modifies the motif of petrifaction (611), and then re-uses it here in its normal form. For the technique, compare the story of Meleager as told by Phoenix. In 9.584–5 Meleager's mother begs him to return to battle: this motif belongs to Homer's peculiar version of the story in which the supplication of the angry Meleager corresponds to the supplication of the angry Achilles, and Meleager's wife Cleo-patra to Achilles' beloved friend Patro-clus. But in 9.564–72 Meleager's mother has cursed him (the cause of his anger and ultimately his death): this is close to the usual version of the story whose essence is that the anger of Meleager's mother causes his end. This motif is relevant to the *Iliad* too, however, because the Meleager-story looks forward implicitly to the future, including Achilles' fated death. See further M. M. Willcock, *C.Q.* n.s. 14 (1964) 147–52; Schadewaldt, *IS* 140–3.

Later writers (see Jebb on Soph. *Ant.* 831; also Paus. 5.13.7; 8.8.4) identify the petrified Niobe with a feature of the landscape on mount Sipylus. So no doubt did Homer, though these lines are quite unspecific.

614–15 For the emphatically repeated preposition cf. 11.163–4; 22.503–4.

616 Ἀχελώϊον: the Achelous, the largest river in Greece, was treated as representative of rivers in general. Thus in the Attic countryside there could be a shrine to the Nymphs and Achelous (Plat. *Phaedrus* 230b, 263d); and later poets use Ἀχελῷος as = 'water'. So Homer may mean by using the word here no more than that the Nymphs habitually haunt rivers. But possibly Achelous is in fact the name of the local river, for other minor Achelouses are attested; or else one of the variant readings is right, and the river was called Ἀχέλης: the epic poet Panyassis speaks of νύμφαι Ἀχελήτιδες. See further the scholia on this line and on 21.194, with Erbse's notes.

ἐρρώσαντο 'spring', timeless aorist (cf. 335 n.). The nymphs move like the streams they represent.

617 θεῶν ἐκ goes with κήδεα rather than with πέσσει: cf. 111, 568 nn.; 5.64; 22.152; Eur. *Ion.* 508 θεόθεν τέκνα ('children with divine fathers'). Niobe's sorrows, like Priam's and all men's (525–6), come from the gods.

πέσσει 'nurses', literally 'digests': cf. 4.513; 9.565. The use of this metaphor here, after 613, suggests it is as natural that men suffer as that they digest after eating.

623–8 623–4 = 7.317–18; 625–6 = 9.216–17 (with Πάτροκλος instead of Αὐτομέδων); 627–8 = 9.91–2, 221–2 (627 often in *Od.*; 628 often in *Il.* and *Od.*). The conventional description of the meal has a peculiar force here, where the social conventions return: cf. 596–620 n.

629–32 The two men look at each other with wonder: this is possible in the calm they have now achieved. This wonder is very different from that of 480–4. In Book 24 as a whole Priam is as much the hero as Achilles is; so here he shares Achilles' stature and beauty (cf. 21.108). The stylistic symmetry brings out their equality.

632 καὶ μῦθον ἀκούων must refer to things said while they ate: for the present participle referring to the recent past cf. Soph. *O.C.* 551, 554. On the position of τε see Denniston 517 and, e.g., 3.80.

635–6 (ὄφρα καί...) = *Od.* 4. 294–5; ~ 23.254–5.

637–8 ὑπὸ βλεφάροισιν ἐμοῖσιν...σῆς ὑπὸ χερσίν: a powerful antithesis, with a slight shift in the sense of ὑπό; for word-play with a preposition cf. Archil. fr. 2: ἐν δορί twice = 'depending on my spear', then = '(leaning) on my spear'.

637–42 Priam has behaved like Achilles: for the defilement see 162–4 n. (also 23.44); for the sleeplessness see 1–5 n.; for the refusal of food and drink see 123–5 n. The two men have shared their grief; they now also share their return to normal life.

642 λαυκανίης καθέηκα 'I have put down my throat'; for the form of the verb cf. 48.

643–8 643 ~ 9.658 (where the subject is Πάτροκλος). 644–7 = *Od.* 4.297–300, 7.336–9 (647 = *Od.* 22.497). 648: cf. *Od.* 7.340, 23.291.

649 ἐπικερτομέων 'teasing', 'mystifying': it is used here of deception, not mockery. Cf. 4.6; *Od.* 13.326; 24.240; Hes. *W.D.* 788–9; Eur. *Hel.* 619; *I.A.* 849; Theoc. 1.62. In fact, the deception is intentionally transparent. For it is quite normal practice to give guests a bed under the αἴθουσα (*Od.* 3.399; 4.297; 7.345); and it is hard to see how Priam by sleeping there would escape the notice of night-visitors. Achilles knows that his guest must leave by night, and his speech hints at the danger of his remaining. He knows too that a god has escorted Priam (563–7); and he guesses that the same god will help him return, as in fact happens. He thus also avoids a farewell in which he and Priam would have to be together in the presence of Hector's body: cf. 583, 587–9 nn. So by making Priam sleep in the αἴθουσα he eases the old man's departure. But it would be undignified and inhospitable for him to do so more openly; hence the polite deception of these lines.

652 ἥ θέμις ἐστί 'which is normal/proper'; the phrase is used to forestall objections: cf. 2.73, 9.33, 23.581. The relative pronoun would naturally be neuter, but is attracted to the case of the predicate (θέμις).

653 θοὴν διὰ νύκτα μέλαιναν: see 366 n.

655 The phrase is euphemistic; and the highly abstract form of expression, with its pair of nouns ending in -σις, brings that out. If Priam really were seen, something worse than 'a delay in the release of the corpse' would happen: see 686–8.

κεν + subjunctive is a potential future, 'will/would happen', like ἄν + optative just before: cf. 18.308; *Od.* 4.692.

661 'You would do me a kindness if you did this', literally 'doing thus you would bring about things pleasing to me'. An everyday form of politeness shows through the epic style: cf. Hdt. 1.90.2; Plat. *Gorg.* 516b; *Phaedo* 115b τί δὲ τούτοις ἢ ἐμοὶ ἐπιστέλλεις...ὅτι ἄν σοι ποιοῦντες ἡμεῖς ἐν χάριτι μάλιστα ποιοῖμεν; (and Socrates' reply there); Theophrastus, *Characters* 24.13: χαρίζοιο ἄν μοι ('please') is a phrase the proud man never uses in letters; P. Cairo Zen. 59251 (*Select Papyri* (Loeb) I 93, a letter of 252 B.C.) χαριεῖ οὖν μοι...ἡμῖν γράφων. The courtesy of this exchange between the two men (cf. 669) is a fine contrast to the abruptness of their opening words at 486, 553, 560: they are now ready, after the emotion and the understanding, to return to everyday politeness.

ῥέξας: the aorist participle is less strongly attested in the manuscripts, but more idiomatic: cf. 170 n.

θείης 'you would do, bring about': cf. 741; 1.2; LSJ s.v. τίθημι c. 2.

662 οἶσθα has a certain finesse, since Achilles is no less than the cause of what Priam describes.

ἐέλμεθα 'we are cooped up'; perfect passive of εἴλω.

662–3 τηλόθι...ὄρεος 'the wood is (too) far to bring from the mountain'; for the use of the infinitive (ἀξέμεν) cf. 369 n.

665 δαινῦτο 'may have a funeral banquet', present optative of δαίνυμαι.

667 The aorist subjunctive (cf. 357 n.), with εἴ περ ἀνάγκη, carries a tone of resignation after κε + optative in 664–6, which expresses a request: 'I hope we may...then let us fight, if it must be.'

669 Achilles' reply is as polite as Priam's request: 'it shall be as you ask'; cf. for the turn of phrase, 21.223; *Od.* 16.31; 17.599. Many examples from fifth- and fourth-century Greek are collected and analysed by Fraenkel, *BA* 77–89.

671–2 The gesture is one of reassurance; cf. 361; 14.137; *Od.* 18.258 (Odysseus took Penelope's hand as he left, warning her he might not return).

673–6 The description has what looks like conventional features: 673 = *Od.* 4.302; 675 = *Il.* 9.663; and in Homeric scenes where a host and guests go to bed it is usual to say that the host slept with his wife or concubine: cf. 9.664–5; *Od.* 3.403; 4.304–5; 7.346–7. But this is a special case, for Achilles had refused sex since Patroclus' death (cf. 129–30); and here it matters that host and guest sleep in quite different parts of the house, because Priam must leave swiftly and in secret. That is another reason why Achilles' 'tent' is such a spacious affair.

673 προδόμῳ δόμου: for the redundant form of expression cf. 17.389 βοὸς...βοείην; *Od.* 17.247 αἰπόλος αἰγῶν; 19.343 ποδάνιπτρα ποδῶν. In prose, e.g. Hdt. 1.5.2 τῷ ναυκλήρῳ τῆς νεός. Cf. 488 n.

677–8 = 2.1–2 (ἄλλοι...παννύχιοι); 10.2 (εὖδον...ὕπνῳ). In both those places, as here, ἀλλά follows, with a verb of thinking. In the story of Priam's journey, this section mirrors 330–3: the gods are watching over the old man all the time from his departure to his return.

680 βασιλῆα: see 483 n.

681 ἱεροὺς πυλαωρούς: cf. 10.56 φυλάκων ἱερὸν τέλος. Here, as often elsewhere in Homer, the epithet is extended outside the religious sphere; it often conveys no more than a feeling of dignity or awesomeness such as is proper to many epic persons, animals, things or places: cf. P. Wülfing von Martitz, *Glotta* 38 (1960) 272–307. A papyrus offers the form πυλαουρούς; this would be more correct, because the simple noun is οὖρος, but for the omega cf. 21.530; 22.69. Such an artificial 'back-formation' from the contracted πυλωρός is not surprising in Homer. But if πυλαουρούς is right, cf. 241 n. (end).

682 = 23.68; *Od.* 4.803; 6.21; the first half of the line recurs in 2.20. Outside poetry the similar ἐπιστῆναι ('stand over') is commonly used of dream-figures, and not only in literature; see E. R. Dodds, *The Greeks and the irrational* (Berkeley and Los Angeles 1951) 105.

683 '*You* have no thought of danger, (to judge by) how you are sleeping...' οἶον, as often in Homer (e.g. 18.95; 22.347), introduces the reason for saying what was just said; cf. 240 n. on ὅτι. Hermes blandly rebukes the sleeper for being asleep: this is typical of dream apparitions (cf. 2.23–5; 23.69–70). Here it also reminds us that Priam really is in danger and that his reconciliation with Achilles does not alter the Greeks' hostility to Troy.

687 παῖδες τοὶ μετόπισθε λελειμμένοι literally '(your) sons, the ones left behind' (cf. 22.334). But παῖδές τοι ('the sons left by you') could be the right accentuation.

688 γνώῃ...γνώωσι: subjunctives in the protasis going with an optative (δοῖεν) in the apodosis. Leaf comments: 'the subjunctive indicates that the discovery of Priam is spoken of as something positively expected, whereas the chance of ransom afterwards is merely a possibility; a rhetorical touch to arouse Priam's alarm'. Homer's usage seems not to confirm this tempting suggestion: see 4.97–9; 9.362–3; *Od.* 1.287–8; and also 586, 655 nn. But the repetition γνώῃ...γνώωσι certainly reinforces the sense of danger; for this kind of emphatic repetition (anaphora) see, e.g., 1.287–9; 6.192–3; 11.660–2 = 16.25–7; 16.14–15; 21.350–1; 23.15.

689 ἔδεισεν...ἀνίστη: for the imperfect coupled with the aorist cf., e.g., 127, 459, 515, 571. In most cases of this kind the aorist seems to denote the more sudden or limited action, the imperfect the more extended one (cf. Chantraine II §287); but the difference, if any, is very slight. See further Palmer in *CH* 146; Wackernagel I 182–3.

690–1 The return journey is described as economically as can be. The emphasis has now to shift from Priam's exploit to the recovered body of Hector and the responses it evokes; cf. 469 n.

691 ῥίμφα 'swiftly': cf. 446, 565–7 n.

692–3 = 14.433–4; 21.1–2. 693 is omitted in some manuscripts and both papyri; it is probably interpolated. At 351, the corresponding point in the outward journey, the name of the river is not mentioned.

692 ἷξον: aorist of ἵκω.

694 Hermes leaves Priam and the herald as they reach Trojan territory; at the same time dawn breaks. The god had come as they reached the same point on their way to the Greek camp, and as night fell (351); the dangers of the night were also his reason for helping them (363, 366).

695 ~ 8.1; cf. 19.1–2.

698 ἔγνω perhaps echoes 688 γνώῃ...γνώωσι, so as to convey a sense of relief at Priam's safe return: he is recognized by his own people, not the enemy.

699 Cassandra now briefly occupies the centre of the stage; she is also spotlighted by the syntax: 'no one else saw them before, man or woman, but Cassandra...noticed them'; for the pattern of sentence, cf. 18.403–5. She is mentioned again in 13.365–6 as the most beautiful of Priam's daughters. That explains her prominence here, as ἰκέλη χρυσέῃ Ἀφροδίτῃ brings out. If Homer knew more stories about her (as he may well have done), they have been allowed to leave no trace in the *Iliad*.

702 τὸν δ': the lack of the name is expressive: 'him' can mean only one person to Cassandra and the Trojans. Cf. 18.257 οὗτος ἀνήρ (Polydamas of Achilles); *Od.* 18.181 κεῖνος (Penelope of Odysseus); Theoc. 2.17 etc. τῆνον...τὸν ἄνδρα (an abandoned woman of her faithless lover); Virg. *Aen.* 4.479 *eum...eo* (Dido of Aeneas).

704–6 The logical conclusion of this sentence ('in order to *mourn* him now that he is *dead*') is suppressed, with a moving economy: it is as if the painful fact defied expression.

In 3.50 Hector called Paris πατρί τε σῷ μέγα πῆμα πόληΐ τε παντί τε δήμῳ (cf. 6.283–4). The hero who gave joy to his parents and his city (cf. 22.431–6) is the one who has had to die: the good-for-nothing who brings disaster on them survives (cf. 253–64). In general on the contrast between Hector and Paris in the *Iliad* see Griffin 5–9. For rejoicing at the warrior's safe return cf. 7.294–5, 307–8; 17.635–6.

704 ὄψεσθε '(come and) see!': here and in *Od.* 8.313 apparently an aorist imperative, like ἄξετε in 778; the future indicative expressing a command, quite common in Attic (e.g. Plat. *Prot.* 338a7), seems to be foreign to Homer. See further Chantraine 1 § 199.

706 χαίρετ': imperfect (without augment).

707–17 Cassandra's appeal is at once answered. πάντας γὰρ ἀάσχετον ἵκετο πένθος in 708 powerfully completes χαίρετε...χάρμα in 706.

707 λίπετ' 'was left'. The aorist middle form carries passive meaning; cf. 1, 709, 789; cf. also 728–9 n.

709 ξύμβληντο 'they met', unaugmented aorist middle/passive of ξυμβάλλω.

710–11 τόν γ'...τιλλέσθην 'they tore their hair...for him'. The accusative is governed by the notion of mourning implicit in τιλλέσθην: cf. Hdt. 2.61.1; Ar. *Lys.* 396 κόπτεσθ' Ἄδωνιν. For the action cf. 18.26; 22.77, 405; and for representations of it in art, see Neumann 86–7, with illustrations; J. D. Beazley, *The development of Attic black-figure* (Berkeley 1951), Pl. 33.

712 ἁπτόμεναι κεφαλῆς : this gesture is customary for the nearest and dearest at funerals: cf. 724; 23.136 (Achilles with Patroclus). For representations in art, see Neumann 89 n. 369: the mourner stands with one palm cupped under the dead person's head. It is also a gesture of protective or motherly love: cf. 18.71: Thetis takes hold of Achilles' head when she finds him groaning; Theoc. 24.6: Alcmena holds her baby children's heads as she sings them a lullaby; Arr. *Epict.* 3.5.12: a milksop wants his mother to hold his head when he is ill.

713–15 Cf. 23.154–5 'the sun would have set on their weeping if Achilles had not spoken to Agamemnon'; *Od.* 21.226–7.

716 'Let me through with the mules!', literally 'Give way, for me, to the mules to go through!' The infinitive expresses the consequence of the main verb (cf. 2–3 n.); μοι is ethic dative (cf. 85 n.).

717 ἄσεσθε 'you can have your fill', permissive future; cf., e.g., 6.71; 10.235.
ἀγάγωμι = ἀγάγω: on the form of the termination see 154–5 n.

720 τρητοῖς 'perforated'; cf. 3.448; *Od.* 3.399; 7.345. The fibres

which criss-cross to make the surface of the bed proper are threaded
through the holes in the bedstead: cf. *Od.* 23.198 (how Odysseus made
his own bed) τέτρηνα δὲ πάντα τερέτρῳ. Cf. S. Laser in *AH* P 31–2.
The epithet is not purely decorative; we are presumably to think of this
bed as something more elaborate and ceremonial than the one on which
Hector's body was carried from Achilles' tent.

721–2 There is a sharp change of construction after ἀοιδήν: οἱ μὲν ἄρ'
replaces the relative οἵ τε, in order to stress the contrast and
correspondence between the singers' and the women's actions; cf. *Od.*
1.115–17 ὀσσόμενος πατέρ' ἐσθλὸν ἐνὶ φρεσίν, εἴ ποθεν ἐλθὼν |
μνηστήρων – τῶν μὲν σκέδασιν κατὰ δώματα θείη, | τιμὴν δ' αὐτὸς
ἔχοι καὶ κτήμασιν οἷσιν ἀνάσσοι; *Il.* 23.181–3. On such phenomena
in Homer see 42–3 n. The variant θρήνους is out of the question; it
would require an unattested sense for the word ('lamenters') and an
inversion (the verb ἐξάρχουσ(ι) placed before οἵ τε) unparalleled in
Homer.

The pattern of the lament seems to be: a song sung by the professional
singers, followed by keening from the women, out of which the
individual laments of Andromache, Hecuba and Helen arise. There is
a similar pattern in Achilles' funeral as described in *Od.* 24.58–61: the
Nereids wail and the Muses sing a lament. In tragedy cf., e.g., Eur. *Supp.*
798–836; *Tro.* 1209–59. Hired mourners are familiar from later
antiquity (e.g. Aesch. *Cho.* 733; Plat. *Laws* 800e); the captive women
in 18.28–9, 339–42; 19.301–2 serve the same purpose for the Greeks.

In general on ancient and modern Greek laments see E. Reiner, *Die
rituelle Totenklage der Griechen* (Tübingen 1938); M. Alexiou, *The ritual
lament in Greek tradition* (Cambridge 1974). When we compare Homer's
laments with some in Greek tragedy (or with Lucian, *De luctu* 13), it
is the more striking how they maintain the formal dignity, and the
expressive fluency and flexibility, of all Homeric speeches. There is deep
feeling, but no strident or stilted pathos here; and the inarticulate cries
of mourners which can be found in tragedy – ἒ ἔ, αἰαῖ, ὀτοτοῖ etc. – are
quite foreign to Homer. One can see from Aristophanes (*Frogs* 1029;
fr. 678) how differently the chorus of Phrygians in Aeschylus' *Ransoming
of Hector* must have lamented. Cf. Deichgräber 82, 120.

723–76 The three laments for Hector follow naturally on the return
of his body. Andromache at length, and Hecuba more briefly, have

already lamented Hector in 22.431–6, 477–514; but though Andromache's lament here in some particulars recalls her earlier one, this scene is shaped by a quite distinct purpose. There she gives voice to the sorrow of the deserted wife and her fears for her son, and Hecuba expresses her own and the city's loss. Here what they say forms part of a sustained and detailed re-evocation of Hector: first as warrior and as husband, then as the gods' favourite and the favourite son, then as the kindly brother-in-law. This is, in effect, a kind of *laudatio funebris*; such praise is a standard element in the θρῆνος: cf. Ammon. *Diff.* 54 θρῆνος...ὀδυρμὸν ἔχει σὺν ἐγκωμίῳ τοῦ τελευτήσαντος ('a *threnos* contains lamentation together with praise of the dead man') and, e.g., Eur. *Alc.* 435–75; Hdt. 6.58.3; Aesch. *Ag.* 1547 and Fraenkel ad loc.

Another distinctive feature of Andromache's lament in this book is its more accurate prevision of the future: she is to be enslaved and Astyanax, if not enslaved with her, to be thrown to his death from a tower. What she foresees for her son in 22.487–507 is designedly put in the form of a description of *any* orphan's sufferings and humiliations. Thus at the end of the poem, just as the memories of Hector become more precise, so the sense of foreboding for Troy becomes more acute. In the same way, the foreshadowing of Achilles' death becomes more and more definite over the last part of the *Iliad* (18.96; 19.416–17; 21.111–13, 277–8; 22.359–60).

The three women's laments could be said to sum up major themes of the whole poem. There has and will be suffering for the Trojans (Andromache); but in the midst of it the gods have shown their friendship (Hecuba); and Troy's greatest warrior in the end, like Achilles, wins praise for his kindness (Helen). This section also looks back to Book 6 and fulfils what was left in suspense there. The three women whom Hector met and spoke to in the earlier book are the three who mourn him here. In 6.500 the slave-women lamented him before his death: here the laments are for the now dead man. In 6.450–65 Hector predicted Andromache's future: here she does so herself. In 6.476–81 Hector fondly imagined that Astyanax would live to be a better warrior than his father: here Andromache guesses the truth, that he will be killed in his babyhood because of his father's prowess in war. Thus the Trojan episode of Book 6, so far from being a mere interlude, creates a tension which sustains the poem to its end: cf. W. Schadewaldt, *W.S.* 69 (1956) 5–25 = *Hellas und Hesperien* (Zurich and Stuttgart 1970) 21–38.

725 ἆνερ 'husband': each of the three laments begins by placing Hector in his relationship to the speaker.

ἀπ' αἰῶνος νέος ὤλεο 'you perished/were lost from life young': a slightly redundant form of expression for which I know of no exact parallel, but all kinds of pleonasm are common in Homer: cf., e.g., 488, 673 nn., and the very frequent ὀφθαλμοῖσιν ἰδεῖν (e.g. 206). For ὄλλυμαι with ἀπό cf. 18.107; *Od.* 15.91.

725–7 Cf. 22.482–5 νῦν δὲ σὺ μὲν Ἀΐδαο δόμους ὑπὸ κεύθεσι γαίης | ἔρχεαι, αὐτὰρ ἐμὲ στυγερῷ ἐνὶ πένθεϊ λείπεις | χήρην ἐν μεγάροισι· πάϊς δ' ἔτι νήπιος αὔτως, | ὃν τέκομεν σύ τ' ἐγώ τε δυσάμμοροι.

727 δυσάμμοροι: the δυσ- reinforces the idea of unhappiness already present in ἄμμορος; cf. in later poetry δυσάθλιος, δυσαλγής, δυσάνολβος.

728–9 The last reminder of what is foreshadowed throughout the poem, that Troy must fall: passages are collected by Kullmann 343–9. In this book, see esp. 245–7, 380–5, 551.

πέρσεται 'will be sacked'. The future passive in Homer, like the present and imperfect passive in all periods of Greek, has no forms distinct from those of the middle; and indeed in origin the passive is merely one sub-category of the middle, which indicates that the subject is in some sense affected or interested by the action of the verb. Cf. Wackernagel I 137–44; cf. also 355, 707 n., 731.

730 ῥύσκευ 'you protected', unaugmented second person singular of the frequentative imperfect (cf. 12 n.) of ῥύομαι.

ἔχες alludes to the origin and meaning of Hector's name ('keeper'); Astyanax ('lord of the city') too is so called because οἶος...ἐρύετο Ἴλιον Ἕκτωρ (6.403; cf. 22.507). For similar word-plays on names see Hes. *Theog.* 775 and West ad loc.; Hdt. 3.62.2; Bacchyl. 6.1–2; Eur. *Bac.* 367 and Dodds ad loc.; *Supp.* 497 and Collard ad loc. They are compatible with moments of great tragic intensity; but they do not seem to reflect a firm belief that a name could determine a person's life in any way.

731 ὀχήσονται seems to continue the word-play, this time with a pathetic contrast: before, Hector 'kept' them, now they 'will be carried (off)'.

732–40 In these lines Andromache addresses Astyanax, no longer the dead man, as is normal in laments. The baby boy is clearly not with her, which enhances the rhetorical and pathetic effect.

732–4 Andromache, who knows the city's days are numbered, foresees her own captivity: in later stories (e.g. Euripides, *Andromache*) she becomes Neoptolemus' concubine. In 727–8 she had assumed that Astyanax would die in the sack of Troy; here she imagines that he may go with her. This wavering is very natural; and thus Andromache's premonition in 734–5 of what is really to come does not seem an implausible foreknowledge.

734–8 This is how Astyanax is said to have died by most later writers from the Cyclic poets onwards, though the deed is ascribed to different Greek heroes (for testimonia see Erbse's note on the scholia ad loc.; Apollod. *Epit.* 5.23 and Frazer ad loc.). The story must have been known to Homer: it is very unlikely that he should have invented *ad hoc* this form of death for the child. For the combination of a true and a false foreshadowing cf. 21.113: Achilles predicts that he will be killed either by a spear, or by an arrow (the truth; cf. 21.278); *Od.* 16.274–7: Odysseus tells Telemachus to endure it if he (Od.) is dragged out of the house by his feet, or if he has things thrown at him. The latter assumption comes true (see 17.463–5; 18.394–8; 20.299–302); the former does not – in fact, it is neatly reversed: it is Odysseus who drags Irus out of the house by his foot (18.100–2), after the beggar had threatened to do the same to him (18.10).

734 πρό 'before', 'in the sight of'.

735 χειρός 'by the arm'; for the genitive cf. 515.
    λυγρὸν ὄλεθρον: the accusative is 'internal': cf. 38, 172 n., and Barrett on Eur. *Hipp.* 752–7.

736–8 In later stories of Astyanax' death, the murderer is Odysseus (the *Iliou Persis* etc.) or Neoptolemus (the *Little Iliad* etc.), neither of whom has the motive which Andromache mentions. It would, of course, be unrealistic if Andromache were to foresee who in particular would cause her son's death; and the point here is in any case to bring out how much the Greeks as a whole hate the son of the man who killed so many of their kinsmen.

738 ἄσπετον οὖδας 'the vast ground'. The phrase is an alternative (scanning ‒⏑⏑‒⏑); to ἀπείρονα γαῖαν (⏑‒⏑⏑‒⏑); it recurs in 19.61.

739 ἐν δαῒ λυγρῇ ('in the grim battle') corresponds forcefully to λυγρὸν ὄλεθρον (735) and ἄλγεα λυγρά (742): Astyanax' death or Andromache's sufferings are a sort of *quid pro quo*. Similarly, οὐ... μείλιχος echoes ἀμειλίχου (734).

741 = 17.37 (said of a killer). 'You have left sorrow behind you' is a theme typical of laments and epitaphs: cf., e.g., Soph. *Aj.* 972–3; (ed.) W. Peek, *Griechische Versinschriften* 1 (Heidelberg 1955) 697.5–6, 2002.7–8. The abrupt return to addressing Hector is expressive: cf. 57 n.

743–5 The last words of the dying person are the subject of some rather sentimental Hellenistic epigrams in the *Greek Anthology*: 7.513 ('Simonides'), 646–8 (Anyte, Simmias (?), Leonidas).

πυκινὸν ἔπος 'a wise word' (cf. 75); for the idea cf. Tac. *Agr.* 45.5 (on his own and his wife's absence from her father's death-bed) *excepissemus certe mandata vocesque quas penitus animo figeremus*. Propertius 4.11 (though spoken by a wife who is already dead) represents in great poetry the sort of utterance meant here; cf. Eur. *Alc.* 299–311.

745 μεμνῄμην: optative of μέμνημαι.

746–56 Like Andromache's lament, Hecuba's contrasts with her more violent outburst of grief in Book 22 (431–6). Here she expresses above all wonder at the gods' preservation of Hector's corpse; and the hatred she voiced against Achilles in 212–16 is replaced by something not far from pity (754–6).

746 = 22.515 (cf. 22.429).

749 μοι is ethic dative: cf. 85 n.

749–50 Cf. 425–31 n. Both Priam and Hecuba come to see that the gods have not been altogether cruel.

περ...περ: the repeated particle stresses the antithesis (Denniston 482–3, 486): 'when you were *alive*...even though it was after your *death*'.

ἄρα has its full sense, 'as it now turns out'; cf., e.g., 11.604.

751–3 We have been reminded in this book by Hecuba herself (204–5 ~ 520–1; cf. 478–9), and before by Priam (22.44, 423), that Achilles *killed* many of their sons. In the period before the action of the *Iliad* he, like other Greeks (2.229–31), took captive and sold some at least of the enemies he defeated: see 11.104–6; 21.34–44, 57–8, 76–9; 22.45; but after the death of Patroclus he is no longer in any mood to spare Trojans, as he says in his great speech to Lycaon (21.99–105). If Hecuba does not here recall the other sons Achilles killed, that is to stress his savagery against Hector.

753 ἀμιχθαλόεσσαν: the meaning and derivation of this word is as obscure now as it was to the ancients, who explained it in various ways, none of them convincing, recorded by the scholia (see also Erbse's notes) and Eustathius. What meaning, if any, Homer attached to the word seems now beyond recall.

755 ἑοῦ περὶ σῆμ' ἑτάροιο: cf. 416 n.

756 Cf. 551 οὐδέ μιν ἀνστήσεις. As those words of Achilles' to Priam suggest, he has in fact learned the lesson implicit in what Hecuba says here.

757–9 Cf. 416–23; see 749–50 n.

759 ~ *Od.* 3.280; 15.411 (preceded by Ἀπόλλων); cf. *Od.* 5.124; 11.173, 199 (with feminine participle, preceded by Ἄρτεμις or equivalent). The phrase is used of a swift, easy death. Rather than being a stock formula, it may well have been invented for this place, where it is peculiarly expressive, and then reproduced more or less appropriately to the context in the *Odyssey* passages. The same almost certainly applies, for example, to Hector's words in 6.492–3 πόλεμος δ' ἄνδρεσσι μελήσει | πᾶσι, μάλιστα δ' ἐμοί, which are echoed with less force in *Od.* 1.358–9; 11.352–3; 21.352–3. See further 339–48, 553–5 nn.

762–3 Helen's opening words correspond exactly to Hecuba's: cf. 725 n.

764 ὡς πρὶν ὤφελλον ὀλέσθαι 'How I wish I had died before!' This is Aristarchus' reading, which brings the verse into line with 6.345–6, where Helen wishes she had died on the day she went off with Paris (cf. 3.173–5); but in 3.428–9 Helen wishes Paris had been killed in the

battle, which corresponds to the variant reading here ὤφελλ᾽ ἀπολέσθαι.
If we could be sure that Aristarchus or someone before him altered the
text because it seemed offensive, then ὤφελλ᾽ ἀπολέσθαι would have
to be accepted; as it is, ὤφελλον ὀλέσθαι seems preferable. Helen's words
in 3.428–9 are a brief outburst of disgust, already softened by what
follows in that same speech; such a feeling is no longer in place here.
And 22.481, where Andromache says 'If only my father had never
begotten me!' (cf. Hecuba's 'Why should I go on living?' in 22.431),
suggests that Homer thought that sentiment proper to a lament.

765–6 This is the tenth year since the beginning of the Trojan war
(cf. 2.134, 295, 328–9). Why then 'the twentieth year' here? Clearly
some time must be reckoned for the gathering of the army (a process
alluded to in 4.28; 11.770), if nothing else; so the figure is 10 + . Such
a 10 + could naturally be extended to 20, given that 'twenty' is often
used in Homer as equivalent to any large number: e.g. 13.260 'you will
find not only one, but twenty spears in my tent, if you want'; 16.847
'if twenty men like you had encountered me, they would all have been
conquered'; and in *Od.* 19.536 the twenty geese in Penelope's dream
stand for the much larger number of suitors (see 16.245–53). 'Twenty'
can also be used as an intensification of 'ten': so in 9.379 'ten, or
twenty, times as much' (cf. 22.349).

It is unclear whether Homer knew of the stories later told in the *Cypria*
(or of others like them) which delayed the Greeks' arrival in Troy – the
campaign against Telephus in Mysia, Achilles' sojourn in Scyros on the
return journey, the unfavourable winds in Aulis before the second
departure; for passages which have been taken to show that he did see
Kullmann 192–200. In the *Odyssey*, at least, they cannot be presupposed
since Odysseus returns after twenty years, ten spent wandering and
ten before Troy.

These lines are very similar to *Od.* 19.222–3 ἤδη γάρ οἱ ἐεικοστὸν ἔτος
ἐστὶν | ἐξ οὗ κεῖθεν ἔβη καὶ ἐμῆς ἀπελήλυθε πάτρης (Odysseus is
disguised, and speaking to Penelope of himself; he is explaining that
his memories of Odysseus may be dimmed by the length of time which
has passed since he saw him). The effect of ἐμῆς... πάτρης is stronger
in the *Iliad*, where Helen is bewailing her own exile; and the following
ἀλλ᾽ οὔ πω σεῦ ἄκουσα... caps lines 765–6 very fittingly: for the
pattern of sentence cf. 2.798–9; 10.548–50; *Od.* 4.267–70. So although
the twenty years of Odysseus' absence are firmly rooted in the *Odyssey*,

it does not seem that these lines in the *Iliad* are affected by that motif. For this whole line of argument cf. Reinhardt, *ID* 485–90.

768 εἴ τις...ἐνίπτοι 'if ever someone spoke harshly to me'. On the use of the optative cf. 14 n.

770 Priam's tenderness towards Helen is shown in 3.161–70. The frankness about Hecuba, in her presence, is natural, and was no doubt tolerable, in a lament.

771–2 A phrase of wonderfully subtle and expressive construction.

(1) The repetition σύ...σῆ...σοῖς stresses the peculiar kindness of Hector and brings out how much he is missed: cf. 6.465 πρίν γέ τι σῆς τε βοῆς σοῦ θ' ἑλκηθμοῖο πυθέσθαι (Hector is declaring his special concern for his wife, cf. 450–5); *Od.* 11.202–3 ἀλλά με σός τε πόθος σά τε μήδεα, φαίδιμ' 'Οδυσσεῦ, | σή τ' ἀγανοφροσύνη μελιηδέα θυμὸν ἀπηύρα.

(2) The repetition ἐπέεσσι...ἐπέεσσι framing the whole is the device called κύκλος; for examples in later prose, see Hdt. 6.86 δ; 7.156.1; and J. D. Denniston, *Greek prose style* (Oxford 1952) 90. Here it brings out how the killer and man of action (cf. 739) used words to protect Helen: cf. 22.126–8 (Hector steeling himself to meet Achilles in battle) οὐ μέν πως νῦν ἔστιν ἀπὸ δρυὸς ἠδ' ἀπὸ πέτρης | τῷ ὀαριζέμεναι ('casually converse with him') ἅτε παρθένος ἠΐθεός τε, | παρθένος ἠΐθεός τ' ὀαρίζετον ἀλλήλοιϊν.

(3) The repetition ἀγανο-...ἀγανοῖς emphasizes Hector's courtesy: cf. 516 n.

(4) ἀγανοφροσύνη makes it plain that Hector's words were a true expression of his nature and feelings.

For the whole cf. 19.295–300, where Briseis recalls Patroclus' kindness to her, in lamenting his death. It is also fitting that this should be the final image we receive of one of the *Iliad*'s great warriors, in a book where the humaner virtues are overtly affirmed.

775 πάντες δέ με πεφρίκασιν 'they all abhor me': cf. 19.325 ῥιγεδανῆς 'Ελένης.

776 ἐπὶ δ'...ἀπείρων: after each lament (cf. 746, 760) the phrase which follows ὣς ἔφατο κλαίουσα is delicately varied. One of many places where it is striking how Homer avoids a mere stereotype: cf. esp.

3.171, 199, 228, where each of Helen's replies to Priam is introduced by a different phrase; see further M. W. Edwards, *C.P.* 64 (1969) 81–7.

778–9 ἄξετε is aorist imperative (cf. 704 n.); δείσητ' is aorist subjunctive.

780 ἐπέτελλε is used in an unusual sense, 'promised' rather than 'prescribed, enjoined'; but a command to the *Greeks* is implicit here. The meaning may have been extended partly in order that this line should echo 1.25.

785–804 The burial rites correspond almost wholly to the practice of the ninth-eighth centuries B.C. in Greece: see Kurtz and Boardman 186–7. In Homer, cf. 7.414–32; 23.250–7. Though what is described is exactly the same as in Book 23, the language is consistently varied: the only phrases which occur there too are lines 791 and 801 (χεύαντες...κίον).

788 ῥοδοδάκτυλος: the metaphor is probably that of a spread hand; but the first strip of light may possibly be compared to a single finger: cf. West on Hes. *W.D.* 610.

789 ἤγρετο 'was gathered', aorist passive/middle of ἀγείρω. Most manuscripts here and at 7.434 read ἔγρετο; but this is probably the false transcription of an original ΕΓΡΕΤΟ: η would have been written E in the earliest texts (cf. 241 n.; G. Murray, *The rise of the Greek epic* (Oxford 1911), Appendix 1). Alternatively, it could be seen as an artificial epic form, generated by confusion with ἔγρετο 'was awoken' (from ἐγείρω).

790 Cf. 1.57 οἱ δ' ἐπεὶ οὖν κτλ., and three times in *Od.* Omitted by the papyrus and some MSS, this line could well be an interpolation: it seems more suitable for an 'assembly' in the strict sense of the term. If it is genuine, for the heavy repetition of words meaning 'assemble' cf. *Od.* 2.8–9.

791 Cf. 23.237–8, 250. The practice of pouring wine over the burnt bones is familiar from Latin sources: see R. B. Onians, *Origins of European thought*[2] (Cambridge 1954) 277–8.

795 χρυσείην: cf. 23.253, where Patroclus' bones are put in a golden jar, and *Od.* 24.74 (Achilles' likewise). The gold belongs to the heroic, as to the divine, world (cf. 20 n.); burial urns of bronze from the Geometric period have actually been found: see Kurtz and Boardman 53.

796   The practice of wrapping the burnt bones in a cloth (cf. 23.254) is the basis for a powerful oxymoron in 21.318–20 'I will wrap him in sand and pour heaps of gravel over him' (the river threatening Achilles with loss of burial); cf. *Od.* 14.135–6.

799   I.e. they poured out (ἔχεαν) earth so as to form a mound which served as a grave-marker (σῆμα = the τύμβον of 666): cf. again 21.319–20 (see 796 n.).

800   πρίν: for this elliptical use – we are not told before *what* – cf. 31 n.; also *ante* in Virg. *Aen.* 9.315; 12.680, where there is intense pathos. This is a tactful remainder of what overshadows the peaceful conclusion of the *Iliad*, war; and in war, there can be no trust in mere agreements.

801–3   For the funeral banquet cf. 23.28–9; *Od.* 3.309. Priam had envisaged a banquet on the tenth day (665); this one comes on the eleventh. The discrepancy seems to be insignificant. Priam also says they will bury Hector on the tenth day, whereas this actually happens on the eleventh.

801   ∼ 23.257. That line, which concludes the burial of Patroclus, introduced the last section of the poem, which ends with the burial of Hector. That section is sharply divided at 24.1–2, lines which likewise look back to 23.257–8 (cf. 1–5 n.). Yet another reminder of how firmly and how delicately Homer holds together his great poem.

802   εὖ 'duly', 'in the proper fashion', Latin *rite*: cf. 2.382–4; *Od.* 20.161; 23.197 εὖ καὶ ἐπισταμένως; also 388 n.

INDEX

This is an index to the Commentary, not to the Introduction, which itself serves as an index on a number of points. Where one note contains cross-references to others on the same topic, only the 'key' note is mentioned here. Numbers refer to the lines of the text as they are recorded at the beginning of each note.

I SUBJECTS

2 GREEK WORDS